On
Education

On Education
by José Martí

Articles on Educational Theory and Pedagogy, and Writings for Children from The Age of Gold

Translated by Elinor Randall

Edited, with an Introduction and Notes, by Philip S. Foner

Monthly Review Press
New York and London

Library of Congress Cataloging in Publication Data
Martí, José, 1853–1895
José Martí on education.
"Selections from La edad de oro (The age of gold)":
p. 197
1. Martí, José, 1853–1895. 2. Education—Philosophy.
I. Foner, Philip Sheldon, 1910-   II. Martí, José
1853–1895. La edad de oro. English. Selections. 1979.
III. Title.
LB775.M3573 1979   370.1   79-2326
ISBN 0-85345-483-3
ISBN 0-85345-503-1 pbk.

Monthly Review Press
62 West 14th St., New York, N.Y. 10011
47 Red Lion Street, London WC1R 4PF

Manufactured in the United States of America

10 9 8 7 6 5 4 3 2 1

Contents

II
For Children
Selections from The Age of Gold
(La Edad de Oro)

Preface

The first volume of this work dealt with José Martí's writings on the United States, and the second volume presented the writings of Martí on what he called "Nuestra América," the America of the Spanish-speaking peoples, and included writings on Latin America and the struggle for Cuban independence. It had been our original intention to complete the series with a third volume which would include Martí's writing on education, his writings for children, on art and artists, on literature and literary figures, and his poetry. However, it was felt that it would be most useful to publish his writings on education and for children in a separate volume for those especially interested in this aspect of this truly remarkable figure in world history, especially since none of these writings have been available in English in our country before. The final volume in this collection will then be devoted to *José Martí: Critic and Poet*.

In this volume all of the translations are by Elinor Randall, but my wife, Roslyn Held Foner, translated excerpts from Martí's writings that are used in the introduction.

In the preparation of this volume I again had the good fortune to be able to discuss its contents, during a visit to Cuba in December 1977, with Roberto Fernández Retamar, director of Casa de las Américas and of the newly established Centro de Estudios Martianos, with Salvador Morales, the director of Sala Martí, Biblioteca Nacional, and with Professor Martin Franzbach of Bremen University in Germany. I wish to thank them for valuable suggestions.

Philip S. Foner

Lincoln University, Pennsylvania
August 1978

Introduction
by Philip S. Foner

Basic to the foundations of liberty, in the eyes of José Martí, was the education of the people. Nothing guaranteed that a government was anxious to serve its citizens as much as the haste it displayed in educating its people.[1] Hence it is not surprising that Martí devoted considerable attention in his writings to education, earning thereby the reputation as the "Maestro."

"Education is a work of constant impassioned tenderness," Martí proclaimed. His great respect for great teachers is reflected in his tribute to Mendive and his article on Amos Bronson Alcott. Martí recorded with approving comment Alcott's opposition to corporal punishment and routine learning for school children, and he expounded on Alcott's insistence on the importance of exercising love in teaching.[2]

Martí's first teaching experience came in Guatemala. During the reform administration of Justo Rufino Barrios, the school administration was enlarged and Martí, who was in Mexico city, learned that teachers were in demand in Guatemala. He was hired by a fellow Cuban, Don José María Izaguirre, Director of the Normal School, to teach literature and history. From March 1877 to July 1878 he was a teacher in

1. José Martí, *Obras Completas,* Trópico Edition, edited by Gonzalo de Quesada y Miranda (La Habana, 1936–49), Vol. XII, p. 136. Hereafter referred to as Trópico Edition.
2. See below, "Bronson Alcott."

11

Guatemala. Then, in a gesture of fraternal protest (or "solidarity," as he expressed it), he resigned his post when Don José María Izaguirre was deprived of his position as Director of the Normal School.

But Martí's interest in education did not cease with his resignation. In the pages of *Revista Universal* of Mexico City, he wrote articles criticizing education in Latin America—an education dominated by scholasticism and narrow formalism from the primary schools all the way up to the university. Martí declared war on this formalism, noting that with its emphasis on theology, rhetoric, and logic, there seemed to be no time for other subjects, especially those which were vital for man. In place of the prevailing scholasticism, Greek, and Latin, he urged the inclusion of physics, mechanical and practical arts, and the study of scientific agriculture. This is not to say that Martí was the enemy of classical languages. Of Celcelio Acosta he wrote: "He spoke a pure, rich, and graceful Latin, not that of the Imperial Forum, but that of the Senate of the Republic; not that of the House of Mecenas. Such language smells of myrrh and milk, and of thyme and verbena." Of Heredia's translation of Horace, Martí rhapsodized that it was "of clear beauty, more beautiful than the Greeks because it has their elegance without their crudeness."[3]

But the teaching of a useless language to a people anxious to find their own forms was a diversion from the basic needs of the times. Compulsory education, schools of art, of occupations, of professions, manual education, scientific education, were the needs of the times. He placed a great deal of emphasis on education in agriculture:

> The teaching of agriculture is the most urgent of all, not in technical schools, but in experimental stations where the parts of the plow will not be described except

3. Félix Lizaso, *Martí Educador* (La Habana, 1962), "Prologo," pp. 6-9.

where the student may see it in operation; and where the composition of the fields will not be explained in formulas on the blackboard, but rather in the layers of the earth itself.[4]

Latin Americans became aware of the educational system of the United States through Martí's journalistic dispatches published in the Hispanic American press. To be sure, his picture of North American education was not an account of its national educational life (even though he referred in his dispatches to "the United States"). He never discussed the little district school that was still an important factor in the public-school system of the United States. McGuffey, Frye, Barnes, and the *Blue-Black Speller* which had sold eighty million copies since 1840, are names that he did not mention. While he did challenge the myth that the public schools were benign institutions that successfully made over poor immigrants into solid middle-class citizens, he did not discuss the way in which the schools had become racist, class-biased servants of the upper classes.

Despite these limitations, and the regional character of his descriptions of education in the United States, Martí's writings are important contributions to our educational history. He was deeply interested in education on all levels, from elementary school to university studies, and in all types, from industrial and commercial training to the liberal arts and sciences, in female as well as male education, in day schools and in night schools where those who could not find time to attend classes during the day could come at their convenience

4. *La América* (New York), June 1884. See also Martí, *La Cuestión Agraria y la Educación del Campesino,* Biblioteca Popular Martiana, No. 5 (Editorial Lex, La Habana, 1959), and "El Proyecto de Instrucción Pública—Los Artículos de la Fe—La Enseñanza Obligatoria," *Revista Universal Mexico,* 26 de Octubre de 1875, in José Martí, *Educación* (Patronato del Libro Popular, La Habana, 1961).

after the day's work was done (and at one of which he himself taught Spanish for a time), in public and parochial schools, the former of which he favored and to which he advised parents to send their children.[5]

It is necessary to know what was, Martí explained, in order to know what is, for the present has its roots in the past. "To be a citizen of a republic is a difficult thing, and one must rehearse for it from childhood." He approved of the fact that in schools in the United States, "the children play at government. A parody on Congress, with its debates on the affairs of the nation, is reenacted in the wake of actuality. A hundredweight is heavy for one to lift, but among a hundred persons it signifies only a pound each. Children grow accustomed to carrying their pound from the time they are able to help choose a captain for a baseball game."

But this positive aspect of education in the public schools he visited was all but destroyed by what was taught. He had hoped to find

> the reading of beautiful things, the contemplation of the harmony of the universe, mental contact with great ideas and noble deeds, intimate dealings with the best things which the human soul has given forth in every epoch—these quicken and enlarge the intellect and place in one's hands the bridle which checks briefly homely pleasures, produce deeper and more delicate joys than the mere possession of fortune, and sweeten and ennoble the lives of those who possess rights, and create, by a grouping together of men of similar mental stature, a national soul.[6]

Instead, Martí found educational practices that bored and alienated the pupils and failed to prepare them for citizenship in a republic. It was September 1886, a cloudy morning made

5. Trópico Edition, vol. XXXIX, p. 109; vol. XXX, p. 177.
6. Ibid., vol. XXXII, p. 69.

bright by the colorful swarms of children, with their arms full of books, flocking out of the side streets to be regimented in the public schools of New York City. Some tarried to examine the billboards of the theaters; others waited submissively in line, carefully arranging their slate pencils and sponges in their pencil boxes; and still others, with stockings falling, shirts unbuttoned, and hats lost, raced through the streets like untamed colts. The big boys sent to bring them in returned red and panting after the fruitless chase.

This tableau was the preface to an exposition of the public school system of New York, with its inability to embrace the many elements of which its student body was composed and its failure to determine an objective. Martí recapitulated some of the problems facing the educational reformers. Should education consist merely of literary subjects, or should there be instilled even in the primary grades the superior spirit of the fine arts? Should education be indifferent, generalized, or specialized, in the teaching of religion? Should not all education be so disposed as to develop equally the intellect, the emotions, and the hands?

New York had many beautiful buildings, efficiently equipped and provided with excellent textbooks by the state, but, withal, there were always between four and six thousand children of the lower grades, largely the children of German and Irish immigrants, unable to attend school for lack of space. The poorly clad and ill-fed urban children who did attend were herded into overcrowded classrooms, were learning by rote, and the teaching was of a fearful and insensate monotony.

The teaching was inferior because it consisted only of counting, spelling, and memorizing maps. Martí registered disagreeable surprise at a boy of five who could count to a hundred. This error of memorizing, he pointed out, instead of facilitating the expression of originality which is inherent in every child, suffocated it and robbed the intellect. This sterile, repugnant uniformity he called a kind of intellectual livery. How could one face existence in this selfish, active city with mere verbal instruction? It produced cold, stupid children who, after six years, at the age of thirteen or fourteen, dropped out of school with uncultivated tastes and no thirst for knowledge, lacking the grace of childhood and the enthusiasm of youth. They had not even mastered the elements of learning, and the few who went on to high school were taught subjects that would be considered elementary by any logical standards.[7]

Martí's remedy lay in changing radically this verbal method of primary instruction into an experimental system, changing from rhetoric to science, from an alphabet of words to one of nature. "Put the entire boy in school," he said, quoting a St. Louis educator. But even this would not suffice. The child must be taught the pride of being a man, with the expression of majesty which comes from a working knowledge of the world. This was the accomplishment of the "saint Peter Cooper," for whom Martí had the highest words of praise. He was one of Martí's self-made men, who had founded a school, Cooper Institute, where might be learned "the practice of life in its beautiful ordinary arts, and the piety and morality which spring spontaneously from this knowledge."[8] Peter Cooper was a self-made man with a fortune from iron rails and glue, and a passionate attachment to New York and its people. In the 1850s he founded and endowed the Cooper Union for the Advancement of the Arts and Sciences, a tuition-free school open to anyone of "good moral character," and housed in the Foundation Building at Astor Place. To Martí, Cooper could not have done more to justify his existence—the provision of a free school for all was the greatest gift a man could bestow on humanity.[9]

The 1887 annual assembly of the American Association

7. See below, "A False Conception of Public Education."
8. See below, "Peter Cooper."
9. See below, "Peter Cooper."

for the Advancement of Science, held at Columbia University, gave Martí another opportunity to criticize education in the public schools of New York City. There was much discussion about the necessity of teaching the physical sciences in these schools, and about the benefit to be gained from the teaching of the industrial arts. The questions were "national and urgent" to Martí, and the very mention of them fired him with argument. Where would the youngster who left school at fifteen go with his reading, writing, and counting, his grammar that he neither understood nor applied, and his geography which he learned by memory? He disdained real work or did not know how to undertake it. Martí approvingly quoted William Arnold Anthony, American scientist and educator, who said:

> It makes the blood boil to see a handsome boy—who might have learned, instead of the pluperfect, what heat is and how man can make use of it—mumbling verbs, which in the street he will conjugate in a barbarous off-hand manner. Until we teach science in the schools we shall not have saved the Republic.[10]

Martí complained that the education which the children were receiving in the public schools was not designed to prepare them thoroughly for life in the United States, and had not been worked out according to the needs of the children. As a result, the education of its children had already become one of the country's major problems. Several factors contributed to this condition. The curriculum had not been planned with the idea of holding the child's interest. Naturally, the children developed dislike for the various subjects, while some who did not actually dislike them were indifferent in their attitude. Small wonder, then, that children always desired to get out of the classroom to play ball in the

10. See below, "The Annual Assembly of the American Association for the Advancement of Science."

streets and spend more time in the park. Of course, lack of discipline also contributed to the vagrant tendencies of the children, and Martí noted that discipline often was absent in the home as well as in the classroom. However, if the children were given the right guidance in the school, juvenile delinquency would be on the decline. The teen-age boys who visited the tobacco stores to buy cigarettes would engage in more wholesome activity, while the girls of the same age group would cease to consider themselves as adults. There was a distinct lack of cooperation between the school and the home, and since the child is reared in both of these institutions, this contributed to the inadequacy of the system of education in the public schools.[11]

Martí's general reactions to the universities and colleges of the eastern United States were quite different from those he revealed to the public schools. In the main, he believed the universities did what the public schools should do. They prepared the student for the type of life he intended to live. The public schools had a curriculum that all pupils must follow despite the fact that it was not suited to each pupil. But the universities had divisions or departments to accommodate students who specialized in different fields.[12] Martí was also impressed by the extent of college education for women in the United States. This comes through in his 1884 report of the graduation exercises at Vassar, the college for women in upstate New York. In an article written for the Spanish-language periodical *La América* of New York, he drew a complete picture of the occasion and elaborated it with his own witty and sagacious observations. The ceremony opened with a convocation by a Protestant clergyman. Here Martí commented that "in the United States every ceremony, private or public, festive or serious, be it a school celebration or a gathering of delegates to a political convention, begins

---

11. See below, "A False Concept of Public Education."
12. Trópico Edition, vol. XXXIII, p. 103.

with a prayer." The pastor, in black attire, raised his eyes to Heaven, and the members of the audience covered their faces with their hands and rested their heads on the backs of their seats or in front of them. "And that spontaneous prayer from free men vibrates," Martí remarked, but much of its impact was canceled for him by the lack of harmony in the churches.

Brief outlines of nine of the speeches of the female graduates were given as an example of what the students were being taught. They spoke on profound subjects in specific terms; they did not repeat from memory—a contrast to the prevailing practice in the New York public-school system. They did not offer proofs that the world is round, debate the capacity of qualifications for learning, nor recite the ancient names of inlets, coves, and river bends of historic Greece, "as we were made to do in our time, to the great satisfaction of parents and teachers (who in truth derived scant satisfaction from it)."[13]

Martí's conclusion concerning the issue of female education was that every nation requires for its salvation a certain portion of feminine intellectuality. Like wandering stars that shed soft light and illuminate the darkness, these "bachelors with long hair and harmonious form" are cast upon the nation each year. Martí assigned to female education the task of sweetening and spiritualizing life around it. Thus, as good wine is enhanced by delicate crystal, the influence of the spirit of a beautiful cultured woman is received with greater pleasure and profit. Not a very radical approach to female education, to be sure, but considering the fact that it was as yet a rarity in Latin America for women to attend colleges and universities, the attention Martí paid to female education in the United States in his dispatches to the Latin American press contributed to advancing the concept that such education was in the best interest of the nation. "Make instruction

13. See below, "The Distribution of Diplomas in One United States College."

so common among women," he wrote in *La América* of June 1884, "that the knowledge they possess will go unnoticed."

The schools that taught the science of life without smothering the imagination and sentiments, the practical institutions of industrial training in which the students' intelligence and character were developed, won Martí's high approval. It was in schools like Cooper Institute and Cornell University that Americans were being formed who would be able to meet and conquer the increasing influence of the

> bureaucratic Yankee, the Yankee who has a mania for holding public office, the hireling Yankee, the weak wasteful Yankee who proudly displays, at childish parties in his room, at a rhetorical university the shoulders that were produced by the excessive playing of polo or baseball.[14]

Cornell University, "a city of universities," where one might study bridge building, decompose bones in the laboratory, decipher Sanskrit, row, run, and jump, was, without doubt, Martí's favorite among the larger colleges and universities. It was the choice, he argued, of all who had a sincere desire to learn both philosophy and the crafts, politics and mechanics, in a methodical yet pleasant way. It was coeducational, and to it flocked the most noble and energetic youth of the nation—men and women—who, from the poverty of the villages or the rude sections of the city, "had given heed to the inner voice which demanded knowledge, and had come to forge for themselves implements with which to carve their passage along the stony path of life."

Cornell, Martí explained, drew its support partly from the productive lands donated by the government to the industrial schools, partly from the gifts of rich friends and funds left by its successful graduates who had been there without the

14. See below, "Manual School for Girls."

ability to pay at a time when the school was not the prosperous institution it was in the 1880s, with its ten buildings that housed classrooms, its eight laboratories, its twelve museums, its famous libraries, and its campus with the military field where "all who carry a book also carry a gun." This, he thought, was a good plan, for "the only way of overcoming imperialism in the larger countries, and militarism in the smaller ones, is for all to be soldiers."[15]

Another thing Martí liked about "natural life" at Cornell was its many trees, for a knowledge of trees and a love of them produced wealth and comfort of spirit. Brotherly trees bring rain from the clouds and offer shade and quiet for study.[16]

In 1890, after ten years in the United States, Martí found the school that almost fulfilled his ideal, and he entitled the article in which he described it "The University of the Poor." The school term opened with the mountain laurel in June and closed with the falling of the acorns in October; its campus was the shores of a lake and the slopes of the hills. There one could learn to cook by cooking and study astronomy by the light of the stars.

This was the free school of Chautauqua, New York, whose sylvan amphitheater was open to all those who, with only "a woman's handful of coins," wanted to live in one of the picturesque houses and learn, for the love of learning, the arts of housekeeping, commerce, painting, music, or any one of

15. Trópico Edition, vol. XXXI, p. 122; vol. XXVIII, pp. 84-85.

16. Ibid., vol. XXXI, p. 123. Unfortunately, Martí never commented on the fact that his favorite university, Cornell, dismissed Henry Carter Adams in 1887 as professor of economics because of his advanced ideas. Adams was dismissed upon the complaint of a wealthy benefactor of the university after he had delivered an unequivocal pro-labor speech. (*See* Richard Hofstadter and Walter Metzger, *The Development of Academic Freedom in the United States* [New York, 1955], pp. 418-19.)

the many subjects taught there. It became a town of ten thousand inhabitants during the summer months, and included those who preferred to read at home rather than attend classes. All over the nation, invalids and laborers registered for the four-year reading course on the classics.

Martí saw farmers' children at the camp, with glasses and round shoulders, who had come to read Horace and Virgil; men with sunken eyes who came to learn mechanics, bookkeeping, politics, declamation, or photography; hotel employees who wanted to read Goethe or Ibsen or learn Hebrew grammar; and women of all ages—mothers, teachers, and ladies, flirts and ugly women with glasses. Silk dresses and rough hands were not uncommon.

Delightedly Martí informed his readers that to matriculate in the literary and scientific circles of the Home University, Chautauqua's correspondence school, which had fifty thousand students, one had only to send fifty cents to John Vincent, Box 194, Buffalo, New York. Martí, who opposed any union of church and education, was pleased that Vincent, a bishop of the Methodist Church, had founded the institution not as a denominational project, but in behalf of the humble, and that leaders of other denominations had allied themselves with him. Here creeds were forgotten, and all applied themselves to the study of Nature.[17] Martí would also have been pleased (had he lived) to learn that the Chautauqua Institute had affiliated in some of its branches with his favorite school, Cornell University.

Despite his respect for many North American universities and colleges, Martí concluded that it would be of doubtful benefit for the youth of Latin America to come to the United States to study in these institutions. For he found much to shun, much to scourge "in the harsh selfish civilization of North America." The excessive covetousness in the United States took away the grace of youth and beauty of character. Moreover, in many of the universities there was

17. See below, "Chautauqua: A University of the Poor."

more ostentation than knowledge. Those institutions that were the favorites of the rich consumed the students' money, through thousands of dollars spent for personal vanity, and diverted them from the pursuit of learning.[18]

Hence Martí advised "Our America" to borrow the best in the educational systems of the "Other America," and develop a system of education for Latin America suited to its own national character. The four main aspects of this system would be:

1. Lay education, the only one that could insure liberty of conscience of both teachers and pupils:

> One has no right to teach the Catholic religion, nor an anti-Catholic religion, in schools; either honor is not one of the religious virtues, or education will be sufficiently religious if it is honest. That, yes, implacably honest. It is not proper for a teacher to claim as the only true religion, one which is held in doubt by the majority of the people, even if he shares it, or offend a religion to which, since the student follows it in free use of his judgment, he already has a right. Or is the Catholic Church so vapid and empty that it will crumble with the study of Nature and the teaching of human virtues? Or is it, perhaps, that it is against these virtues, that it fears them? Or has it come to so little that, although it be a divine doctrine, and therefore eternal, as its supporters affirm, this work of centuries cannot be sustained even by the prestige of tradition, or the influence exerted by solemnly lit churches on the imagination and the senses, the terror aroused in souls by the threat of damnation, its practice and reverence in all homes, or with the permission to teach its cult in schools to all boys and girls whose parents ask for it? [19]

18. Trópico Edition, vol. XXVIII, pp. 47, 52, 54.
19. *Trajectory and Actuality of Martí* (Center for Studies on Martí, La Habana, 1961), p. 31.

2. Scientific and technical education. The teachings of science constituted one of the basic aims of education, Martí emphasized, and modern technology in all its aspects ought to be taught from the elementary school on. Scientific and technical education was what assured the true growth of nations. Indeed, "the scientific element must serve as the backbone of the education system."

> Like the one who turns the sheath of his sword inside out, the entire transitory and unstable system of modern education must be completely changed. But there will be no true growth for a nation, or any happiness for men, until basic education becomes scientific—until a child is taught to manage those elements of the earth which are to nourish him when he is a man; until, when he opens his eyes to see a plow, he will know that a flash of lightning can draw it as an ox used to do in bygone days! For within a short time electricity will move plows.[20]

3. Education for life. To Martí the main function of education is to prepare the pupil for life. School must be like a shop, where the student may learn about the forces with which he will have to struggle later on. The foremost aim of education was to make the student fit for his or her historic moment and circumstance. "Education has an unavoidable duty to man—not to fulfill it is a crime—to make him fit for his times without causing him to deviate from the great and final living." And

> Since man's destiny is life, education must prepare him for living. He must learn in school the handling of the forces with which he will struggle in life. One should not call them schools, but shops. And the pen should be used in schools during the afternoon; but during the morning the hoe.

20. See below, "Classical and Scientific Education."

Again:

> To educate is to deposit in every man the whole of
> human effort preceding him; it is to make every man the
> totality of the living world up to the day in which he
> lives; it is to place him at the level of his time so that
> he may float above it, and not to leave him below his
> time so that he will be unable to keep afloat; it is to pre-
> pare the man for life.[21]

4. Education must have a national content. It was this,
Martí believed, that insured the ties of the student to his
social environment and to the nation. The danger of educating the students in foreign countries was that knowledge
acquired in these lands would make them look upon their
own nation with contempt and drive them to adopt a superior attitude to the institutions of their native land.

> The education of the sons of these smaller countries
> (of Latin America) in a country of an opposite character
> and superior wealth, can bring the student into a fatal
> opposition to his native country where he is to make use
> of his education—or into the worst and most shameful
> of human misfortunes, contempt for his own country—
> if when nourishing him with practices and knowledge
> unknown or underdeveloped in his native country, he is
> not taught how they relate to him, and if love and
> respect for the country where he is going to live is not
> maintained in the student. Let not the water he drinks
> be poisoned.[22]

In applying these four principles of education, Martí
stressed that the elementary—urban or rural—school was the
backbone of the nation. To serve this function it must

21. *Trajectory and Actuality of Martí*, p. 31, and see below, "A
School of Electricity."
22. Ibid., pp. 32-33.

provide compulsory, free, and universal education for everyone, an education which would insure the happiness, progress, and intellectual and material improvement of the nation,
by creating valuable and healthy men and women. Education
was a natural right, and by being born, everyone acquired
"the right to be educated, and then, in turn, the duty of
contributing to the education of others." Education was the
one fundamental necessity for democracy and freedom, for
"an educated country will always be free."[23]

When Martí spoke of universal education, he included the
female sex. "Education should be so common among women
that the one who has it is not noticed nor does she herself
notice it."[24]

The struggle against illiteracy was a cardinal feature of
Martí's educational philosophy. The men or women who
lacked elementary knowledge would not be able to fulfill
themselves, either individually or socially. "Knowing how to
read is knowing how to walk. Knowing how to write is
knowing how to ascend. Feet, arms, wings, all these are given
to man by his first and most humble schoolbooks."[25]

Martí had only a limited opportunity to put his educational theories into practice. He did teach classes to black
Cuban tobacco workers at "La Liga" ("The League") in New
York City, the classroom located close to Cooper Union.[26]
For a brief period, too, he produced a monthly magazine for
children which contained examples of what he believed
should be presented to young people. Named *La Edad de Oro*
(The Age of Gold), the magazine was founded in New York
in 1889. Four monthly issues appeared, all written exclusively by Martí, and then the magazine for children was

23. Ibid., p. 33.
24. Ibid.
25. Ibid.
26. See below, "Mondays at The League"; "A Beautiful Night at
The League."

discontinued owing to a disagreement between Martí and his partner A. de Costa Gómez, who was also the financial backer. The conflict arose when the sponsor insisted that the pages of *La Edad de Oro* reflect religious opinions. Martí, of course, refused.

But during the brief period of its existence, Martí wrote fairy tales, related the lives of Latin American liberators, summarized the *Iliad,* wrote several poems specifically for his young audience, and translated a few poems and tales from the French and English. In keeping with his theory that scientific and technical knowledge must be part of elementary school education, he wrote a detailed account for his young readers of the Industrial Exposition in Paris, marking the centennial of the French Revolution. "We must go to see the greatest marvel of them all," he told his young readers as he escorted them through the exposition grounds, "and feel the daring that melts when we see the human heart and makes us want to embrace all men and call them brothers. ... We enter ... the portico of the Palace of Industry."[27]

"Ignorance and superstition makes barbarians of men in every nation," he told his readers in "The Indian Ruins" as he described the barbarity of the Europeans toward the Indians of South America.[28] The lesson to be learned from studying the history of man (told by way of his houses) was that "man is the same everywhere, and appears and progresses in the same way, and makes and thinks the same things, their only differences being those determined by the lands in which they live." He was pleased to inform his young readers that today "all the peoples of the world know one another better and visit back and forth," and he predicted

27. See below, "The Paris Exposition."
28. See below, "The Indian Ruins."
29. See below, "The History of Man, Told By Way of His Houses."

that it was "as if a happy time were to come in which men treated each other like friends and are coming together." [29]

Recounting the contributions of great musicians, poets, and painters during the early years, Martí brought home to his young readers the fact that there were "more young people than old in this world. Most of humanity is composed of youths and children. Youth is the age of growth and development, activity and liveliness, imagination and impetuousity. When you have failed to take good care of your heart and mind while young, you may well fear that your old age will be desolate and sad." [30]

In his letter to María Mantilla (published below), Martí noted that he had tried to write in "pure and simple Spanish" in *The Age of Gold.* He succeeded admirably, and at the same time avoided writing condescendingly. He sought to raise their standards. Moreover, although Martí dealt at length with ancient times, he did not neglect contemporary issues. In "An Excursion in the Land of the Annamese"—Annam was later to become part of Vietnam—he described how the French, "waist-deep in blood," had "been robbing the Annamese of their country." Prophetically, he quoted an Annamese as saying of the French occupation: "Now they are our masters; but tomorrow, who knows!"

In the vehicle of expression he directed to children in the pages of the magazine, Martí included five poems that were to carry a message to the younger generation. The poem "Cado Uno a Su Oficio" (Each One to His Work) is a fable by Ralph Waldo Emerson that Martí translated. "Los Dos Príncipes" (The Two Princes) is an idea derived from the poet Helen Hunt Jackson (whom Martí admired for her devotion to justice for the Indians of the United States), [31] and put into Spanish verse to suit the purpose of the maga-

30. See below, "Musicians, Poets, and Painters."
31. Martí translated into Spanish the novel *Ramona,* by Helen Hunt Jackson.

zine—to combine a cheerful sense of play with the teaching of a lesson to the youthful readers.

The most famous poem of the group is "Los Zapaticos de Rosa" (The Rose-Colored Slippers), dedicated to "Mademoiselle Marie," one of the women who inspired Martí to write verse. It tells of the loss of the small rose-colored shoes, and what had happened to them. The child who possessed them had presented the shoes to another youngster whose feet were bare and cold. While her mother was scolding Pilar for the loss of the slippers, the mother of the other child explained that Pilar had given them to her little girl. Pilar's mother opened her arms and held her daughter close. Afterward she advised the child to give her cloak, ring, and purse to the other, less fortunate, young girl. When Pilar obeyed her mother, she not only gave her material possessions, but also a kiss to the other child. The moral of the story, of course, is human kindness. Probably more children in Cuba (and perhaps in all of Spanish America) have learned this poem by heart than any other.[32]

"With his monthly for children," write two distinguished critics, "Martí left us the only example of children's literature produced in the Spanish language, worthy of being compared to the most admirable in other languages. Never before or after 1889 was there published in Spanish such a beautiful and edifying review for children."[33] Hermanio

32. In her article, "Martí Intimo," Blanche Zacharie de Baralt includes an incident revealed to her by Ubaldina Guerra de Pujol which related to her childhood association with Martí and the poem. At three years of age, Ubeta (the nickname of Sra. Guerra de Pujol) could already recite "Los Zapaticos de Rosa," and one day when Martí visited the home, the young child sat upon his knee and gave the recitation. Martí was so impressed that the next day he sent the child a doll with rose-colored shoes, and with the gift a dedication in verse. (*Archivo José Martí* [La Habana, 1944], vol. VII, p. 398.)

33. Ivan A. Schulman y Manuel Pedro González, *Martí, Darío y el Modernismo* (Madrid, 1969), p. 33.

Alendros, a leading Spanish educator, writing in his study, *About "The Age of Gold,"* develops this theme further:

> ... *The Age of Gold* is the best-written work for young people in the Spanish language. To the universal collection of classics of literature for children and youth, France would contribute Perrault and Verne; Italy, *Pinocchio* and Cuore; Germany, Grimm; Denmark, Andersen; Sweden, the marvelous voyage of Nils Holgersson; the English-language countries, Nursery Rhymes, *Robinson Crusoe, Tom Sawyer,* Kipling. The countries of the Spanish language will point with pride to *The Age of Gold* of José Martí.

After voicing his regret that he had been deprived of the opportunity to read Martí's magazine when a child, the distinguished Spanish educator concludes:

> The writings of Martí for *The Age of Gold* are the most clear and truthful ever published in Spanish for children and young people. In the general climate of untruth and bias in which children's books have flourished, *The Age of Gold,* so frank and human, is like a miracle.[34]

In the preface to the Argentinian edition of 1953 (reprinted in the 1955 edition published in El Salvador), Fryda Schultz de Mantovani refers to *The Age of Gold* as a work "which has no equal in Spanish or Hispanic-American literature." Martí, she notes, liberated himself, in writing for children, "from the dry scholarly teaching and post-Romantic and domestic sentimentalism, whose boring models dominated the field." *The Age of Gold,* she concludes, is "a soliloquy to sons and

---

34. Hermanio Alendros, *Sobre "La Edad de Oro"* (Madrid, 1956), pp. 165, 223.

daughters: a voice which must not be lost in the wilderness."[35]

It is a miracle, moreover, that is constantly being renewed, for *The Age of Gold* continues to be reprinted in book form and is read not only in Cuba but in every country of Latin America.

On receiving news in Paris of Martí's death, Rubén Darío, the great Nicaraguan poet, called the New York journalist who sent "these kilometric epistles" to the Latin American press, "Martí, the thinker, the musician, Martí the poet always." There was also, of course, Martí the educator. As a journalist Martí read copiously almost every subject that was to occupy his pen. Márquez Sterling says of Martí:

> He went to bed with a book by Wendell Phillips and got up with another by Waldo Emerson. . . . In his room there was nothing but books, piled on chairs and on his night-table. He was reading at the time (1882) the pantheistic poetry of Bryant, the verses of Josiah Holland, and a large volume of Henry Ward Beecher. Upon the death of Darwin, he brought out a complete study of his work, proving his admiration for men of thought. He visited the study of the sage philosopher, commenting on the gruff Flourens and the scholarly Hechel; and in a general résumé he defined the origin of species.[36]

José Martí knew that his role was not merely to report—but to educate—and as a journalist, a pedagogue, an educational theorist, a teacher and writer for children and youth, José Martí ranks among the outstanding figures in the field.

35. José Martí, *La edad de Oro,* prólogo de Fryda Schultz de Mantovani (San Salvador, El Salvador, 1955), pp. 14, 33.

36. Rubén Darío, in *Archivo José Martí* (La Habana, 1944), vol. VII, pp. 325-26; Carlos Márquez Sterling, *Nueva y Humana Visión de Martí* (La Habana, 1953), p. 375.

It would be a mistake, however, to isolate Martí's educational principles from his other social ideas. He knew and he said that it meant little to poor peasants to teach them scientific agriculture if land was monopolized by a few wealthy aristocrats, or to teach mechanical education to workers if they were forced to endure hunger and unemployment. The great Cuban student activist, revolutionist, and one of the founders of the Cuban Communist Party, Julio Antonio Mella, makes this clear in his seminal essay, "Glosas al pensamiento de José Martí" (Interpretations of the Thought of José Martí). Mella points in this connection to Martí's famous assertion: "There can be no political democracy where there is no economic justice."[37]

Contrast between the old and new Cuba is nowhere more evident than in education. At the triumph of the Cuban Revolution of 1959, 23 percent of the population was illiterate and average school education was below third grade. In 1958, one year before the takeover by the revolutionary government, only 717,000 children attended primary schools; in 1973, the figure was 1,898,000. Before the revolution only a few thousand children attended secondary schools, but in 1973 there were more than 470,000. In 1958 there were 15,000 university students and in 1973 more than 60,000. In 1974 there were 758,000 workers taking continuation and technical courses. The real contrast is illustrated in the fact that in 1958 there were 811,000 students all told in Cuba while in 1973 the figure had leaped to almost three million, located all over the island, including the remote rural regions where hardly any schools existed before the revolution.[38] "In the basic secondary schools in the countryside,"

37. Julio Antonio Mella, "Glosas al pensamiento de José Martí," in *Siete enfoques marxistas sobre José Martí* (La Habana, 1978), pp. 13-14.

38. *Cuba Today: Sixteen Years of Socialist Construction* (La Habana, 1975), p. 24; Karen Wald, *Children of Che: Childcare and Education in Cuba* (Palo Alto, California, 1978), pp. 10-12.

wrote the late Juan Marinello, the great Cuban poet, critic, and revolutionary, "there has evolved a coordination between intellectual work and manual labor, a permanent attention to the works of Marx, Engels, and Lenin, and a tireless attention to the teachings of our José Martí."[39]

In a 1961 publication issued in Havana, two years after the triumph of the revolution and entitled *Martí Educador: Ideario Pedagogico,* the point is stressed that already the revolution had undertaken serious steps to wipe out illiteracy and to provide universal, free education, education which would combine the fundamental ideas of Cuba's greatest teacher—José Martí.[40] Indeed, the *Manual Para Alfabetizador,* issued to teachers in the celebrated, successful anti-illiteracy campaign by the Comisión Nacional de Alfabetización, Ministerio de Educación, features as its fundamental theme the following words of Martí:

> . . . Y me hice maestro,
> que es hacerme creador.
>
> . . . and I became a teacher,
> in other words a creator.[41]

39. *La Educación en Revolución,* prólogo para Juan Marinello (La Habana, 1974), p. 12.

40. *Martí Educador: Ideario Pedagógico* (La Habana, 1961), p. 43.

41. *Manual Para el Alfabetizador* (La Habana, n.d.), p. 4.

I

On Education

Popular Education[1]

I. Instruction is not the same as education: the former refers to thought, the latter principally to feelings. Nevertheless, there is no good education without instruction. Moral qualities rise in price when they are enhanced by qualities of intellect.

II. Popular education does not mean education of the poorer classes exclusively, but rather that all classes in the nation—tantamount to saying the people—be well educated. Just as there is no reason why the rich are educated and not the poor, what reason is there for the poor to be educated and not the rich? They are all the same.

III. He who knows more is worth more. To know is to possess. Coins are minted, knowledge is not. Bonds or paper money are worth more, or less, or nothing; knowledge always has the same value, and it is always high. A rich man needs money with which to live, but he can lose it and then he no longer has the means of living. An instructed man lives from his knowledge, and since he carries it with him, he never loses it and his existence is easy and secure.

IV. The happiest nation is the one whose sons have the best education, both in the instruction of thought and the

1. This selection is considered to be so reflective of Martí's deep concern for popular education that it is usually included as an introduction to that section of his collected works dealing with education.

direction of feelings. An instructed people loves work and knows how to derive profit from it. A virtuous people will live a happier and richer life than another that is filled with vices, and will better defend itself from all attacks.

V. Every man when he arrives upon this earth has a right to be educated, and then, in payment, the duty to contribute to the education of others.

VI. An ignorant people can be deceived by superstition and become servile. An instructed people will always be strong and free. An ignorant man is on his way to becoming a beast, and a man instructed in knowledge and conscience is on his way to being a god. One must not hesitate to choose between a nation of gods and a nation of beasts. The best way to defend our rights is to know them well; in so doing one has faith and strength; every nation will be unhappy in proportion to how poorly educated are its inhabitants. A nation of educated men will always be a nation of free men. Education is the only means of being saved from slavery. A nation enslaved to men of another nation is as repugnant as being enslaved to the men of one's own.

Guatemala (Mexico), January 1878

Itinerant Teachers

"But how would you establish that system of itinerant teachers we have seen mentioned in some book on education, the system you recommended in the last year's number of *La América,* which I have before me?" An enthusiastic gentleman from Santo Domingo respectfully asks us this question.

We will tell him briefly that it is an important matter, but not how to accomplish it.

There is a heap of essential truths that can fit upon the wings of a hummingbird, and yet they are the key to national peace, to spiritual advancement, and to the greatness of one's country.

Men must be kept in the knowledge of the land and of the durability and transcendence of life.

Men must live in peaceful joy, a natural and inevitable outcome of Freedom, the way they live in the joy of air and light.

A nation in which a taste for wealth and a knowledge of the sweetness, needs, and pleasures of life do not develop equally is condemned to death.

Men must know the composition, enrichment, changes, and applications of the material elements from whose development they derive the healthful pride of one who works directly with Nature, the bodily strength derived from contact with the forces of the land, and the honest and secure wealth produced by its cultivation.

Men need someone to stir their compassion often, to make their tears flow, and to give their souls the supreme benefit of feeling generous; for, through the wonderful compensation of Nature, that which is given increases; and whoever withdraws within himself, lives for small pleasures, is afraid to share them with others, and thinks only of greedily satisfying his own appetites, is gradually changing from a man into pure solitude, carrying in his heart all the gray hair of winter time. He becomes within, and appears to others—an insect.

Men grow, they grow physically and visibly, when they learn something, when they begin to possess something, and when they have done some good.

Only fools or egoists talk about misfortune. Happiness exists in the land, and it can be won by means of the prudent exercise of reason, the knowledge of universal harmony, and the constant practice of generosity. He who seeks it elsewhere will not find it, for, after having drained all the cups life has to offer, only in the aforementioned will he find flavor. It is a legend of the Spanish American lands that at the bottom of ancient cups there was a picture of Christ, so that when one of them was drained, people said: "Until we meet, my Lord!" For at the bottom of those cups a heaven unfolded—serene and fragrant, endless and overflowing with tenderness!

Being good is the only way of being happy.

Being cultured is the only way of being free.

With human nature in general, however, to be good one has to be prosperous.

And the only open road to a constant and facile prosperity is that of knowing, cultivating, and profiting from the inexhaustible and indefatigable elements of Nature. Nature, unlike men, is not jealous. Unlike men, she has no hates or fears. She does not bar the way to anyone, for she is not afraid of anyone. Men will always need the products of

Nature. And since every region produces only certain products, its trade will always be kept active, thus assuring wealth and freedom from want for all peoples.

So now there is no need to engage in a crusade to reconquer the Holy Sepulcher. Jesus did not die in Palestine; he is alive in every man. Most men have gone through life half asleep. They ate and drank but learned nothing about themselves. Now one must go on a crusade to reveal to men their own natures, and give them, with plain and practical scientific knowledge, the personal independence that fortifies a man's kindliness and gives rise to the pride and decency of being an amiable creature and a living force in the great universe.

This, then, is what teachers must take to the rural areas. Not merely explanations in the field of agriculture and mechanical implements, but the tenderness which is so lacking in men and does them so much good.

The farmer cannot leave his work to go so many miles to see some incomprehensible geometric figures, to learn the names of capes and rivers and peninsulas in Africa, and to be provided with empty didactic terms. The farmer's children cannot leave the paternal farm and day after day go mile after mile to learn Latin declensions and short division. And yet the farmers comprise the most valuable, healthful, and red-blooded segment of the population, because they receive directly and in full measure the emanations and the affable relationship with the soil from whose friendly intercourse they live. Cities are the minds of nations; but their hearts, from where the mass of blood is sent in all directions, are in the countryside. Men are still mechanical eaters and the shrines of worry. We must make every man a torch.

For we are proposing nothing less than a new religion with its new priests! We are describing nothing less than the missions by means of which the new era will soon begin to spread its religion! The world is changing; the regal priestly vestments, so necessary in the mystical ages of man, are lying upon their deathbed. Religion has not disappeared, it has been transformed. Above the affliction into which a study of the details and slow evolution of human history plunges observers, one can see that men are growing, and that they have already climbed halfway up Jacob's ladder; what beautiful poems are in the Bible! If huddled upon a mountain peak one suddenly glances at human progress, one will see that people have never loved each other as they do now, that in spite of the painful disorder and abominable selfishness to which a momentary absence of ultimate beliefs and faith in Eternal Truth is leading the inhabitants of this transitory age, the benevolence and impetus to expand, now burning in everyone, will never be of greater concern to human beings than they are today. They have stood up like friends who knew one another and wanted to meet and move forward to a mutually happy encounter.

We walk upon the waves, and, tossed about and caught in their swirling motion we fail to see, and perturbed by their action do not stop to examine, the forces that move them. But when the sea is calm, we can rest assured that the stars will be nearer to the earth. Man will finally sheathe his sword of battle in the sun!

The foregoing is what we could call the spirit of itinerant teachers. How happy the peasants would be if some good man arrived now and then to teach them things they did not know, and with the warmth of a communicative manner leave in their spirits the quietude and dignity that always remain after seeing an honest and loving man! Instead of talking about cattle breeding and crops, there would be an occasional discussion—until the subject could be covered constantly—of what the teacher taught, of the curious implements he brought them, of a simple way to cultivate the particular plant they have been working so hard to develop, of what a fine good man the teacher is. Because he makes them impatient, they would talk about when he would come again so they might ask him what has been occurring to them ever since they began to acquire knowledge; for their minds have been expanding incessantly, and they have started to think. How happy all of them would be to leave their hoes and shovels, and, filled with curiosity, take refuge in the teacher's campaign tent!

Extensive courses obviously could not be given, but if their propagators made a thorough study, they could certainly sow and cultivate the seeds of their ideas. They could awaken the appetite for knowledge. There would be some encouragement.

And this would be a sweet intrusion, carried out in agreement with what is a common concern of the human soul; for since the teacher would instruct the peasants in practical and profitable things in a gentle manner, those peasants would gradually and without effort absorb a body of knowledge which begins by flattering and serving their interests. For whoever attempts to make men better must not disregard their evil passions; he must consider them as an extremely important factor and see to it that he does not work against them, but rather for them.

Instead of sending pedagogues through the rural areas, we would send conversationalists; instead of pompous schoolmasters, instructed people responsive to the doubts presented to them by the ignorant, or responsive to the questions prepared for when those people should arrive. They would observe when the farmers made mistakes in agricultural procedure, or when they overlooked some source of wealth that could be developed, so they could be informed of these things and at the same time told how to remedy them.

In short, it is necessary to engage in a campaign of gentleness and knowledge, and give the farmers a body—not yet in existence—of missionary teachers.

The itinerant school is the only kind that can eliminate peasant ignorance.

And in the rural areas as well as in the cities, it is urgent to replace sterile and indirect book learning with the direct and fruitful knowledge of Nature.

It is urgent to open normal schools with practical teachers, to then scatter them over the valleys, mountains, and outlying regions, much as the Amazonian Indians tell us that to create men and women Father Amalivac scattered the seeds of the tropical palm over all the earth!

Time is wasted upon elementary literary education, for it creates people aspiring to pernicious and fruitless values. The establishment of a fundamental scientific education is as necessary as the sun.

La América (New York), May 1884

Rafael María de Mendive[1]

Sr. Enrique Trujillo[2]
My noble friend:

How do you wish me to say, in a few lines, all I might be able to say that is new and different about that man who loved beauty both in literature and the affairs of life, and who never wrote anything but the truths of his heart or the sorrows of his country? I will not discuss his life as a man, for anyone unaware of how he fought for Cuba with his clandestine sonnets and his printed satires, ever since the days of his youth; how he set the example in Spain, more necessary now than ever, of acquiring fame in Madrid without sacrificing faith in his own country; how he used his wealth more than once to enhance the life around him so that every bit of it shone like a work of art; how the loyal Cubans and liberal Spaniards could find a place at his table at all hours; and how

1. Rafael María de Mendive (1821–86), romantic poet, translator of *Irish Melodies* of Thomas Moore, and works by Byron, Longfellow, and others, founder of *Revista de la Habana,* was appointed director of the Elementary School for Boys in Havana when it opened on March 19, 1865. Martí, then twelve years old, was one of his students, and his contacts with Mendive, a backer of Cuban independence, left an indelible imprint on the future Cuban liberator. In this biographical sketch, Martí paid tribute to a great teacher.

2. Enrique Trujillo was the editor of *El Porvenir,* organ of the Cuban Revolution published in New York.

their country as much as he, and who, like himself, were writing about it, whether those people were thankless or sincere—anyone ignorant of all these things knows little about Cuba. I will say nothing here about the *Revista de la Habana,* or about his translation of Thomas Moore's[3] *Irish Melodies,* or about his filial fondness for José de la Luz[4] and his brotherly fondness for Ramón Zambrana; or about the tender affection felt for him by both the young and the white-haired men who carried Cuba in their hearts even when disappointments soured their dispositions a bit—the men who saw their brave and elegant country reflected in his fine poetic soul. How can I forget those nights in the Calle del Prado at the school he called San Pablo because la Luz called his El Salvador? José de Armas Céspedes hid in Rafael Mendive's own room to escape from the Spanish police. In the courtyard under the banana plants the boys recited Señor Mendive's sonnet to Lersundi.[5] Always dressed in his white drill, he could hear, albeit faintly, the play which Tomás Mendoza was rehearsing for him in the lecture hall. Or he changed the line "the glory of Bolívar[6] and Washington,"

3. Thomas Moore (1779–1852), Irish poet.

4. José de la Luz y Caballero (1800–62), professor of philosophy at the College of San Francisco, and later founder and president of the College San Salvador, one of the great intellectual influences in Cuba. He was accused in the so-called slave plot, "La Escalera," of 1844, but was acquitted.

5. General Francisco Lersundi, reactionary captain-general of Cuba, ex-Carlist and Minister of War, who had suppressed a revolt in Spain in 1848. This was a satirical sonnet.

6. Simon Bolívar (1783–1830), named El Libertador for having rescued South America from the Spanish yoke, and often described as the George Washington of South America. In 1825 Bolívar visited Upper Peru, the name of which was changed in his honor to Bolivia. For Martí's discussion of Bolívar's career, see *Our America: Writings on Latin America and the Struggle for Cuban Independence,* by José Martí, edited with introduction and notes by Philip S. Foner (New York, 1978), pp. 98–108.

which the censor had stricken from Francisco Sellén's "Elegy for Miguel Angel,"[7] to "the glory of Harmodius and Aristogiton"[8] in such a way that the censor failed to notice that the original meaning remained intact. Or, à propos of one or another Sedano, he dictated some sextains about "the undecided ones" which exploded like the crack of a whip. Or he defended the glory of Cuba from hispanophobes and petticoat authors who wanted to steal it from the poetess Avellaneda. Or, his elbows upon the piano, he and the engineer Roberto Escobar, and the lawyer Valdés Fauli, and the landholder Cristóbal Madán,[9] and the student Eugenio Entenza followed the march of Céspedes[10] on the map of Cuba. One day he gave me his watch to pawn for six *onzas* to help a needy poet, and then, in tears, I presented him with a new one that we students had bought for him.

Or I could talk about some of his former life, when he had just been named headmaster of the school and had recently married for the second time, into a houseful of angels. These angels used to sit with us at night, whispering over their embroidery, to hear the history class that Rafael Mendive taught for the sheer pleasure of teaching it. Or they would

7. Martí's discussion of Francisco Sellén will appear in the next volume, dealing with his literary criticism.

8. Harmodius and Aristogiton, according to popular but erroneous legend, freed Athens from the tyrants.

9. Cristóbal Madán was a powerful merchant and planter of Matanzas (owner of the Rosa sugar mill, Cimarrones), who made himself an American citizen, became a leading advocate of annexation of Cuba to the United States in the 1850s, and later of Cuban independence from Spain. Martí's first revolutionary poem, "Abdala," was published in *La Patria Libra,* a journal edited by Mendive and Cristóbal Madán.

10. Carlos Manuel de Céspedes (1819–74), Cuban revolutionist, planter in Oriente, who issued the call (*Grito de Yara*) from his sugar farm, La Demajagua, which opened the Ten Years War for Independence. For Martí's estimate of Céspedes, see the previous volume, *Our America,* pp. 193–200.

listen from behind the shutters to what we had to say before
the board of examiners, composed of Valdés Fauli, Domingo
Arosarena, Julio Ibarra, the Count of Pozos Dulces,[11] and
Luis Victoriano Betancourt, on the subject of "the sorrowful
Alcibiades" or "the magnanimous Artaxerxes" or "the
sublime Graco brothers," whereupon they would be expelled
for being mischievous little girls. It was marvelous—and I do
not use this word lightly—how Mendive's power of understanding was able to detect a man's true character at a glance;
how, knowing so little about the sciences, he would sit down
and talk to us about physical forces when poor Manuel Sellén
was absent. Mendive fascinated us. In the evening, before his
friends arrived, he used to dictate to his young amanuensis
some scenes from his unpublished play *The Black Cloud,* or
some chapters from his novel of Havana society in which he
scourged with roses the heroes of gossip and dandyism in
such a manner that their scheming, eye-winking ways were
exposed to the reading public.

Shall I describe him as a prisoner in a cell of the Prince's
castle,[12] waited upon by his faithful Micaela and his children
and students? Or in Santander, where the Spaniards welcomed him with palm leaves and banquets? Or in New York,
where he came to escape from Spain, to share the lot of the
Cubans there, and to celebrate with his vehement winged
poetry the hero who fell upon the battlefield, and the good
Spaniard who had no desire to rise up against the land that
gave him his bread and his children? Or in Nassau where,

11. Francisco de Frias y Jacob, second Count of Pozos Dulces
(1809–77), educated in Baltimore, succeeded his father in the family
estate in Cuba. A student of science in Europe, he was a Cuban
reformer who favored abolition of slavery and edited the reform journal, *El Siglo.*

12. Mendive was imprisoned for his revolutionary activities, and a
visit to his imprisoned teacher when he was thirteen years old left a
deep impression on Martí.

dressed in white as in Cuba, silent and ill-humored, he finally rebelled, whip in hand, against *Les Misérables*?[13] Or in Cuba after the truce, when he gave this reply to an anxious student: "Do you believe that if there had been some hope for at least ten years, I'd be here?" But why repeat what everybody knows; why think that the ten years have passed? I prefer to remember him when on his long and lonely walks from the shed, or in his quiet house, he would spin his poetry out of the moonlight or starlight and the rustle of leaves; or when, talking of those who died upon the Cuban scaffold, he would rise angrily from his armchair, his chin trembling.

Your
José Martí

El Porvenir (New York), July 1, 1891

13. *Les Misérables*, published in 1862, was Victor Hugo's best-known novel, and by the end of the century had sold over seven million copies.

Bronson Alcott[1]

Some famous men have died recently: William Corcoran,[2] who ennobled his advanced years by employing for the good of the public the fortune he acquired in his courageous enterprises; the satirist David Locke, renowned under his pseudonym of Petroleum V. Nasby,[3] who contributed to

1. Amos Bronson Alcott (1799–1888), educational pioneer and transcendentalist who, in his schools, attempted to treat children as individuals. Alcott was the progenitor of the progressive educator, but was a failure in all of his projects and was rescued from financial distress by his daughter, Louisa May Alcott, and her successful book for children, *Little Women,* published in 1863. Alcott is satirized in Henry James's *The Bostonians* (1886), but was honored by his contemporaries in Boston and esteemed by posterity.
2. William Wilson Corcoran (1798–1888), banker and broker in Washington, D.C., in 1840 formed the banking firm of Corcoran & Riggs, which has continued under various changes of name and organization to the present day. On April 1, 1854, he retired from active business and devoted himself until the time of his death to the management of his properties and to his philanthropic interests. Among the latter, the Corcoran Gallery of Art, in Washington, ranks high.
3. David Ross Locke (1833–88), journalist and political satirist, who, under the name of Petroleum V. Nasby, achieved fame during the Civil War. His creation, Petroleum V. Nasby, was a caricature of the pro-slavery, pro-Southern Copperhead, whom Locke depicted as an illiterate, hypocritical, cowardly, loafing, lying, dissolute country

the winning of the war against the South, and to the benevolence of the victors, with critical letters that delighted Lincoln, and in which his extraordinary wit was an effective vehicle for his just ideas—like a jester with bells and cap in the ancient courts, he was the spokesman of oppressed freedom; the botanist Asa Gray,[4] who began life as a tanner and farmer and died well known to every scientific circle for having been Darwin's[5] greatest deputy and of most help to him in demonstrating the theory of evolution in the realm of plants where, in the constant struggle for existence, the superior excludes the inferior and the predominant species survives.

But none of these men, although they were all creators and worthy of veneration, lived as pure a life as did that little old dreamer who used to sit at the window of his celebrated but humble parlor every morning in the philosophical town of Concord, to wave at everyone who passed by as though giving a benediction. What person, even the most hardened merchant, would fail to tenderly return the greeting of that stainless idealist, friend of the trees, who never put meat upon his table, companion of Thoreau[6] the hermit and of the august Emerson—Amos Bronson Alcott?

---

preacher. Abraham Lincoln was one of Locke's most fervent admirers, and frequently read from Nasby's letters.

4. Asa Gray (1810–88), noted American botanist and author of five important textbooks in the field of botany. Charles Darwin first outlined his theory of the evolution of the species to Gray, and the American botanist became Darwin's chief advocate in this country.

5. Charles Darwin (1809–82), British naturalist, renowned for his theory of evolution, published in his 1859 work, *On the Origin of Species.*

6. Henry David Thoreau (1817–62), social rebel who is best known for his masterpiece *Walden* (1854) and for his essay "Resistance to Civil Government" (1849), which influenced Ghandi. In 1848 Thoreau refused to pay a poll tax because the money went to a government which was waging war on Mexico in the interest of the slave owners.

Just as poetry—pure restraint—bursts forth more musically and brilliantly when, because it is not a common quality, it is purified by solitude and indignation on the part of anyone who possesses its terrible inspiration, so the idealistic life of this Platonic philosopher, who went out to sell books as a boy and returned from his sally writing them, reached a celestial repose and the whiteness of snow in his harsh and busy country. The more brutal it was, the clearer was his duty not to be. For whiteness to be seen, let it shine forth! If men encourage their beastliness with bad behavior, I shall use mine to encourage whatever they have of the dove. Since there are so many men with mouths, from time to time there should be a man with wings. Duty is fortunate, though it may not seem so, and simply complying with it lifts the soul to a perennial state of kindness. Love is the bond of men, the way to teach, and the center of the world. What Plato[7] said must be repeated until men live according to his doctrine. Teaching must be done by conversation, the way Socrates[8] did it, from village to village, field to field, house to house. Intelligence is only half of the man, and not the better part. What kind of schools are these where only the intelligence is trained? Let the teacher place himself on equal terms with his pupil, and man be in friendly cooperation with his fellow creature, and may they learn in strolls through the countryside the soul of botany which is no different than the universal, and by studying their house plants and animals and the celestial phenomena confirm the identity of creation. In this knowledge and in the happiness of goodness, let men live without the childish quarreling and meaningless torment—heavy as

7. Plato (427–347 B.C.), a disciple of Socrates, one of the great philosophers whose idealistic views inspired many social reformers in the United States, most notably the Transcendentalists, who advanced the ideas of Neoplatonism.

8. Socrates (466–399 B.C.), Athenian philosopher and leading figure in Plato's *Dialogues;* suffered death by drinking hemlock for having been accused of fostering impious notions among his students.

iron and vain as froth—which is the result of that bestial state of spirit dominated by sensuality and arrogance. Anyone who disregards the reality of idea and the spiritual fruition that comes from the constant practice of love knows nothing of the world's delight!

Alcott prefers the soul of the heart to that of the mind and to that of the realm of desires; hegemony must not come from the soul alone, but from a healthy relationship of these three. Satisfactions that make death unnecessary come from the spirit, for they contain the loftiness of pleasure and luminous rest which, because of hope rather than certainty, one assumes to be a part of death. But just as judgment matures sensibility, and by known sentiment the human being rises to pleasure, so must one recognize and observe the law of the body whose harmony leads to spirituality; for in the corporeal as in the spiritual, health is indispensable to beauty, and the latter—in man as in the world of which he is the sum and substance—depends upon balance. That is what Bronson Alcott preached, and that is how he lived. His house was a cenacle, his family a garland, his existence a lily.

Where did such a pure man come from if not from work and a natural life? He was not born in the city, which misleads one's judgment, but in the country, which puts it in order and cleanses it. His father was a farmer. A dog and a horse were his first friends. He ploughed, planted, and harvested. The refined ear that he drew to himself from Nature he laid close to the harmony and teachings of the world, so that when his father, seeing how intelligent and talkative he was, believed—as fathers usually do—that he ought to put into practice these blessed gifts in the profitable deceptions of commerce, he did not engage in trade with his trunkful of books. They had been put upon the back of a little nag so he could tour the villages for a purchaser, but he himself was a living book. That beardless one, who was so willingly given a bed to sleep in and bread and butter to eat, talked to the peasants in such heartfelt language about the poetry of his labors and about how to be spiritually happy that they listened to him with pleasure and amazement.

The trunkful of books returned little less than full; and Bronson Alcott established his first school, and with it the groundwork for his fame and his renown as an innovator. For if now there is corporal punishment in the public schools here, in those days it was a matter of drawing blood from the buttocks and hands, which so infuriated Alcott that, in order not to inflict torture upon his pupils, he did not even impose the torture of books upon them, preferring to impress them —by a love not exempt from firmness—with the knowledge he imparted to the child by talking to him about knowledge as a whole and its results, a pleasurable and profitable method for children. He did not indulge in long and disjointed studies of mere methods of how to gain knowledge, which neither accommodate the mind to its natural impatience nor discipline it easily and efficiently; nor do they reveal to the child, with the adjustments and understanding of all he sees, the law of his own happiness and that of the world.

His fame and his critics increased at the same time. It is painful to read what priests, poets, and teachers wrote—when Alcott founded his celebrated Temple School—in defense of corporal punishment and routine education.

Develop the whole man, said Alcott thirty years ago— morally, intellectually, and physically—by gentle means which dispose him to gentleness, thus building him up instead of tearing him down, while at the same time revealing to him the universal law of his destiny, which is either a crime of nature, or love. Train the citizens of a republic in the habit of investigation, in communication with men, and in the constant use of words, for that republic will collapse if its sons are lacking in those virtues. What we are creating are lawyers, doctors, clergymen, and merchants; but where are the men? Christianity itself will vanish from the world because the ministers who live by interpreting it are transmitting its inert and obscure letter, not the spirit that reveals the pettiness of those ministers and the greatness of Creation, for the knowledge of that spirit and the faith that comes from it are indispensable to man's happiness! "Your system is a fair one," Emerson told him, for he never feared to plead for abandoned reason. "Do not let the enemies of kindness discourage you; do not forsake your preaching for a single minute."

He had to abandon the school, but not his preaching or that purity of soul which, in the daily communication of these noble ideas, gave his life such splendor, his schoolhouse such fame, his discourse such magic, that people came from everywhere to hear the author of *Tablets,* which were like maxims of this Neoplatonism. They came to hear the man who wrote ideas that shone like lights in that historic *Dial,* where Transcendental Philosophy was left more beautiful after he endowed it with his Orphic Sayings. They came to hear that philosopher, famous among transcendentalists, who wanted to make the world's chance events conform to its essence, man to the universe, and life to its end. They came to hear him talk, the way the disciples of Socrates listened to their master whom Alcott resembled in this and in the clarity with which he explained his ideas of the world—but not in Socrates' irony, which in Alcott's case was indignation, nor in Xanthippe's either, because a woman who did not object to his apostleship, but understood and encouraged it, made his life pleasurable in its poverty, as did a chorus of faithful daughters. He finally had to set aside days, almost always during the summer, for those philosophical conversations whose subject matter circulated in advance and which Alcott developed most fully in his monologues, at times so sublime that a friend knew somebody who came away from one of them "because of the glare from his face." He retired to Concord like Plotinus[9] to his Campania, and like Plotinus,

9. Plotinus (205–270 A.D.), philosopher and religious thinker who

and with no better luck, in a country house surrounded by a small amount of arable land, tried to establish among men a model for the ideal life. But by then he no longer had any enemies as did the one from Lycopolis; nor, like Plotinus, did he discredit with school texts and fallacious eloquence the dignity and simplicity of that happy and to a certain extent brilliant doctrine. With that doctrine upon his lips, he died. He was a bad businessman.

La Nación (Buenos Aires), April 29, 1883

---

transformed a revival of Platonism in the Roman Empire into what modern scholars call Neoplatonism, and exercised great influence on the thought of the Islamic world and on European thought until the seventeenth century.

Peter Cooper[1]

To the Editor of *La Nación:*

Flags are at half staff—and so are hearts: Peter Cooper is dead. What he leaves behind is a nation of sons. I was not born in this country and he never knew of me, yet I loved him like a father. If he had crossed my path I would have kissed his hand. And when the fragrant spring flowers upon their newly grown stems open to the air and sunlight of May—not those pale and sickly hothouse blooms of winter—I shall pick a bouquet of wildflowers in some nearby field and leave them at the grave where, like the robe of an angel fallen to earth when the winged owner begins his flight, lies the body of that gentle and loving old man. He is dead, and those who knew him well have placed a lyre upon his breast amid the praises of the entire city. So it was at his grave. Oh, that marvelous breast upon which, after ninety-three years of earthly life, a lily is opening! Life is now like the battle of a white-robed youth who with feeble hands is arguing in the

---

1. Peter Cooper (1791–1883), manufacturer, inventor, philanthropist, founded Cooper Union or Cooper Institute at Astor Place, New York City, in 1857–59 "for the advancement of science and art." Free courses were given in general science, chemistry, electricity, civil, mechanical, and electrical engineering as well as in art. There were also free lectures, and the Institute maintained an excellent reading room and library service.

middle of the night to prevent armies of abject and satanic beasts from soiling his white robe with their vicious teeth—beasts that had attacked him at every turn in the road, dragging their heavy bellies, their human faces glowing from the sinister flash of their eyes, a muddy liquid dripping from their eager fangs, ravenous for robes. The world justly prostrates itself to see a man die who has kept his robe immaculate in his passage through the army of wild beasts.

He loved, founded, comforted. He practiced the human Gospel. He put peace into rancorous hearts, bread into outstretched hands, sustenance into eager intelligences, dignity into life, happiness into himself, and glory into his people. He leaves a school where two thousand artisans are learning, where thousands of men are calmed by reading; for there is no altar in any cathedral which raises its saint higher than Peter Cooper raised this college! During his lifetime he plowed the earth, cleared the woodlands, mended cloth, invented machines to cut it; machines to calm the sleep of children, empty mines, navigate canals, and put brakes upon steamboats, which before his day rebelled as if angry to be stopped. Like a provident mother the earth bared its breast to him. He boiled ores, an exercise bestowing an unusual strength; new worlds seem to be boiling in the big ovens whose splendor gives men the aspect of gods.

He lived serenely because he lived without sin. For him his wife was not an impious amazon leading her horse by the bridle badly, like other wives; she was a wing. He was so tender that he appeared weak, but he had that magnificent energy of gentle men. He would weep when he heard a child, but he started the first locomotive in its successful run across the forests of America. And from making a cap for an aged neighbor lady, with his skill as a hatmaker, he rose to draw with a steady hand a machine to subdue and utilize the power of the tides.

He attended school for only fifty-two days, but every year hundreds of men and women leave the school he founded, prepared with arts and sciences like shields for the battle of life. His parents were impoverished. At the age of five Peter Cooper helped his father sell beer. At ten he was making hats; at fifteen, when he wanted some shoes he made the last with his own hands, and then the shoes. Soon he was making carriages, and the savings he gave to his indigent father. The war with England caused a national shortage of clothing and cutting machines, so he made the latter—that poor little beer seller! With his earnings from the machines, and despite all he gave away—for he lived by giving—he came to New York to sell spices on the site where today his generous Institute rescues souls. He built and purchased factories, invented industrial chemicals, drained swamps, excavated sand pits, broke up woodlands, supported thousands of men, discovered where there was need, overcame everything that stood in his way, built colossal iron mills, abandoned all his inventions so that others could profit from them, gave his property to his children and accumulated more, and grew like a ground swell. And he always held his calm and patriarchal hands over the tormented heads of men!

For Peter Cooper, it was not a sign of virtue to do good, but a crime not to. He would have trembled with fear, as if some huge monstrous hand had vented its fury upon him, on a day when he had failed to do some good deed. He believed that human life is a priesthood, and egoistic well-being an apostasy. He never faced God because he was angry at feeling Him but not seeing Him, nor did he shake his fist at disdainful Heaven; but he lived a gentle life, like someone who caught a glimpse of supreme pleasures, and he was successful because he knew the object of life. Only one key unlocks the doors of happiness, and that is love. He who loves does not suffer even when he is suffering, because intoxicating aromas issue from the love that devours men's souls as from a bowl of burning incense. He saw that the greatest pleasure comes from doing good, and the greatest torture from being unable to do so; that pure grief nourishes, but impure or niggardly grief, like the height of human suffering, lashes the soul like handfuls of bristling wire upon the flanks of crazed horses in the barbarous races of Roman carnivals.

And he saw that whoever locks himself up lives with lions, and whoever is open and outgoing and gives himself to others lives among doves. When evil people sank their furious teeth into him, he felt no pain from having been bitten, only from the fact that there was still a tooth left to do the biting. And he would lay his hand upon the brow of the attacker and look him in the eye in such a gentle way that the defeated attacker finally withdrew his teeth from the wound.

In short, Peter Cooper lived certain of a later life whose beginnings were already flooding him with light. No earthly pleasure whatever, nor any orchestral music at all, seemed comparable to those melodies and pleasures of his spirit. "Why do you give me this title of Doctor of Law?" he once asked the chancellor who brought him the honored Latin inscription upon parchment with which the university rewarded that man who had received such high marks at the University of Nature. "If you give it to me because I've preached how to be successful, which is to be good; because I'm proving by my long life that to give strength to others fortifies one's own strength; because I'm still teaching, with my pure white hair and my still-rosy cheeks, that whoever feeds upon young ideas is always young himself; because I'm spreading the fact that learning is not the mortarboard of a professor, or the mystery of initiates, or the privilege of mental aristocrats, but rather man's only way of understanding the laws of life—then give me your generous parchment, despite the fact that I am not a scholarly gentleman and that all Latin is Greek to me." And this man who said those things was ninety years old!

He was never strong of body, which did not mean that he was weak of spirit. He never left one purpose until he had accomplished it, and only then did he move on to another. To every marvel of natural force he opposed another marvel of mental force. As the sun warms fish eggs, his hand warmed inventions. Whatever he touched turned out improved. During his years of stale bread and a pine-board table, he had to rock his baby's cradle as his wife watched over the stew; and out of his fertile mind came a little contraption to rock the cradle, chase the flies, and be a music box. He was made to buy a long stretch of coastline which everyone looked upon as a ruinous thing to do, but he made it fertile. A railroad would be good for taking ore out of the ground, but those forested regions are full of curves, and the engines of those days, like iron crocodiles, took the curves badly. So Cooper examined those engines, rebuilt their insides, created the tubular boiler, and started the first locomotive running across America. People paid dearly for produce shipped by rail—produce which they could buy for less if it came by canal—but horses on the banks pull the produce-carrying barges up the canal very slowly. So Peter Cooper devised a Cyclopean system of chains running along the banks of the canal and enabled the barges to travel a mile in six minutes. Ore had to be taken down from a very high mine over a steep grade to a distant depository, and no one knew how the bucketsful of ore would go, or how the empty buckets would be brought back. But he invented a rotary apparatus that hauled the buckets above the slope and was three miles long; the full buckets at the mine traveled on the apparatus by gravity down the steep grade as the lightweight empty ones returned on the rebound, propelled by the buckets again leaving the top. He heard that Turkey was suffocating Greece and staining it with blood; why must a nation boasting of independence change its own evil men into apostles and its doves into ravishing lions? Peter Cooper sat down to devise an apparatus of destruction, a torpedo that could be guided from the shore by many long wires, the way a horse's reins guide the horse, and by impact knock a Mohammedan ship to pieces. He thought it would be good—so that log fires would not put out the flames upon the altar where spiritual fires must burn—to erect the Institute of Arts and Sciences as an acid test, and to spend seventy-five thousand dollars on preparatory machinery to produce iron girders. And it produced them . At times he was regarded as a Satan of good. Whenever he overcame some malignant natural force, his wide lips spread into a smile filled with angelic malice. He enjoyed shutting himself up by himself among the retorts and blow-torches. He was not looking for gold because he had that within him, but he was looking for a means of snatching some secret from Nature, after which he would laugh glee-fully like a player satisfied that he has won a hard-fought game, or a child who finally finds the toy its mother hid. He sought a way of producing expensive spices at small cost so the poor could enjoy them, for the poor were his friends. He was always seated among his workmen, asking them if they wanted higher salaries, or if their work was very tiring, or what they wanted him to do to lessen their suffering; but at his lathes, nobody suffered. Everything his genius produced he dumped onto the pillows of the unfortunate. He considered every cent he earned an obligation to give. He viewed himself as the administrator of his wealth, not as its owner. With every profitable business transaction he added another good classroom to his Institute. His industriousness brought him millions, and millions he put back into charity. Quietly, and never permitting any ostentatious reward or formal recognition or public praise. He headed all the great enterprises; because of him, telegraphy was improved. Because of him. When he noticed an occasional broken wire, he did not become discouraged and anticipate astronomical sums of money, and the wire was finally repaired. He immersed himself in his private affairs, in his school, which he watched over daily, and in public concerns. Do not ask if he had children, for I shall tell you that all his workers were his children. He carried his wounds in his heart, he begged the wealthy to be merciful, he entreated the discontented to be patient, and he showed them and gave them as proof all the treasures which, like magic ribbons out of a magician's hat, came out of that poor cap he stitched in his youth for the old neighbor lady. He never believed in the efficacy of anger, only in that of knowledge. He preached that ignorance sometimes goes as far as to make justice abhorrent. He announced to all those people that there is no power that can combat a cultivated human intelligence. From the harmony of all known laws, and of the imperfection and brutal rudeness of present-day human life, he inferred that man does not yet glimpse all of life's tractable and ample rules, and that the earth keeps a surplus of easy benefits from which to calm the desires of all its inhabitants. To study the forces of Nature and learn how to manage them is the most direct way to solve social problems. Intellectual intercourse ennobles. The ignorant man has not begun to be a man. Man carries all his swords and all his spears in his mind.

But it was not enough for Peter Cooper to alleviate; he had to redeem. Beneficence is a narcotic, not an effective medicine. It dries the tears but not the source of the tears. And Peter Cooper, who had once begun the tearful working day unshod, tried to strengthen men's feet for the working day. Why learn in the schools words whose sense is not understood, numbers whose capricious combinations sit idly in the mind like cold and disjointed bones in a physician's cabinet, and various geographical boundaries which one flight of the mind brings to the brain and another carries away? So take the unfortunate ones out of those urns of life—for that is what the schools ought to be—and see if with those shields and bucklers the battle can be well fought! Men live by chance alone and the kindness of others, and by laboriously creating for themselves in greater times what should have been learned with preparation in lesser times with no work whatever. Since man is living, he must be prepared for life by education. In school he must learn to manage the forces against which he has to struggle in life. Workshops, not schools, should be indicated. The pen should be wielded at school in the afternoon, but in the morning the hoe.

Thus Peter Cooper, who yearned to learn but had no place in which to do so, when he had already counted off seventy-four years of his beautiful life, thought of opening a house of industry, arts, and sciences for those who must live from the labor these require. Will you not teach riding to a man who intends to be a desert horseman? Well then, teach the Land, the varied and throbbing living Land, to him who must live upon it and from it! Solemn arches were built, spacious pavements were laid out, bookshelves were filled with thousands of volumes, eminent teachers were given professorships, doors were flung wide open, and uncultured workers filed through them as if through the waters of a river of redemption. There go some to the School of Chemistry! There go others to the Schools of Wood Carving, Photography, Practical and Mechanical Drawing, Machinery! A crowd of men and women who are learning the arts of life in that noble school are coming in together to receive their year-end degrees, and leaving—the reins of fortune in their hands—to serve in the positions which the school itself provides! Enter. What silence! Two thousand men are reading. Keep on going. What loveliness! Three hundred young girls are studying. And look down those vast corridors and into those magnificent classrooms. Excited groups are waiting for the Institute's teachers to come and explain to them how to manage such instruments, or drive such apparatuses, or how social forces move, or how electricity is stored and carried, or why Peter Cooper wants it said that the only religion worthy of man is that which does not exclude anyone from its fold.

And now he is dead, now he is dead! No longer will he come every Saturday, leaning upon the arm of his daughter, to visit his beloved Institute as was his custom. No longer will that grateful crowd of young people look into his eyes as they wait for him at the foot of the stairs, and stop him in the street, and fill the air with their cheers, and wave their hats frantically in his praise. No longer will those uncouth and not very ceremonious men who drive loaded carts and wagons greet him respectfully, moving aside to let his carriage go by. No longer will those multitudes of the poor wait for him and hang onto the door of his carriage, sure of his bounty, as they used to do every day. No longer will he step down from his old and rickety carriage and, with his ninety-three-year-old hands that have amassed millions, mend a broken rein with cord and a wooden needle; or talk from the footboard of his carriage to the crowds of people congregated there and moved at the sight of him—people who shouted praises to their simple benefactor loudly and long! The entire city walked behind his casket. An assemblage of people, so large that it seemed as if they wanted to carry off upon their backs the church in which he lay, crowded around that church in the rain. Fifteen thousand New Yorkers saw the body of that old man in six hours.

The church was a basket of flowers, the streets a carpet of bared heads. Senate and House, City Hall, and Chamber of Commerce, all announced their mourning, proclaimed him father of the nation, and wore black armbands.

When men, women, and children—and servants—heard his name spoken in their homes, they stood up. And because of a sensitive and unheard-of allegiance, women at the windows removed their plumed and gaily colored hats when they saw his casket go by!

José Martí

La Nación (Buenos Aires), June 3, 1883

The False Myth
of Latin Inferiority

Of the many books which have interested the monthly *La América,* one of them must gladden the heart, and it is nothing but a college catalogue.

We do not like that catalogue merely because it furnishes us with subject matter for empty and facile celebrations of new advances, which are celebrated better with arduous toil than with brainless words that simply by repetition rob the ideas they embrace of energy and prestige; but because in the pages of that little book the Latin intelligence springs to the fore in humble but eloquent proof.

Nature did not give us the palm trees of our forests and the Amazon and Orinoco that water our lands, in vain. The ample Hispano-American mind comes from those rivers, its fame from those palm groves, its wisdom from what is preserved of the Indian culture, its ostentatious and volcanic characteristics from the fruits of the earth, its qualities of indolence and the artistic from what the Spaniards brought of the Arabic. Oh, the day when the Hispano-American mind commences to shine, it will shine like the sun—the day when we consider our present provincial existence as dead. Academies of Indians; expeditions of farmers to the agricultural countries; periodic and constant voyages, with serious purposes, to the more developed lands; incentive and science in the planting of seeds; opportune presentation of our products to foreign countries; an extensive network of railways within each country and from one country to another; an absolute and indispensable dedication to a respect for foreign ways of thinking—this is what is coming, even if in some lands it can only be seen from afar; this is the new spirit taking shape.

We do not lack enterprise. Look at the college catalogue. It is a North American college where scarcely a sixth of the students are of Spanish blood. But not in awards: there the percentage is growing, and if for every Spanish-speaking student there are six who speak English, for every six North Americans who win awards there are six other Americans from the South.

Upon that simple list of classes and their titles, carelessly passed over by vulgar eyes, *La América*'s glances tarry. In this immense total of analogies composing the universal system, in every small event there is, in short, a great event either in the future or past. Should it not make us happy to see that when a son of our lands, spare of flesh and thin of blood, engages in combat with his fully fleshed and rich-blooded rival, he wins the battle?

In this college under discussion, students of Spanish blood rarely enroll in classes other than elementary or business ones. For in the catalogue of business courses, two out of every three favored students come from our countries.

The best bookkeeper is one Vicente de la Hoz. The student who learned most about business law is one Esteban Viña. The student who won every award in his class, not leaving a crumb for the formidable all-powerful Yankee, is one Luciano Malabet; and the three awards in English composition did not go to a Smith, an O'Brien, or a Sullivan, but to a Guzmán, an Arellano, and a Villa!

Oh, if only these intellects of ours were put abreast of their times; if only they were not educated for judges' robes and cardinals' caps as in the days of audiences and potentates; if only in their eagerness to learn they were not left to feed upon the vague and galvanic literature of half-dead foreign peoples; if only the happy consortium of intelligence which must be applied to a country would match the country to which it must be applied; if only the South Americans were not prepared to live in France when they are not French, or in the United States—the most prolific exponent of these bad procedures—when they are not North Americans, or in colonial times when they are living away from the colony, in competition with active, creative, vital, free peoples. On the contrary, they must be conditioned to live in South America . . .! He who gives his son merely a university education, in South America, kills him.

Campaigns for political freedom are expanding; they ought to expand more vigorously for spiritual freedom, to accommodate man to the land in which he must live.

La América (New York), November 1883

Education for the Masses

And this vast Guatemalan Republic, this land of fertile expanses and generous spirits, how did it live before, under its oligarchic government? The students in their wretched schools used to be taught the bare principles of doctrine and of Fleury and Christian morality and Christian saints, and they learned to read and write in just such a superficial manner. My mission here is neither to harm nor poetize; it is to report. Today every village has a school. Parents build the teacher's house with their own hands; the peasant is deprived of the possession of his young ones because they are learning their alphabet; serious institutions in the city are increasing; an already full program in the University is being expanded; students in the Polytechnic School are learning mathematics in military dress; the Normal School, by a practical system of reason and one's own judgment, teaches its pupils to be teachers. Five hundred children are enrolled in the classrooms of the large National Institute; teachers receive good training in San Francisco, and men and women teachers are brought in from abroad; all of them teach religious tolerance, give truly useful instruction, and popularize the most recent American and European systems.

The ears of grain in those minds are mature. In the lands of America, maturity is not difficult to achieve. Indian-like, unshod, shy, sullen, and crude, children and farmhands come from the lonely interior, and suddenly, through innermost revelation and wonderful work, through contact with cultural superiority and with books, bushy hair settles down, pigeon-toed feet are set straight, hard hands are cared for, mournful aspects are ennobled, bent shoulders are straightened, averted eyes awaken: the wretched larvae have become men.

Shortly afterward they assault the rostrum, the history books, the books on agriculture, the flute and piano. They devote themselves to thinking about serious things, to doubt, inquire, and examine. They talk of Bolívar, of patriots, of the good government that is educating them, of the vast future which is awaiting—as they say—their beloved Guatemala! I see them and encourage them. Some great figures will emerge in time from among these men.

The University, which is certainly spacious and beautiful, has just reformed its various departments, improved its medical courses, liberalized its law school, established its school of literature and philosophy, the great study of origins, hopes, developments, and analogies.

From agricultural Costa Rica, ultra-intelligent Honduras, nearby San Salvador, conservative Nicaragua, come many students to become scientists in the Central University.

The medical students have an excellent hospital in which to practice; for being humanitarian, methodical, clean, and well endowed, European travelers consider it a rival of the best.

The students of jurisprudence hold philosophical discussions with distinguished professors in vast classrooms lining the spacious corridors, and these discussions aid in the eternal broadening of thought.

And the young people feel encouraged. They argue with the teacher about the subject matter and the textbooks. They have a certain Voltairean spirit, which is good. They reject the imposition of dogmatism, which is also good. In order to believe, they long to know. They long for truth through experience, through a way of solidifying their talents, energizing their characters, and stabilizing their virtues.

But a great revolution lies within the people. Education for the masses has just saved France; I saw this three years ago, and I reliably predict its triumph over any new reaction, even if this is believed by very few.

The reaction came, and France has triumphed.

Education for the masses holds pleasant Switzerland in respect abroad and in honor at home.

Education for the masses, solid as well as rancorous in Germany, has given that country its present great power.

Knowing how to read is knowing how to act. Knowing how to write is knowing how to ascend. Those first lowly schoolbooks put at man's disposal feet, arms, and wings. Man then flies off into space. He considers the best way to plant seeds, the useful reforms to make, the applicable discovery, a new recipe, a way to turn bad soil into good, the history of heroes, the futile reasons for wars, the great results of peace. One sows chemistry and agriculture, and reaps greatness and wealth. A school is a forge of the mind; woe to peoples without schools! Woe to minds without a temple!

This redeeming rebirth has taken five years to come about. It is the work of the liberal government exclusively. Barrios[1] is never approached by a grieving mother who does not immediately have a bed or clothes or a book for her children. In the city and in the outskirts, in the Polytechnic School and the Normal School—everywhere—rather than just thinking about the good, he predicts it. He knows that this is redemption, and naturally, without any effort at all, he is angered by the oppressors and he comes to the rescue.

Much is spent upon schools. The teachers are well paid; no steamer arrives without its cargo of equipment—at times material for calisthenics, at times astronomy apparatus,

---

1. Justo Rufino Barrios (1835–85), president of Guatemala from 1873 to his death in 1885. During his administration, Barrios became known as the "Reformer." Among other reforms, he enlarged and secularized the school system.

books, collections, and models. Upon entering the National Institute, one hears an excellent band. Going to the Normal School with a spirit of love for Spanish American things, one sees a remarkable institute in the New York style. A shaping of men mentally by the contemplation of objects, and morally by daily example.

The revolution having triumphed, it was like a plethora of good desires. It overflowed with productivity. It strung telegraph wires, contracted for railroads, opened roads, solicited educators, subsidized promoters, funded schools. In this last, its ardor still has not cooled. Nor will it cool, because its results are visible, and those very results encourage it. How warmly the young teacher is welcomed back to his distant village; to receive him his mother dons her finest corals and winds her head with her most carefully braided hair, and the good old man—Indian or Spanish-speaking Negro—dons his whitest cotton shirt! The teacher left home in rags and returns with his dreams, his benches, and his books; with his dearest musical instruments and his spiritual riches. He went away as a rough character and returns as a polished man. He went away stammering and returns eloquent.

Formerly he would dream about cows; today about the future, about great work, glory, the heavens. He is the editor of all letters, the manager of all love affairs, the respected scholar, the dependable mayor, the steadfast teacher. New souls will grow in his warmth, without his having to move away from his pleasant home.

He was made in the likeness of others, and he will make these others in his likeness. Education is like a tree: a seed is sown and it bursts into many branches. It may be the people's gratitude, the gratitude of men who do them so much good today, that trains the protective tree in storms and in rains. Whoever plants schools will harvest men.

Guatemala (Mexico), January 1878

A False Concept
of Public Education

To the Editor of *La Nación:*

September is always a very spirited month in North American life. Hunting matches follow bathing in the sea; great yacht races between the English and Bostonian sailboats, in which the Bostonians win, follow fishing contests.

Abandonment and flirtations at the beaches, a principal and sinful occupation here, give way to elegantly attired strollers along the seaside boardwalks and at the horse races where, at Narragansett Pier and Bar Harbor, the showiest and most daring clothes are fearlessly displayed from morning until evening. People are now returning to their city homes, more honestly dressed, to lose at champagne suppers, fashionable luncheons, balls, and winter rivalries the roses which the bracing sea and country air brought back to their cheeks.

Theaters are opening; schools are brushing the dust off their benches; the dance-master convention announces three new dance steps; political figures who have counted up their constituents again and mended their banners, during the summer months, are returning to their elections and battles with all the ardor of summer.

One need only go out this morning at an early hour to understand that North American life is changing.

A leaden veil covered the sky; a subtle wind ruffled the branches of trees; carrying their overcoats, men assaulted the shaky stations of the elevated railroad with heavy steps;

bands of children came out of the intersections like colored bees, their arms full of books, bound for school to take their places there.

Some went out of their way to feast their eyes upon the large playbills posted upon all the walls and fences at the street corners; others, crowded at their classroom doors waiting for the time to enter, carefully arranged their slate pencils and sponges in their Japanese pencil boxes; still others, almost all of them dark-skinned, as if there were some innate rebellion in a certain color, were running away like untamed colts—their socks fallen down, the uppers of their shoes half off, clothes torn, hats lost—fleeing from the blond and red-cheeked older boys whom the schoolteachers of the poorer neighborhoods had sent out to corral the fugitives. Drill jackets, rope hammocks, and straw hats were no longer seen in the cupboards; only rubber raincoats, fur caps, and sturdy camel's hair gloves.

But this spectacle, which shrinks the little that remains of a soul in the tropical breasts here, seems to swell and rejuvenate the spirits of the country's sons. One hears the sound of joyful voices and the sleigh bells that flood the city at the first snowfall. Now one can see shining in the air the red, yellow, and blue plumes they use to decorate the horses.

Schools, theaters, elections—there you have the great festivities of September.

There is much discussion here about schools, their inadequacies, the inefficiency of importing for education new and strange systems from peoples made up of different ingredients; discussion about the incomplete, rhetorical, and artificial aspect of the present system, and the need to reform it.

Must education consist solely of literary components or, as the Englishman Matthew Arnold[1] wonders, does not the

1. Matthew Arnold (1822–88), British poet and critic who covered in his criticism not only literature but also theology, history, art, science, and politics.

nation which, even in its primary education, fails to inspire
the superior spirit with beautiful subjects for study, run the
risk of losing its way?

Will education have to be indifferent, general, or special in
its religious teachings?

Others wonder if all education, from its first impulsive
start in the primary grades, should not be resolved to develop
children's intelligence, feelings, and hands in a free and
orderly manner?

What is known as industrial or manual training has many
advocates—even fanatics—blind to the fact that it is only a
partial education, good mainly for a country of industrial
workers, rather than being general and incorporating all the
elements common to the country's life, which is what public
education must be.

We are in New York. Let us see how the problem is
presented in New York.

The schools are numerous; handsome, by and large, and
monumental. Others are more neglected and dingy. But
although there are so many, there is still not enough space for
all who want to enter.

In the grades known here as upper classes, although in
many of our lands they would only be elementary, there are
plenty of places; after the age of fourteen here, few children
go to school.

The Irish and German children flock to the lower grades,
for they form the bulk of the school-going population here,
especially the German.

There are a hundred and fifty thousand places in the
primary schools; five more of these are going to be built this
year; the city spends an annual four million dollars for
education, yet every year from four to six thousand children
cannot find room in the schools.

How is this growing number of pupils viewed in people's
minds? How do the generous school system and the luke-

warm and individualistic spirit of the country struggle or coincide?

What defects in method has the practice revealed in this gigantic educational effort in the United States? What radical structural defects of the system are discovered by observing it?

Must judicious men be contented with the formal, outward, and apparent greatness of the systems, or study them sincerely in their administration, operation, and results?

The large number of schools and students is a great blessing, but it would be a greater one if the education provided to the children would represent as much of the solidity, amplitude, and spaciousness as the buildings where it is distributed; if the character, habits, and formation of the teaching corps would be in keeping with the beauty, independence, and order abounding in those prudent and elegant texts given to the children by the state. It would be a great blessing if the schools here were like most of those in Germany—houses of reason where with judicious guidance the child is accustomed to develop his own thinking, and where objects and ideas would be set before him in an orderly relationship so he could deduce by himself the direct and harmonious lessons that leave him both enriched by their facts and strengthened by the practice and pleasure of having discovered them.

The secret of the adaptability and success with which the Germans get ahead in the world, in spite of their native slowness and obduracy, lies in that methodical and inventive development of their intelligence.

But because of the lack of agreement between those charged with educating and the generosity of the system and texts, the schools here—with their beautiful books, their grand facilities, their outward order, their pencils and slates, their grammars and geography books—have become workshops for memorizing where children languish year after year in sterile spelling lessons, maps, and calculations; where corporal punishment is authorized and practiced; where time is wasted copying words and listing mountains and rivers; where the live elements of the world we inhabit, or how the human creature can improve himself and serve in his inevitable contact with those elements, are never taught; where teacher and pupil do not share that warmth of affection which enlarges to giant size the student's desire and aptitude for learning, and which remains in their souls as sweetly as a vision of paradise, comforting and gladdening their paths in life's unavoidable spells of dejection.

Things should not be studied in the system directing them, but in the manner of their application and in the results they produce.

Education—who can deny it? —is above all a labor of infinite love.

Reforms are productive only when they penetrate the spirit of nations; they slide over them, like dry sand over sloping rocks, when the rudeness, sensuality, or egoism of the public soul resists the reforming influence of practices which that soul respects in form and name only.

How does it happen—with such obvious care given to public education here, with such vast resources, so many teachers, such capable and handsome books—that the usual results are to turn out dull and indifferent children who, after six years of schooling, leave their benches without having acquired any cultured tastes, or grace of childhood, or enthusiasm of youth, or a liking for knowledge, and generally knowing no more—even when they know a lot—than to read passably, write crudely, calculate in elementary arithmetic, and copy maps?

It comes from a false concept of public education; from an essential error in the system of education stemming from that false concept; from a lack of a loving spirit in the teaching force. Like all those evils, it comes from a niggardly sense of life, which is a national cancer here.

Life in these parts is viewed not as a discreet partnership between the needs which tend to demean it and the aspirations which extol it, but rather as a mandate of pleasure, like an open mouth, like a game of chance where only the rich are the winners.

Men never stop to comfort and help one another. Nobody helps anybody. Nobody waits for anybody.

There are no people to give rewards, so there is no stimulus to ask for them.

Everyone is on the march, shoving, cursing, fiercely elbowing people out of the way, sweeping everything aside—everything—to reach their own objectives first.

Only in a few sensitive souls does some enthusiasm remain, like a dove upon a ruin.

No no, it is not malevolence, but a painful truth, that here one does not even notice in children any further desires than those of satisfying their own appetites and stepping upon others to do so.

Can this be enviable? One must shudder to think so!

This is the destination of the fully matured man, the woman, and the child born to them.

What is coming in from the outside? How is this enormous abundance of egoism increasing? How is immigration influencing the people's culture?

There are hungry generations of men coming, men abandoned to themselves who anxiously employ the second half of their lives in freeing themselves from the misery in which they spent the first. Here they do not have their own country which nourishes with its tradition and warms with its passions the spirits of the most wretched of its sons. Here they do not have the family circle which preserves a man in its own strength, and gives him the certainty of not being abandoned in his hour of agony. Here they do not have their native people whose esteem helps them to live and whose censure is feared.

With no direction or rest or aid, with only the pleasure of

being alone in the house, poisoned by the fatigue it costs to keep it, and by the frustration of never seeing his native land, a man is hardened in the fears of others and the contemplation of self, and in this state of hotheaded and sickly individuality he begets children who grow up in the atmosphere of his ambitions and disappointments, and heedless of the noble causes that give to human nature its energy and charm.

These masses of men are colossal rows of teeth.

The soul dies here from lack of use.

Such is the concept of life; such are the fractional ideas about its conduct, and they stem from it.

The old puritanical spirit, surrounded by this constant invasion, tries in vain to hold fast to the reins that are gradually slipping out of its hands. In vain do farseeing men attempt to direct, through culture and a religious sense, this vigorous mass of people who freely seek a quick and full satisfaction of their appetites.

In vain do the generous innovators and concerned teachers contrive plans to perfect public instruction and prolong its courses in the upper grades.

The crude spirit of the masses sweeps away these attempts at refinement, neutralizes or annuls their influence, and invades and starts corrupting the very teachers charged with leading those masses.

Why must the law have one spirit if those whose duty it is to carry it out have another?

Why improve public instruction in its outer form and in the material resources—a labor of constant and impassioned tenderness—if the teachers who transmit it, even though they are women, have not been able to save themselves from the malign influence of this national life so lacking in expansion and love?

Why accumulate rules, distribute texts, grade courses, erect buildings, pile up statistics, if those occupied in this work are women defeated in the battle of life, which hardens and embitters, or discontented or impatient young people who are like a flock of birds outside of school, and work inside it as if school were an unfair punishment for being poor, as if it were a hateful prison of their youth, as if it were a troublesome and temporary preparation for the real and happier purposes of their lives?

From that sparse concept of existence comes the imperfect way of preparing children for it.

Not only is existence viewed principally as the necessity of satisfying its needs by work; it is viewed exclusively as such.

That situation is everyone's concern, fear, and anxiety. The people have been suffering from this constantly, and so has the legislator who arranges the courses, the expert who recommends them, and the teacher who has to teach them.

Therefore they are resolving to avoid the anguish that they themselves have felt, and to give the child the rudimentary means of fighting somewhat successfully for his existence.

Reading, writing, and arithmetic—that is all they think that children need to know. But why should they read if it fails to instill in them a taste for reading, the conviction that it is both useful and enjoyable, and the pleasure of gradually building the soul with the harmony and greatness of knowledge? Why write if the mind fails to be nourished by ideas, or stimulated by the taste for them?

Arithmetic indeed—they teach that extensively.

Some children still do not know how to read a syllable when little five-year-olds have already been taught to count to a hundred by heart.

By heart! That is how they shave intellects like heads. That is how they suffocate people from childhood on, instead of facilitating the movement and expression of originality which each child carries within him. That is how they produce a sterile and repugnant uniformity, a kind of liveried row of intelligences.

Instead of setting before children's eyes the living elements of the earth they tread, the produce it grows, and the riches it stores, the ways of furthering the former and extracting the latter, some manner of freeing their bodies in health from the agents and influences that attack it, and the beauty and finer totality of life's universal forms—thus pledging in the spirit of children the poetry and hope which is indispensable for courageously enduring human toil—they stuff them, in these schools, with states' boundary lines and columns of numbers, with spelling facts and word definitions!

And so, with merely a verbal and representative kind of instruction, how can a person confront existence—an existence in this active and egoistic nation which is all action and deeds?

Not in vain do the majority of children who leave school at the age of thirteen or fourteen—children with no more talent than a bad handwriting and a little reading and arithmetic—wander weakly and aimlessly through the streets; or else they are reduced to running errands in the shops. This land derives its driving force and momentum from people formed and raised in the countryside with the vigor given by direct work; from those genuine spirits who carry within themselves an original and insuperable strength—not from these impotent hordes raised by anxious parents and irascible school teachers in schools of mere words where one learns barely more than an apparent way of satisfying the needs that stem from instinct.

This system must be overturned from top to bottom. Here this is beginning to be vaguely seen. Its failure is recognized and a remedy is being sought. "Put the entire boy in school! " a defender of industrial education in St. Louis has just said, and rightly so, but this is still not enough.

The remedy lies in developing the child's intelligence, at the same time as his qualities of love and emotion, with orderly and practical teachings of the active elements of existence in which he must struggle, and the manner of utilizing them and setting them in motion.

The remedy lies in courageously changing primary instruction from verbal to experimental, from rhetorical to scientific; in teaching the child the ABC of words at the same time as the ABC of Nature; in deriving from Nature, or arranging some way for the child to derive it, that pride of being a man and that sound and constant impression of majesty and eternity that comes—like aromas from flowers—from a knowledge of the world's causes and functions, even in the simple terms to which they would have to be reduced in rudimentary education.

Diligent men, direct men, independent men, loving men—these are what the schools must turn out, for now they do not.

But that saintly Peter Cooper did: he who suffered from ignorance and abandonment, and built a school where one might learn how to practice life in its usual and beautiful skills together with the religiosity and morality that arises spontaneously from the knowledge of them.

Still gropingly, that is what the more judicious reformers might want to make of the public-school system here—to reconstruct it so that man will not be destroyed, and so that all the gold in his nature will appear in the sunlight.

José Martí

La Nación (Buenos Aires), November 14, 1886

The School for Deaf Mutes

Gloominess has its poems, the spirit its disturbances, and compassion its tears. All this is felt, and many things are loved, in the presence of those beings burned by their own light, without the sense-perception to transmit that light or the ability to receive the life-giving warmth of others. Born like corpses, love transforms them, because teaching the deaf and mute is a sublime profession of love. This term "sublime" is wrongly used, but all tenderness is sublime, and teaching the deaf and mute is the stubborn work of tenderness. Exquisite patience, aroused ingenuity, words eliminated, eloquent gestures, Nature's mistakes defeated, and the benevolent spirit victorious over torpid matter, by virtue of the power of calmness and kindness.

The professor is transformed into a mother: the lesson must be a caress; every boy carries within him a sleeping man; but the deaf and mute are locked into a perpetual triple prison. When the deaf and mute took their examinations the day before yesterday, copious tears brimmed unavoidably from their eyes.

There is a boy in the school by the name of Labastida, with shiny black hair, eyes lively with candor, broad forehead, smiling mouth, and a meek and frank expression. He was writing scientific definitions with remarkable speed, filling his slate rapidly, and asking for more to do when the other students had not yet finished.

Labastida is twelve years old, and since the light of his soul is forcibly dimmed, he wears all of it upon his face—a beautiful, animated, and shining childish face. That boy is captivating; he invites embraces.

Beside him worked Ponciano Arriaga, son of the distinguished man who added some magnificent principles to the beautiful Mexican Constitution. Arriaga will soon be eighteen. He has learned all there is to know in the primary grades, easily expresses the thoughts he conceives, studies botany under the skilled instruction of Mr. Huet, solves complicated problems in upper-division arithmetic, and draws with a purity of outline and with delicacy and softness of shading. His brow is ample, and as if descending in a thoughtful attitude, above his small but lively eyes; his aquiline nose and finely chiseled lips reveal a natural distinction. They say that Arriaga has an extraordinary facility for comprehension, and that brow of his certainly seems made for serious thought.

At the side of these two is another boy solving problems in arithmetic with a speed which even in children endowed with all their senses would attract attention. He is Luis Gutiérrez, the student most advanced in calculus. His voluminous forehead rises in a curve from his stern and inquiring eyes to his thick, curly hair. He is a serious boy in whom one can foresee the man.

We are unjust without meaning to be. There are probably other children who deserve special mention, but in Sunday's examinations we were only able to see these.

In those tests the second aspirant, Dámaso López, was asked questions by means of sign language, one of the three systems used in education at the school. The fastest system is mimicry; the most difficult, the grammatical; the most solid, sign language. The students immediately wrote upon their slates both question and answer. Not an accent or punctuation mark or particle was missing. They understand the value of every word and have clear and elementary notions of geography, history, natural history, arithmetic, and grammar.

The professor wrote a problem and all the students wrote it at the same time. Labastida was writing numbers with extraordinary speed, and in the meantime Ponciano Arriaga was explaining the names and classifications of flowers.

And at the back of the hall were the girls who had taken their examinations the day before. Far greater is the unhappiness of these beings, endowed with a useless beauty and with treasuries of candor by which human love would not have the courage to profit. Women, seldom happy, are unfortunate in everything, and yet always able to bring happiness to others. These girls are lights perpetually burning in lamps perpetually closed, which not one merciful hand will come near enough to open. They will have compassion, which suffers; but not love, which invigorates, inflames, and makes fruitful.

The news bulletins of periodicals do not like these kinds of reflections, which are anxieties rather than thoughts. That spectacle is a sad one, and yet one comes away from it with a strange joy: the fact is, we have just attended a redemption. Creation produces man, but man is gradually gaining strength against his mother, Creation. Those living men are born dead, and education exposes them to life and makes them bountiful in the building of patience and kindness.

We were told there that the deaf and mute cultivate gardens for vegetables and flowers, a new fraternity that gives pause for thought. Every man is held fast to the earth with terrible roots; we are shrubs that drag our roots along the ground: the deaf and dumb, because of being held more firmly than ourselves, are fond of flowers because the flowers are as firmly rooted and enslaved as are they.

There is a professor in this school, young and filled with self-denial. Everyone there is good and merits respect, but the prime aspirant, Luis Jiménez, is deserving of special mention. He has the habit of benevolence; he loves those he teaches and it pleases him to talk about them. We have already said that in this school one must profess love above teaching.

The school is well attended; Mr. Huet is a good head-master. The students are hale and hearty and seem happy; they have their vegetable garden and their drawing class, and they exercise their bodies in the gymnasium. Nature alone is not our mother; who wants to have an unfair, criminal, stupid, and crazy mother? Blessed be the hands that rectify these mistakes and sweeten these sinister errors of blind Mother Creation.

Revista Universal (Mexico), November 30, 1875

A Spanish American University

In nations composed of cultured and uncultured elements, the uncultured will govern, because of their habit of resolving doubts with their power wherever the cultured have failed to learn the art of governing. The uncultured masses are lazy and timid in matters of intelligence, and they want to be governed well. But if the government offends them, they are aroused, and then they are the ones to govern. How are the rulers to be graduated from a university if there is no university in America where they teach the rudiments of the art of government, which is an analysis of the elements peculiar to the nations of America? Young people go out into the world wearing Yankee or French spectacles to solve problems, and aspire to rule in a nation they do not know. Political careers should be denied to those who disregard the rudiments of politics. Prizes in competitions should not be for the best ode, but for the best study of the elements of the country in which one lives. In journalism, among the university faculty, and in the academies, the study of a country's true elements must be carried on. Just knowing them, in plain language and without beating about the bush, is enough, because anyone who lays aside part of the truth, either intentionally or due to forgetfulness, fails in the long run because of the truth he lacks, which thrives upon neglect and overthrows what is built without it. To solve a problem after knowing its elements is easier than solving a problem without knowing them. The strong and indignant natural man comes and overthrows the justice accumulated from books, for that kind of justice is not administered in accord with a country's patent needs. To know is to solve. To know a country and govern it in conformity with knowledge is the only way to free it from tyranny. The European university must yield to the American university. The history of America, from the Incas to the present, must be taught down to the fingertips, even if the history of the Greek archons[1] is neglected. Our Greece is preferable to a Greece which is not ours. We need it more. National politics must replace foreign politics. The world must be grafted onto our republics, but our republics must be the trunk. And let the defeated pedant hold his peace, for there is no country in which a man takes more pride than in our afflicted American republics.

El Partido Liberal (Mexico), January 30, 1890

---

1. Archons were the chief magistrates in many ancient Greek city-states. During the fifth century B.C. the institution spread widely in the Aegean islands, mainly under Athenian influence.

Learning on the Farms

Our extremely fertile soil, rich in all kinds of crops, yields little produce, and less than it should, because of the routine and outdated systems of plowing, planting, and harvesting in our countries, and because of the use of decrepit farm implements.

An immediate need arises from this: new implements must be introduced into our lands; our farmers must be taught the tested methods by which other peoples achieve such astounding results in their own productivity.

What obstacles will remain, what competition will not be overcome, what rivals will maintain their jurisdiction, when modern farm implements, and the best methods now in use, enrich the American lands? Buenos Aires knows this—Buenos Aires which is taking out of these ports five or six shiploads of agricultural implements a month.

But not all of our nations enjoy the same prosperous conditions as those of the Plata, nor is it possible to introduce such large quantities of fine new farm implements that save so much time and effort; merely introducing them into lands unprepared to receive them and put them to good use is not enough to change, as if by magic, the rudimentary state of our agricultural methods.

Nor are there sufficient funds everywhere to purchase the necessary new farm implements. It is not enough to acquire these implements if they are not accompanied by people to manage them and condition the soil to make good use of them. Even with the special compliments given to them by the expositions, their manufacturers do not always dare to send their products to nations where there is fear that their sales will not compensate for the costs of shipment.

So, if these implements are not sent, one must come to look for them.

But as we have already said, even when the implements do go, the new agricultural practices to encourage the growth of crops do not go with them. In books this is not understood, or it is misunderstood. This factor cannot be set forth in the expositions. Only in part, and at great expense, can this be taught in the agricultural schools. One must start learning it where it is in full practice and practical development. Spanish American children, perhaps insanely, are sent to well-known schools in this land where they exchange the tongue they know inadequately for the foreign tongue they never learn well, and where—in the conflict between the childlike but sensitive civilization which comes with them and the virile but crude, peculiar, and foreign civilization awaiting them here—they leave with their minds confused and filled with memories of what they brought and with imperfect thoughts about the new things they see, perhaps unqualified for the spontaneous, ardent, and exquisite life of our countries, and yet unfit for the fast-paced, crowded, and impetuous existence of this land. The trees of one climate are rachitic, faded, deformed, and sickly when grown in another.

So then, just as the sons of Spanish America are sent to learn what they would learn better in their own lands, no matter how elementary that knowledge would be, with the risk of losing the aroma of their mother country which gives to life a perpetual charm and a healthful atmosphere; just as one works in commercial offices to acquire after long years a handful of common routines that can fit into a nutshell, which can be learned just as easily in one's own home without losing what is always lost abroad—so without so much risk and more profitably the governments must send able farmers, and the parents must send sons for whom they want to do a real favor by teaching them in the cultivation of the land the only honest source of wealth. And those governments should also send planters to study the new agricultural methods used upon productive farms, to live during the times of one to several harvests upon farms where the recent systems are followed, to acquire in all their details a personal and direct knowledge of the advantages of modern methods and farm implements, leaving aside the unproductive, and then these men will be able to take back to their plantations the improvements which they have seen in agriculture here.

It is urgent to cultivate our lands as our rivals cultivate theirs.

These farming methods do not travel; one must begin learning them upon the farm, wearing the wide-brimmed hat and the farmer's loose shirt.

This may be the only easy, productive, and perfect way to bring the new agricultural methods into our countries.

Apprentices are sent to the machine shops, which is good; let us send apprentices to the farms, which will be better.

Patria (New York), August 1883

Man and the Land

Honduras already has its School of Arts and Crafts.

Honduras is a noble and congenial nation in which one must have faith. Its shepherds talk like academics. Its women are affectionate and pure. There is volcanic substance in the spirit of its people. In Honduras there have been revolutions born of more or less visible conflicts between those enamored of a superior political state that is a natural outcome of the social state, and the feudal appetites that are naturally aroused in countries which—in spite of having capital cities with universities embedded in them—are still patriarchal and rudimentary.

But once opened, men's eyes do not shut. The very sufferers for the attainment of freedom become fonder of it, and the very tranquility given by a tyrannical rule allows people's spirits to be purified and fortified in its shade. Honduras has not suffered much from tyrants because its sons of Nature, with a natural wisdom that is to hasten their definitive well-being, have a certain indomitable courage that does not let them endure restrictions that are too severe.

There, as everywhere, the problem lies in planting. The School of Arts and Crafts is a very good invention, but the country has only one, and it is not enough to make an entire new nation. The teaching of agriculture is the most urgent of all, not in technical schools, but in experimental stations where the parts of the plow will not be described except where the student may see it in operation; and where the composition of the fields will not be explained in formulas on the blackboard, but rather in the layers of the earth itself. The students' attention should not be cooled down with the merely technical rules of farming—rigid as the lead type that printed them—but kept entertained by curiosity, desires, surprises, and experiments—delightful payment and a lively prize for those who are dedicated to agriculture of their own volition.

Whoever wants a nation must habituate men to create.

And whoever creates is respected and seen as a force of Nature against which to attempt a crime or deprive it of its will would be illicit.

A seed sown is not merely the seed of a plant; it is the seed of dignity.

A nation's independence and good government come only when its inhabitants owe their subsistence to a labor which is not at the mercy of a bestower of public offices who takes them away as he gives them, and who always keeps those whose lives depend upon him—when they are not armed against him in a war—in a state of alarm. Those people are free in name, but in their inner selves they are quite dead, even before dying.

People of importance and foresight from these countries of ours must work incessantly for the immediate establishment of practical locations for agriculture, and for a corps of traveling teachers to go through the fields instructing the farmers and villagers in what they need to know about the human being, government, and the land.

La América (New York), June 1884

Obligatory Education

Yesterday a beautiful campaign was to have begun in the Mexican Chamber of Deputies. The deputy Juan Palacios was preparing to explain the groundwork for a Public Instruction project which is a result of two years of preparation and study. Intelligence and imagination have essentially different qualities; reflective study, which would harm the imagination, is necessary and useful to the intelligence.

The commission has done much reading, engaged in discussion, and thought out its project. This project is probably fallible—it certainly is—but it will always be respectable. It ends by overturning the present order of teaching, but what this overturning means is that it establishes order. It rudely stirs up the present system, but does so for the benefit of the country and under the protection of the logic and practice in other nations.

I do not wish to dwell upon the project's defects. I believe that these do exist, but its excellent qualities are greater and more important.

It establishes two great principles; even if the entire project were unacceptable, it would be saved by these two principles, which sustain it and have brought it into being: freedom of education and obligatory education. Or better still, obligatory education and freedom of education; because the former healthful tyranny is worth even more than the latter liberty.

91

Can a reason be advanced for obligatory education? One can only bring up in argument one nation: Germany; and one propagator: Tiberghien.

Every idea is sanctioned by its good results. When all men know how to read, all men will know how to vote, and—since ignorance is the guarantee of political misconduct—conscience itself and the pride of independence guarantee the appropriate practice of freedom. An Indian who knows how to read can turn out to be a Benito Juárez[1]; an Indian who has not gone to school will perpetually carry a useless and lethargic spirit in a rachitic body. I think even these words are useless; to my mind an obligatory education is unassailable, and so useful. The articles of faith have not disappeared, only changed form. The teachings of reason have replaced those of the Catholic faith. Obligatory education is an article of faith of the new dogma.

Here it is necessary to interrupt these reflections and joyfully set apart one fact which is a veritable guarantee. In itself it is trivial, but in its results it will be fruitful. I have wanted to reminisce about the Catholic articles of faith. In contemplating all religions my memory has forgotten the forms of one of them. I have asked coeditors, employees, domestics, compositors. *La Voz* will suffer from this, but those who deeply love Mexico will probably be satisfied with it; there is not a single individual on *La Revista* who knows the articles of faith. They know one article, the primal cause and savior; that which reconstructs and invigorates us; the Messiah of our free age: work.

This fact would take us to different considerations than those which have commenced this bulletin.

We were talking about obligatory education. Prussia's bru-

---

1. Benito Juárez (1806–72), president of Mexico from 1861 to 1871. Born among Indian priests in Oxaca, Juárez is one of the heroic figures in Mexican history.

tality has prevailed because it is an intelligent brutality. The minister has so informed the parliament; every Prussian[2] knows how to read and write.

And what forces would not be discovered in us by throwing great quantities of Victor Hugo's[3] light upon our eight millions of inhabitants? And as upon us, upon all of South America. We are not yet sufficiently American; every continent must have its own expression; we have a deputized life and a stammering literature. There are men in America who are letter-perfect in European literature, but we do not have one exclusively American writer. There ought to be a poet who soars above the summit of our Alps, of our rocky heights—a mighty historian more worthy of Bolívar than of Washington, because America is the violent, the gushing forth; it is revelations, vehemence. And Washington is the hero of tranquility, formidable but calm, sublime but composed.

Why will we not adopt the new system of education? The natives bring us a new way of living. We study what is brought to us from France, but the natives will reveal to us what they take from Nature. A new light will shine from those copper-colored faces. Education is going to reveal them to themselves. We shall not be ashamed to have an Indian come and kiss our hands; we shall be proud to have him approach us to give us his.

---

2. Martí is referring to the Prussian mentality in which ideas of German superiority, historical mission, etc., had been drilled into people through regimented and propagandistic education, through a militaristic use of education. This program was advocated by Prime Minister Otto von Bismarck in his message to the Reichstag.

3. Victor Hugo (1802–1885), French poet, dramatist, and novelist, who was the most important of the Romantic writers. A lifelong supporter of Republican ideals, Hugo exerted great power in shaping public opinion in France, and Martí was desirous of having these Republican ideals widely spread in the education of young people.

This is not a dream; it is the positive result of the law. By what means, one wonders, will the obligation be discharged? By imprisonment or fine.

Habit creates an appearance of justice; advances have no greater enemy than habit; compassion is sometimes a great obstacle.

And how will these men of the fields, who earn so little, pay the fine?

They will pay it because they will prefer this to stopping work for a few days; and since they will not want to pay a higher fine, they will send their children to school. One makes use of the only perceptible things: daily concerns, daily food. The Indian will see these threatened and will do what the law demands.

A project of public instruction is a seedbed of ideas; every glance at the project gives rise to new thoughts. But the times teach, and I, an experienced writer of bulletins, have learned that bulletins must be simple and easily read. I obey practice and leave for coming bulletins the reflections which congressional discussions of the project will be awakening in me.

Revista Universal (Mexico), October 26, 1875

A French Normal High School

Near Paris there is a normal high school for women teachers, built a short while ago by the enterprising Minister of Public Education, Jules Ferry.[1] Of course the objective of this school is to educate women teachers who will later serve in the normal schools as teachers in the various departments. So large a nation requires such complicated organization. To educate is to place a shield against life's imperfections. Crime and the desires leading up to it easily nibble away at the ignorant, or at those whose minds are unaccustomed to thinking and who have no taste for the pleasures that arise from exercising thought—those who employ all the active forces of their nature in the mere animalistic satisfaction of their instincts. That high school in Fontenay-aux-Roses receives from the state all the resources that the Paris environs can offer. The instruction received in it by its forty students, who have attained this privilege through competition, is solid and profound and directed—as all good education must be—

1. Jules Ferry (1832–93), French statesman of the early Third Republic, notable both for his anticlerical educational policy, his reactionary policy of extending the French colonial empire, and his despotic policy toward the people of Paris during the siege of Paris in the German invasion of 1870–71. This siege policy won him the nickname "Ferry-la-Famine." In education he sponsored the free compulsory secular educational law of 1882.

toward preparing normal-school principals to teach how to struggle fruitfully and honestly in life. Practical things are taught there, and more science than literature, and more medicine than geography, and more the art of living than the art of dreaming unproductively in a false and impossible life. One notable professor, among others, teaches in the Fontenay school: he is Marion, author of a recently published book in which he sets forth his *Lessons in Psychology* which he taught in the school last year, lessons just as valuable as those on *Morality* which he is teaching in the same institute this year. The laws of public instruction in force in France demand that morality be taught in all state schools. This morality taught by Marion is that essential and undeniable morality of human nature. He analyzes every one of our aptitudes and functions, and regulates the use of each of our powers as well as that code of justice which changes in every human being, always identical to the person himself, who becomes alarmed at the great number of his violations that are so well disguised by the intelligence in need of excuses that the rights which are no more than the conquest of vice over our souls end by seeming to be our own rights. Practical people, in keeping with their principles, want it known so that it may be anticipated and adjusted. This seems still more important to us in the moral realm than in the physical. To guard against dangers it is necessary to know where they lie. We cannot overcome the obstacles and dangers inherent in life because, due to a blameworthy sense of charity, life keeps our eyes bandaged to prevent our seeing or knowing anything about them. It is very useful for us to read that book by Marion. The professor explains in great detail the special psychology of the child, points out the mysteries of his sensitive soul, and offers counsel so that teachers will make no mistakes in the way they guide him. Marion states practical things simply. The moral problems touched upon in education are courageously treated, and treated closely, in those *Lessons in Psychology,* which do not attempt to delve deeply into that confused and impenetrable soul, for which the metaphysical contrives laws and shackles analogies, but to observe sincerely and methodically all that is visible, undeniable, usable, and active in the human spirit.

"Sección Constante" (Caracas), 1882

The New School

In agriculture, as in everything else, a good preparation saves time, disappointments, and risks. Real medicine is preventive, not curative; hygiene is the true medicine. Rather than mending the broken bones of a person who falls bouncing down a precipice, it is better to show him how to avoid the precipice. The schools teach classes in ancient geography, rules of rhetoric, and similar things of long ago, but in their place there should be: courses in health; advice on hygiene; practical counseling; clear and simple studies of the human body, its parts, functions, ways of adjusting one to the other, economizing one's strength, and directing it well so that there will be no reason to restore it later. What is needed is not the student's desire to learn, but a teaching corps able to teach at least the sciences one cannot do without in this new world. In order to teach it is no longer enough—no, indeed—to take a pointer and indicate cities upon maps, or analyze the rule of three or of interest, or recite in chorus proofs of the earth's roundness, or line up a makeshift *romancillo* in the style of the Esculapian priests, or know that worthless chronological history which one is obliged to learn in our universities and colleges, for it is both useless and false. What should be taught, on an elementary level and in simple terms and with practical demonstrations, are the nature and composition of the earth and its crops, the industrial application of the earth's products, and the natural and scientific elements which work upon them and can contribute to their development. In the primary schools themselves there should be a great reduction in the stale and musty programs that make men pedantic and useless.

Let us hoist this flag and never lower it. Primary education has to be scientific.

The new world requires the new school.

It is necessary to replace the literary spirit of education with the scientific spirit.

A new program of education must be adopted: one which begins in the primary grades and ends in a brilliant, useful university in accord with the times, state, and aspirations of the countries where it teaches; a university that is for today's man the alma mater which in Dante's[1] or Virgil's[2] times prepared its students in arts and letters, in theological debates, and in legal sophistry—subjects which gave to the men of those days, for they still knew no better, prosperity and employment.

Like the man who takes off one cloak and puts on another, it is necessary to put the ancient university aside and build the new.

La América (New York), August 1883

1. Dante Alighieri (1265–1321), the greatest poet of Italy and an important political thinker whose Christian epic, *The Divine Comedy,* is one of the great works of world literature.

2. Virgil (full name Publius Virgilius Maro, 70–19 B.C.), the greatest of the poets of ancient Rome, best known for his epic, the *Aeneid,* which was unfinished at his death. The epic traces the history of Rome from its legendary founding by Aeneas of Troy to the Roman unification of the world by Augustus.

Physical Education

In these times of anxiety of spirit, it is urgent to fortify the body that must maintain the spirit. In the city especially, where the air is heavy and miasmal, the work excessive, where pleasure is violent, and the reasons for fatigue great, the organs of the body—for all these causes impoverish and are harmful—need to be assured of a comfortable dwelling place in a well-developed muscular system. The exercise of all the faculties must be balanced so that too much exercise of a single one of them does not pose a threat to life. With a healthful system of blood circulation, and by distributing strength in the use of all the body's organs, one must moderate the risk of having all of one's strength accumulated in the brain from much thinking, or in the heart from much feeling, thus causing death. For children especially, it is necessary to strengthen their bodies at the same time as fortifying their spirit. Today, passions awaken early, desires begin from the moment the eyes fall upon the ground, and everyone knows so much that it is necessary to learn a great many more things quickly, by some marvelous skill, in order to avoid being pushed aside and thrown in the dust in the magnificent competition. These concerns of modern life make it absolutely necessary to distribute one's bodily strength—accumulated in a flame in the brain from the beginning years of life—and to prepare early and expediently the edifice which must sustain such affliction, because the body has to be a theater for those battles of the spirit.

On this very page we are today publishing several prints of a Household Gymnasium which will be viewed as a good work rather than as a business venture. And in Havana it can be seen in the establishment of the agents, Mr. Amat and Mr. Laguardia of American Agency.

Enumerating its good qualities would be endless. It is useful and it is artistic, another way of being useful. The human being has powerful desires for grace and harmony, and just as one complains and is hurt by not seeing them realized, so one is happy and strong every time they are detected. The apparatus is white and pleasing to the eye. It is slender and well built, useful as well as decorative. In addition to being a complete gymnasium, it fits into a small room among the rest of the children's toys, or upon a yard of wall space, or in a bend of the garden, or in a corner of a courtyard. It has everything, even a trapeze on which to commit follies. Although the trapeze is not the most useful of exercise equipment, it is a learning device of the gymnasium, because people are not interested in what they do not consider brilliant and somewhat dangerous. But here the trapeze offers no great risk, because it is only a yard from the floor or the ground. The gymnasium has everything: parallel bars which can be removed and replaced, and which serve to increase chest expansion and develop the muscles of arms and shoulders. It has parallel and perpendicular bars to strengthen the arms, chest, and thighs; a horizontal bar to aid in the elasticity of the waist and power of the arms; all the many exercises to be done with the pulley, so varied and beneficial. From head to toe there is no part of the body that fails to benefit from them, and the body benefits more from this piece of equipment than from any other, because the weights of the pulleys (which can also be used separately) do not drop suddenly, jolting the weary arms that are straining to hold onto them and pulling the body behind them, thus causing the body to quickly tire. On the contrary, the weights descend gently along an inclined plane, allowing the arms to rest in the second part of every movement and therefore permitting the arms to repeat this movement in a more restful, useful, and pleasurable manner, and a greater number of times. The pulley ropes may be lengthened or shortened with no difficulty whatsoever, and are arranged so that with their help, and with the child seated at the bottom of the apparatus upon a comfortable stool that runs on well secured wheels, the feet upon stationary pedals, he can do every beautiful and healthful exercise that can be done with a pair of oars. These exercises, in addition to giving the body a notable grace and enticing one to the ocean and rivers to enjoy the pure air, have the advantage of not leaving a single muscle inactive, and of developing all of them at the same time. With the pulley handles themselves, grasped by the hands from the horizontal bar that completes the contrivance at the top, and seated upon another bar parallel to this one and supported between the two perpendiculars, every movement required by velocipedes can be made. If one suffers from curvature of the spine, the Household Gymnasium has a flexible board adjusted to curve the spine outwardly, placed between the top and bottom of the apparatus. The person so afflicted lies comfortably upon it and goes through his health-giving pulley exercises without any effort. To stimulate the circulation, by jumping lightly upon the little movable planks of which the gymnasium floor is made, one soon feels the benefit of this exercise. To develop the shoulders, give strength and impetus to the arms, and put one in an attitude of defense against some sudden attack from somebody else's fists, the contrivance has a small bag hanging from the horizontal bar where the fists gain strength by punching it again and again. Since the wrists need to develop, the handles of the pulley cords can be turned, this for the sole purpose of developing the wrists. In short, there is no bodily exercise—whether of the easy kind called calisthenics, or of the most strenuous which are taught for gala events in the schools—that, thanks to Gifford's excellent and successful device, may not be done in one's own home with no inconvenience at all. For our modest women, whose understandable reasons forbid their attendance at public gymnasiums but who nevertheless need these exercises just as much as do the men, the Household Gymnasium is of inestimable benefit. Without exposing themselves to the eyes of others, and in their own homes, they can exercise daily in all the health-giving movements that will increase the strength of their muscles and the grace and harmony of their figures.

Consumption mows down our gardens; how many less flowers would consumption snatch from us if our children and young people were accustomed to gymnastic exercises, for this disease often comes from the fact that the lungs which seek development cannot fit into a chest that is constricted and feeble. Gymnastic exercise is a special need in our lands where conventionality on the one hand, and the sanctity of women on the other, bring them inside from the streets and promenades—places, after all, that do help to strengthen the body—and confine them to the house, where the strongest body soon becomes sluggish and sickly.

For the children, Gifford's gymnasium equipment is a delight, because it not only enables them to row a boat and ride a velocipede, but to play at what in Cuba is known as *cachumbambé* and elsewhere as a seesaw, thanks to a plank where a child sits at either end, the plank being balanced upon a bar supported by perpendiculars. And this is not the only game of the contrivance; the Household Gymnasium also has a swing hanging from the high bar and carrying those playful angels as high as they wish to go—even up to the sky! although it makes the spectators tremble and weep.

What more? The apparatus even serves as an easel for paintings; when the pulleys are removed, what remains is like a trim but simple easel upon which a painting by Melero in Havana, or by Ocaranza, Rebull, Parra, or Pina in Mexico, would not be badly placed.

And everything described above fits into a nutshell. In a space two yards long by three quarters of a yard wide this small magic factory can be built, for it is truly a life-giving factory because it gathers together all the equipment and allows one to do all the exercises for which it has been necessary until now to have vast courtyards or great halls. This gymnasium is not even costly; its reasonable price is astounding. Nor is it deceptive, for the wood used in its construction is as strong as it is delicate. Nor does it need teachers, for it alone does the teaching. And it is not dangerous, for everything in it is near the floor.

There is no school that does not desire a gymnasium, but even the wealthy schools hesitate at the expenses which their establishment incurs, and at the difficulty of finding a suitable instructor, and at the costs of maintaining him. Now, when a simple gymnasium apparatus to attach to a wall costs fifteen dollars, or when a complete gymnasium costs thirty-five—the kind that easily fits into the middle of a small room—there is no school that cannot acquire a gymnasium. In the larger schools, from ten to twenty of these gymnasium contrivances would suffice, adding a handsomer aspect to the hall, being of far greater benefit and less risk, costing much less, and replacing the costliest and most complicated gymnasium equipment.

That is why we said that the Household Gymnasium is a good thing to have. A house of firm foundations and strong walls must be given to the tormented soul or the soul in constant danger of misfortune. *Mens sana in corpore sano* (a sound mind in a sound body) is a well-known Latin phrase.

Here is what the prominent North American thinker, Professor Hall,[1] has just written in the *North American Review:*

1. Granville Stanley Hall, psychologist, philosopher, and educator, who established himself as the foremost educational critic in the country. He was the author, among other works, of *The Contents of Children's Minds,* published in 1883.

"I consider hygiene the principal need in the education of children. And perhaps the first thing I would teach them, and that most energetically, would be the development of their muscles. Few people are aware of the very close relationship between physical weakness and moral iniquity, or how impossible is the healthful energy of the will when it is not sustained by the strong muscles which are its natural implements, and to what extent qualities as beautiful as self-denial, self-control, and serenity in misfortune depend upon good muscular development."

La América (New York), March 1883

Variety in Teaching Oral Classes

Would it not be a good thing, if instead of serious and unstimulating lectures, there were vital and interesting classes, where greater variety would be permitted in relation to the subject matter being explained? Would not interruptions for questioning, prompt additions, occasional recollections, appropriate natural language, add a great amount of pleasure to the dry questions which must be dealt with in the Law School?

Perhaps it was not a mistake on the part of the School to reflect a bit upon this humble opinion. Variety must be a law in the teaching of dry subject matter. The attention tires of concentrating for a long time upon the same material, and the ear enjoys the fact that different tones of voice surprise and charm it in the course of the harangue. How one speaks heightens the value of what is said, so much so that it sometimes takes its place.

A lecture does not subject a person, it diverts him. Human nature and especially American natures need some imagination in what is presented to their reason; they take pleasure in lively and turbulent expression; they need a certain brilliant form to encompass what is essentially dry and serious. This does not mean that American intelligences reject the profound; they merely need to take a bright and shining road to it.

It might be said that one tries to have one's lectures give a certain respectable character to the oral classes, but the classes are not in need of that. Knowledge is better established in proportion to the pleasanter form given to it.

Those entrusted with the School's teaching certainly have nothing to fear regarding the success their words might have there. All of them are distinguished lawyers, appreciated for their worth, and most of them are loved by the young people who are to attend their classes. In Mexico one notes with pleasure that the young are quick and eager to bring to light and to praise the talents of those who judge their teachers and talk warmly and enthusiastically about them.

Classes in which there are incidents and animation are alive and endure. At times the weary attention needs some accidental recourse to jolt and revive it. Concepts expressed in a daily natural way are better impressed upon the intelligence than are those presented wrapped in the diluted form of written perorations—always severe and detailed, of course. The student who writes what he is to read aloud in class knows that, because it is not improvisation, he is writing what will be submitted to judgment; therefore he wants that judgment to find nothing to censure in it.

It must not be like a lecture.

A knack with words is frequent in the American lands; as a matter of fact it is difficult here to find anyone who considers them labored; the exuberance of these virgin peoples is powerfully manifested in all forms. Besides, it is a sure thing that nobody deprecates that which is well known. The ability of those who have been chosen to make practical the beautiful idea of the Law School is well known. The public knows, for everyone honors the Mexican legal profession and its eloquence alike; so then, the condition is fulfilled, and words about known material must be, without any doubt at all, pleasing and facile as well as sound and instructive.

And thus the field would be opened to eloquence and stimulus; thus the one who explains would be more closely identified with his audience. Thus, in the teaching of law, the professor would be able to expand his recollections into all kinds of allusions and memories which create in his classes a noble atmosphere of learning and respect forever bound up in memory with the recollections with which he enlivened and treated affectionately both forces in our intelligence and hearts. It is a lecture hall rather than a court of rhetorical speech; it is a simple blending, a mutual and gentle affection, an intimate and most beneficial communication, a fruitful identification between the cultivated intelligence and those opened to hope, to broad avenues, to luminous precepts, to growth and culture, to a beautiful union of affections never forgotten when once enjoyed, never fully experienced when lost.

The classroom is a placid time of life. The Law School is opening a most useful pathway now in which there might be greater progress if the manner of available teaching methods were attractive and pleasant.

It is not a mistake, then, to believe that such lectures would give brilliance, an agreeable individuality, a new charm, to the lessons of the School—in short, forms and a response that are common to the lively and animated Mexican intelligence. There are those who listen to the lectures because of these desires: an overabundance of fitness on the part of their instructors, and a greater guarantee of results from the thinking of their assiduous institution. Would this humble opinion deserve the attention of the School's faculty? Failing to study or think would certainly not be useful to their tasks. Perhaps this exhilaration will be unattainable or inopportune, but even if this is so, it stems from the pleasant affection which the purpose of the Law School arouses and deserves.

Revista Universal (Mexico), June 18, 1875

Equality of Women

In the United States of North America the headmaster of a coeducational school states that, at least from what he has observed in a dozen years at Swarthmore College,[1] there is no difference at all in the intellectual capacity of the sexes, provided that both are exposed to the same system, the same type of education, and the same outside influences. He has had to distribute school awards between boys and girls with complete equality and fairness, and when there has been an excess of prizes in some area it has been in favor of the girls. With regard to his pupils' capabilities this observer sees no more difference because of sex than because of the color of their hair. He believes that if boys profit greatly as a result of mixing with girls, from whom they acquire perspicacity, generosity, and gentleness, it is even more useful for girls to mix with boys, who free them from the awkwardness, lack of social behavior, and ignorance of men's spirit that generally cause such great and irremediable misery later on in their lives.

"Sección Constante" (Caracas), April 1882

1. Swarthmore College in Pennsylvania was founded by the Society of Friends (Quakers).

Manual School for Girls

Cornell University, a model school in this age of men; Cooper Institute, out of which the student comes with gratitude in his soul and a chisel under his arm; Felix Adler's[1] well-rounded school where, without any loss of feeling or imagination, the child is taught the qualities of habit and agility that life demands; the practical school of industrial education where students fight each other to be admitted, and their intelligence and character are visibly growing; a sound but humble school run by one of our own countrymen in a corner of Orange County,[2] where the bearded headmaster, who goes out at sunrise to milk his cows and currycomb his horse to a brilliant sheen, explains a marvelous arithmetic; those lively schools where there are teachers who have struggled for what is needed to cut a brilliant and honorable figure in the world, to earn their bread without subjugating their honesty and talents to unjust class interests or culpable political conniving—those workshops of honesty are launch-

1. Felix Adler (1851–1933), educator and founder of the Ethical Movement, established the Society for Ethical Culture in New York City in 1876. The aim of the movement is to emphasize the importance of moral factors in all life's relations. The society established a school, which is the one Martí refers to.
2. The reference is to the school operated by Tomás Estrada Palma. See "Education and Nationality."

ing the American who may in the future make a stand against the growing influence of the bureaucratic Yankee, the Yankee who has a mania for holding public office, the hireling Yankee, the weak wasteful Yankee who proudly displays at childish parties in his room at a rhetorical university the shoulders that were produced by the excessive playing of polo or baseball.

It is holiday time now for all those institutions of learning. This is the month of degree-giving and vacations. Cadets leave as lieutenants, lawyers and doctors receive their diplomas, in ceremonies open to the public. When the teacher Peter Cooper's name is heard, five hundred students—those men who will owe their happiness to him, and the women whom he always addressed on foot, hat in hand—all stand up and sing "Hail to the Chief" for their dead chief, so that it might be readily seen that he was a person versed in noble gallantry as well as a wealthy man of industry. Because Peter Cooper understood how to truly educate women, giving them the habit of living honorably and doing work in keeping with their comely sex, without robbing them of the charm, queenly grace, and general strength of their feminine qualities; for the one who wants to kill a nation educates its women as if they were men. Bestiality and egoism are the world's enemies; one must create courage and unselfishness in peoples; woe to Zoraida, who threw a pearl into the sea and then spent the rest of her life on the shore, weeping for that pearl!

But this year's innovation has been the practical school for girls, or the "manual school" as it is called here, and it could be called that in Spanish too because what is educated most is the hand, whether in culinary skills that pacify the indigent husband and amuse the rich man's wife, or in the drawings and decoration that teach the young girl the essential lines to enable her to ingeniously construct her designs according to what she sees in Nature and in good models. It amazes one to note that these advanced young people are not fatigued by physical effort; instead, they seek it as recreation, and their minds are strengthened and clarified rather than confused by instruction in literature. They make better inferences, combine facts more quickly, relate them, and create. Being productive affords satisfaction, even if only producing a modest fritter. "Look at the fritter I made! " says a girl to her mother, showing her the respectable result, her eyes sparkling with joy. "Look at the lace I ironed! " says a perspiring Cinderella, not at all flustered from having scorched the most important part. But work with the hands must be done precisely and beautifully so that skill hides fatigue, and so that the pleasure of making the lives of the household servants more bearable by pleasing domestic chores will not be too costly. Gratitude is of so much help in maintaining love! When life slaps one in the face, it is so pleasing to be able to kiss an obliging little white hand in one's own home! Anyone who gives a woman these charms gives her happiness. The world is not a gilded cage of masters who fritter away their time, and of servants who hate. When the weary man is cleansing his spirit of blood, his wife must lay her hand upon his forehead alone where nobody sees him, and must bring to his lips a cup of well-boiled sugar water. And these girls are beginning to be taught all this—to thoroughly boil the sugar, mix flour into dough for bread, make tasty sauces and simple vegetables, and roast meat properly so that the mistreated husband will not have to go into the street to find digestives in the beer hall. She who will run the house is learning to see, and she who must wait upon herself is learning to be less unhappy.

It is in drawings and decorations that the benefit of freedom in education and in spontaneous work is most evident. There are quirks and vagaries in those unsure lines which reveal the lively impressions gained from summer strolls along the rivers, from mountains sleeping upon the sky, or from moonlight chats when curious eyes follow the exquisite embroidery with which the light upon the sidewalks delineates the foliage of trees. And that is where art originates: in direct impressions. Study is the rails, but the child's character and individuality is the engine. And it is evident that, even in girls who are less involved in occurrences, the freedom to invent and the pleasure of creativity stimulates their own ingenuity and strength of character.

La Nación (Buenos Aires), August 2, 1889

The Education of Woman

Like the land, human life is full of mountains and plains. And sometimes of sinister crypts and chasms! And at every step of the way it is necessary to take one's eyes from the mountains—the eminent men—and place them upon the plains. The lady from Massachusetts is in the Congress for discussions and festivities. Congress is looking into whether or not it is to profit by so many men from Europe as they arrive at these shores, and it was said in the Massachusetts Assembly that ladies can plead cases in the courts of the state. In this new land one notes a great urgency to give to woman the honest and ample means for her existence, means which come to her through her own labor and which shall assure her of happiness, because by uplifting her mind with solid studies she will live as man's equal and companion, and not at his feet like a beautiful plaything; and because, being sufficient unto herself, she will not be in a hurry to attach herself to anyone who happens by, like a wild convolvulus to a wall, but she will know and choose and rebuff a base and deceptive man and accept an industrious and sincere one. For in that very state which now accepts ladies as attorneys in its courts, there is a Miss Robinson who manages her lawyer's office with noteworthy success. This is an honor in Boston, the capital of Massachusetts, where the young lady works, because Boston is the center of critics and know-it-alls, and it is by ability, not wishing, that one cuts a figure there. One of the law journals that enjoys the highest reputation in all this land is also controlled by a cultured lady. In nine of the states of the union a woman can adjudicate as a lawyer both civil and criminal cases. In another state—Vermont—women who pay taxes, vote for the school-employee candidates to their liking, and those candidates can also be women; although the detractors say that this gives the ladies of Vermont little satisfaction, for this year there was a town where only five women voted.

But it is not only in the courts and ballot boxes that the thinkers of this land want to see women. It is in public administration, in the management of every house of charity, and on the advisory board of every correctional institution. For did not two New York governors name two ladies for high positions? This they did, and there are no more intelligent officials in the state, or posts better served. Who fails to see in the homes—and more in ours than in these—the ever timid and thrifty wife, and the ever prodigal and conceited husband, as if the land were Sesame and he Montecristo, and as if at each of his outcries—those terrible ones that find no answers—the obedient land were to reveal to his eyes its golden breast? Regarding good fortune we are somewhat Hebraic, and we are always waiting for a Messiah who never comes. There is only one way to see the Messiah arrive, and that is to sculpture him with one's own hands. The only wealth in the land is that which comes quickly by means of indecorum, or slowly by means of work. Who is to be a better adviser to misguided women than a kind lady? Or what person who sees a mother, and sees how she loves, predicts, sweetens, and forgives, can question that treasury of marvels that lies hidden in every woman's soul? It is a woman's hand, a magician's wand, that drives away owls, and snakes, and the touch of Midas that turns everything into gold. So why must it be unjust that in meetings where advice is given on how to manage women teachers or students or poor prisoners, it is the women (who are familiar with their monthly times of indisposition and with ways of reforming or healing) who are the advisers? A man is rude and impatient, and loves himself more than the rest. And a woman is tender and enjoys the giving of herself, is a mother since birth and lives by loving others. Summon her, then, to be a counselor in all these counseling meetings, and wherever there are women or children to manage or care for or heal, let a woman take charge, and thus the healing will be faster and gentler!

And in the colleges? Are those schools of higher learning to be closed to these women who must later become companions to men? For if their feet are not made for the same road, or their tastes for the same inclinations, or their eyes for the same light, how will they be companions to men? Every human being lives to reveal himself, and communication among souls is the mellowest of pleasures. What is an intelligent husband to do but take his frightened and saddened eyes away from the wife who fails to understand his language, or esteem his longings, or reward his noble characteristics, or divine his sorrows, or follow with her eyes the things he regards? And so comes this intellectual divorce, the most terrible kind.

According to what teachers and observers say, there is no proof that the feminine mind is too weak to carry within itself the deeper aspects of the arts, laws, and sciences. England has opened its colleges to women, and the English colleges are proud of them. Women study deep subjects at the university in London, where a third of the students are attentive and studious young ladies, and there is no year when they do not gain some relative advantage over the young men students. The English have four old and famous universities, and in those of London and Dowham the female students have been invested with the doctoral gown. At Cambridge they are admitted to the lecture halls and examinations, which enables them to graduate with honorary degrees, although this gives them no rights. At Oxford, a strict and stubborn university, they are admitted to professorships, which they gladly accept. It is a joyful sight to see spirited young men approach the doors of the college while the young women gravely step down from their carriages to make a serious study of the arts and sciences there. Excellent teachers have come out of Cambridge University. In this very land, Harvard is a much celebrated university and has a professorship for women, whose progress and application it extols. And at Cornell University, which also enjoys fame, there is no memory of any of its numerous female students ever having failed an examination. And now, like proud Harvard and famous Cornell, it is desired that the highly esteemed Columbia College will throw open its doors to young women. These things can have extraordinary significance for those who live upon other shores, but if it is true that this coming and going through lecture halls and along campus walks might seem to our countries like casting fragile flowers to the wind, they must be blind to the method of teaching, or to the fact that the institutes where it is practiced belong to men; rather, it must be anticipated in a way that harmonizes the extremely urgent need of that kind of education with our own customs. For husbands do not generally fly from the vernal golden cage in search of another spring, or from new beauty; they do so because a mindless lady is like an empty glass, and the thirsty man tries to find a place to rest his ardent lips. Souls are like roses; they need a burning sun and new dew to fall upon them with every dawn.

La Opinión Nacional (Caracas), April 11, 1882

Classical
and Scientific Education

New York, July 8, 1883

To the Editor of *La Nación:*

College quadrangles are beautiful these days. Before the students return to their homes, all of them are beginning to row, which they do well; to hunt, which they do poorly unless they hunt foxes or wolves; to swim, discuss their love affairs, dance, and run. All the colleges are inaugurating their classes now, distributing their prizes and degrees, calling their friends together, and holding their fiestas.

In this land the colleges are as old as the churches! Whoever mentions the name Harvard, the great college in Massachusetts which is the Oxford of North America, as it were, says a magic word that opens all the doors, takes all the honors by the hand, and draws to himself a fragrance of long ago. Whoever mentions the name Yale utters wisdom that tints the fair hair of its young doctors with gray.

Who is the counter of colleges here? There once was one who was said to have counted the dreams of the women in a harem; another the dreams of the spirit of an enslaved hero, and they were considered great enumerators. But those who did all that counting would never be able to count the colleges in the United States. Open any fine-print newspaper now, in this great month of the year when the joyful events in the schools are listed there; to admire, the heart is superfluous, but the eyes grow weary from reading about all the various kinds.

And do not let it be said that these colleges could not be better; they could; but it cannot be denied that their pruning hooks are lifted and are trimming the sickly classical tree—a good thing for stimulating the growth, as if with a rare and notable plant in a conservatory—of all the twisted branches and dry leaves which prevent the human sap from flowing unobstructed through the ample veins.

Since one is alive, it is fair that where teaching is done it is done for the purpose of knowing life. In schools it is necessary to learn to bake the bread which is later to be one's sustenance. It is good to know Homer[1] by heart, and he who has not read Homer or Aeschylus[2] or the Bible or Shakespeare[3] is a man who does not think, nor has he seen the whole of the sun or felt his own wings fully unfold from his shoulders. But men must learn this by themselves, because it is taught spontaneously and inspires love, and no teacher is needed for the arts of grace and beauty. And it is good —inasmuch as he who penetrates language penetrates life—to possess the culture of Greek and Latin, in what they hold of the rudimentary and primitive tongues, and serve to show the origins of the words we speak: seeing their innermost recesses explains things.

But since the earth puts forth forces, rather than rhymes and short stories, which are usually fabulous and meaningless outcries, and masses of visibly unconnected events without a cause, it is therefore urgent to study those forces. When the

1. Homer, the Greek poet who lived in the ninth or eighth century B.C., is traditionally believed to be the author of the *Iliad* and the *Odyssey*. For Martí's discussion of the *Iliad,* see "Homer's *Iliad"* below.

2. Aeschylus (525-456 B.C.), the first of ancient Athens's great dramatists, author of tragedies, of which seven are extant.

3. William Shakespeare (1564-1616), British poet and dramatist, generally viewed as the greatest writer of all time.

sun is very bright, let the Bible be read; and when its rays weaken, let one learn to scatter clusters of grapes like those of Canaan[4] which annihilated men with their weight.

Like the one who turns the sheath of his sword inside out, the entire transitory and unstable system of modern education must be completely changed. But there will be no true growth for a nation, or any happiness for men, until basic education becomes scientific—until a child is taught to manage those elements of the earth which are to nourish him when he is a man; until, when he opens his eyes to see a plow, he will know that a flash of electric power can draw it as an ox used to do in bygone days! For within a short time electricity will move plows.

La Nación (Buenos Aires), August 15, 1883

4. Canaan was the land in ancient times which covered the whole area of Palestine west of Jordan and Syria.

A Scientific Education

How can we fail to view with pleasure the fact that what *La América* has been advocating for months is today being confirmed by heated discussion and special attention in the most important periodicals of United States industry, mechanics, and trade? Two fields of activity have arisen: in one, the few calm and comfort-loving but ill-conditioned men are entrenched, sure of the noble and placid joys which give them the right to ardently love Greek and Latin; in the other, the new men, tempestuous and fervent, are cleaning their guns, for they are now in the midst of the struggle for existence, and are everywhere stumbling against the obstacles which the old type education is accumulating along the way in a new world. And they have children, and they see what they are coming to, and they want to free them from the hazards of working in twentieth-century factories with the rudimentary and imperfect tools of the sixteenth.

An outcry rises from everywhere, perhaps not well defined or reduced to concrete proportions, but loud and imposing and unanimous; a scientific education is demanded everywhere. No one knows how it is to be given, but all agree that it is indispensable and cannot be delayed. They cannot yet find a remedy for the wrong, but all know where the wrong lies and are diligently and vehemently searching for the remedy.

Broadstreet's, the most highly qualified and judicious

periodical of trade and finance published in New York; *Mechanics,* the most widely read journal by those who are dedicated to the skills of tool making; *The Iron Age,* an excellent magazine specializing in mechanical and metallurgical interests in the United States; these advocate with intense determination, in this August's issues, a technical education so that it may become something of general and common import. The speaker at a university festivity—one of those liveliest of universities where the students celebrate the beginning of classes—in words that have traveled over the nation amid applause, said something like this: Instead of Homer, Haeckel;[1] instead of Greek, German; instead of metaphysical arts, physical skills.

And today it is like a word said in passing, and a countersign of the times, in every good newspaper and important magazine. One fact is known, and it is enough to decide the contest: out of every hundred criminals locked up in prisons, ninety have never received a practical education. And it is natural: a pleasure-filled land kindles the appetite. In an age that pays well only for practical knowledge, in days of luxury when appetites are easily sharpened, he who has failed to learn the practical skills, which supply him with what is needed to satisfy those appetites, either struggles heroically and fruitlessly and dies a sad man, if he is honest; or is disheartened and kills himself, if he is weak; or looks for some way to satisfy his desires, if these are stronger than his idea of virtue, in fraud or crime.

Raw recruits fight badly in battles against veterans inured to war; whoever has to fight must learn well in advance, and with utmost perfection, the use of arms.

One feels the need, but cannot yet find the remedy. England has already named its Royal Commissioners for the study of technical education, and has established very suc-

1. Ernest Haeckel (1834–1919), German zoologist and evolutionist, a strong proponent of Darwinism.

cessful scientific schools; but in order to have good schools where one can go to learn science—this is not to be. May the spirit of education change from scholastic to scientific; may courses in public education be prepared and graded in a way that, from the primary classes all the way to the final conferring of degrees, public education will be developing—without the waste of spiritual elements—all those elements required for the immediate application of the forces of men to the forces of Nature. To divorce man from the land is a monstrous transgression. And that is merely scholastic: it divorces birds from their wings, fish from their fins, men who live within Nature from the knowledge of Nature: his wings.

And the only way to attach them is to arrange things so that the scientific element is a sort of core of the public education system.

May scientific teaching, like the sap in trees, rise from root to the topmost branches of public education. May elemental teachings be elementally scientific: so that the formation of the land is taught instead of the story of Joshua.

Sometimes men demand this: guns for the battle!

La América (New York), September 1883

A School of Mechanics

To learn petty office skills and the knowledge of a sales clerk, which fits into an anise seed, it seems unnatural for the young people of our American lands to be taken away from under the paternal wing to roam the streets, cease loving their own country, and grow used to living without it in a foreign land that neither loves nor adopts them. We have not come from Spanish America to North America for this, a futile and pernicious reason, but rather to learn about farming on the farms, unlocking a kind of instruction never started, so to speak, as we said in our last issue; to learn mechanics in the workshops; to learn, together with worthwhile habits and the extolling of work, how to manage the real and permanent forces of Nature—forces which assure man of knowing a real and permanent sustenance. For that, one must indeed come to the United States.

We therefore call your attention to a St. Louis company, The Excelsior Manufacturing Company, which gives good training to mechanics' apprentices. It deserves to be known. A radical revolution in education must be brought about in our countries if we do not always want to see, as we still see today in some of them, abnormal, atrophied, and deformed men like Horace's[1] monster: colossal head, immense heart,

1. Quintus Horatius Flaccus (Horace) (65–8 B.C.), outstanding Latin poet and satirist.

arms withered to almost skin and bones, and dragging their feeble feet. Instead of theology, physics; instead of rhetoric, mechanics; instead of the precepts of logic—because the rigor, stability, and union of skills are better teachers than the degenerate and confused texts of schoolroom opinion—the precepts of agriculture. Like a way-shower, then, we point to The Excelsior Company of St. Louis. Nor because of the adult workers' resistance to the apprentices, because the former are afraid of being out of a job, is it an easy thing to find workshops today where young apprentices are willingly received and fully trained.

In The Excelsior Company, all of the youths who desire to learn foundry skills, as long as they possess the necessary strength, are admitted to the factory. Since those who live far from their parents usually find too much pleasure in the vulgar and costly privileges of being their own masters, the factory prefers those who live with their parents, or who have someone to look out for them. Those who are still under age enter into regular apprenticeship; if they are already of age they are obliged by contract to work in the factory for three years. Each new apprentice is put to work beside a worker proficient in the branch which the newcomer is going to learn, thus greatly helping the theoretical and practical explanations of the instructors. The instructors are a perfect staff there, overseen by a superintendent who heads and directs this department of master workmen, and looks after the apprentices' good training and treatment. If after two weeks the beginner has shown good work habits, he is placed among the regular workers, in contact with whom he enters fully into the feverish and healthful work activity of these great factories whose astonishing animation, which at first causes amazement, later fills those who live in it with confidence and daring. The spectacle of the great tempers the spirit for producing the great.

If after eight weeks the apprentice shows the same promise, he begins to be recommended for small jobs and paid for them. Since the factory wants and needs the apprentices to promptly become good mechanics, it is a carefully observed rule that his training be facilitated on all counts, and in no detail hindered or delayed. The instructor is obliged to respond extensively and without delay to all the consultations the beginner desires of him, for his progress is being recorded by the expert as in our public schools, and submitted to the superintendent, who is thus authorized to reward the superior apprentices with distinction, and raise their wages.

In each of these instructors' notebooks, somewhat like the service records of soldiers, there are five different columns, in each of which goes one notation. In the "punctuality" column is entered the number of times the learner is absent from his work. In the "advancement" column, whose notations are based upon the examination of work done by the apprentice, are marked down the progressive merits of his work. In another column goes a notation of his conduct. In another, whether or not he takes good care of his tools. And in another, the care he takes of the models and the factory space in his charge. The apprentice who attains the number 1 in every column is outstanding. He who at the end of six or eight weeks has not reached an average grade—3 to 4—is dismissed and replaced by another who may be more apt.

Especially and above all, the factory demands punctuality of its pupils. It wants the work to be a natural occupation for them, not a burden. The day they fail to come to work it wants them to feel alone, unhappy, and guilty, as it were. Every week their work is examined and graded, and the instructors say that it is a beautiful thing to see how the students keep an eye on each other and nobly vie in doing the best work.

Nearly all the factory apprentices range from eighteen to nineteen years of age, although there are some who are sixteen.

As for salaries, the factory does not abuse: it pays four

dollars and a half per week to beginners, and five or six later on, until, as generally happens at the end of two months, they can now make machine parts, which are worth higher pay. And the company's books show that after seven months many of those apprentices turn out as good quality work as the oldest foundryman.

Good instructors, the vigor of youth, stimulus, and the accumulation of learning perform the miracle.

And through this kind of factory, where the tasks are hard and the greatest difficulties are overcome, must pass all who aspire to a solid education in mechanics.

La América (New York), September 1883

A School of Electricity

To the New World belongs the New University.

To the new sciences which invade, reform, and consume everything, the new professors.

Divorce between the education received in one epoch and the epoch itself is criminal.

To educate is to deposit in every man the whole of human effort preceding him; it is to make of every man the totality of the living world up to the day in which he lives; it is to place him at the level of his time so that he may float above it, and not to leave him below his time so that he will be unable to keep afloat; it is to prepare the man for life.

In theological times, a theological university. In scientific times, a scientific university. So then, what does it mean to see something and not know what it is? To group "Baralicton" syllogisms together, and declaim *"Quousque tandem,"* leaves no qualified men to move ahead in the world and be abreast of these men of the new breed who mount their steam engines and hold aloft, like lances, a sheaf of electric lights.

For such campaigns one needs a school of electric light.

When thinkers are dedicated to thinking about the capability of every people's real and permanent progress—which is different from the brilliant, false, and transitory—and about the relative solidity and inner force of the nations of this earth, England amazes them. She rules the seas. From her semiexhausted carboniferous cliffs she pours colossal ship-loads of inexpensive and useful products over the globe. She goes from the Old World to the New with the firmest step of any nation alive. She manufactures knives and recites the classics. Together with creating industrial arts and artistic industry, she spreads love through beauty, thus improving men. Just as a spacious room invites majesty, a beautiful object invites culture. The soul has an atmosphere of its own, and beautiful objects breathe this atmosphere from them-selves. Prudent, active, and without shouting, England is moving.

And beside every discovery she founds a school.

The universities of London, Cambridge, Liverpool, Bristol, Nottingham, and Glasgow for a long time have had special courses for the detailed and practical education of the new physicists, and have the equipment they use. Vienna, Munich, Berlin, St. Petersburg, all have already instituted similar courses. Not all make a business of closing their doors to the coming light!

In every nation there are cities of bats, or a good copy of bats, that live from the dark and are kings of it, but it is useless to shut the doors on that beautiful light which shines through walls!

And reform is not complete just by adding isolated courses of scientific education to the literary universities, but by creating scientific universities without in this way eliminating the literary courses; by taking a love of the useful, and an abomination of the useless, to the schools of letters; in teaching all aspects of human thought on every problem, and not merely a single aspect—for high treason is committed in that; in taking to literature scientific solidity, artistic solem-nity, architectural majesty and precision. Only such a litera-ture would be worthy of such men!

The literature of our times is ineffective because it is not the expression of our times. No longer is it Velleda who leads into battles, but a kind of Aspasia![1]

New blood must be taken to literature.

These universities, which we have been calling scientific, in Europe are beginning to be called "technical schools."

Darmstadt[2] has a perfect one, from which a student is graduated in all the new sciences—not to lead, as from so many universities of ours, the existence of a pettifogging or intractably poetic lawyer, the wretched fate of grandiose souls, but to occupy with the natural right of useful producers a seat in our creative age.

To be recompensed one must be useful.

And an electrotechnical subschool has now been added to this good technical school in Darmstadt. What do they teach in it? Simply what the name implies: the electrical sciences. In four years one will come out of it an expert. The students will use the first two years studying mathematics and the natural sciences in the mother school. And in the two remaining years, which they will spend among all the apparati and electrical equipment that is there or may be there, they will learn, in doctrine and application, everything important to know about this new agent.

Would you like to read the new school's prospectus? The very names will be unknown even to men who enjoy the wide fame of the well informed; nor do we know the names of the forces acting in our world!

Here is the prospectus:

1. Aspasia, fifth century B.C., mistress of the Athenian statesman Pericles and an influential figure in Athenian society, who was accused and acquitted of the charge of impiety.

2. Darmstadt, a city in central West Germany, capital of the state of Hesse, noted for its development of a chemical industry. A technical university was founded in 1836.

Magetism and electrodynamics.

Magnetic and dynamoelectric mechanics: conveyer of forces.

Electric lighting.

Principles of the telegraph and telephone.

Theory of potential, with special application to the science of electricity.

Electric signals for railroads.

Elevated electric railways.

Practical electrotechnique; galvanic machinery, determinations of differences in potential, of forces of currents and resistances.

Arc and incandescent lights.

Research on cables.

Conclusions on work transmitted by motors and electric machines.

Photometric research.

And those are only the subjects listed in the prospectus for the first fiscal year. So much do we seem like travelers lost in an immense forest—to so many other qualified men!

La América (New York), November 1883

Manual Work in the Schools

The United States schools of agriculture have just presented reports of their last year's work, and one can see from all of them that the theoretical laws of farming taught in these schools are less emphasized than the knowledge and direct management of the land. It is clearly the land which, at first hand and with inimitable geniality, teaches lessons that are always learned in a confused form from books and professors.

Physical, mental, and moral advantages come from manual work, and from that habit of method—a healthful counterweight, especially in our own lands, to the vehemence, restlessness, and deviation in which our imagination, with its golden inducements, holds us. Man grows by the work of his hands. It is easy to see how useless people are impoverished and vilified for some generations until they are pustules of clay with slender extremities which they cover with delicate perfumes and patent-leather buttons; whereas the one who owes his well-being to his work, or has employed his life in creating and transforming forces and in using his own, has a joyful sparkle in his eye, a profound and picturesque manner of speech, broad shoulders, and a sure hand. One can see how these are the ones who are shaping the world: exalted by the practice of their creative powers, perhaps even without knowing it, they have a certain air of happy giants and they inspire tenderness and respect. More—a hundred times more—than

132

entering a church, it stirs the soul to see those mechanics, tanned and healthy-faced and in soiled clothing, enter one of the wagons taking them from their poor neighborhoods to the factories on an early morning in this February cold. And even at this hour they have newspapers in their gnarled hands. Here are great priests, vital priests: workers.

The principal of the Michigan School of Agriculture ardently defends the advantages of manual work in the schools. For Principal Abbott there is no agricultural virtue that does not aid in the school's manual work. The farmer needs to know nature, the diseases, whims, freakish habits themselves of plants, in order to manage his farming in a way that takes advantage of the vegetal forces and avoids their aberrations. He needs to be in love with his work, and to find it nobler than any other whatsoever—and so it is, even if only because it permits him the most direct mental exercise, and with its copious and constant results provides him with a fixed and free income that allows him to live decently and independently. Oh, if only our vote were heard, we would put beside every Spanish American cradle a plot of ground and a hoe. In addition, the farmer should be intimately acquainted, in their effects and work methods, with the sciences which are today aiding and accelerating the science of agriculture. And because nature is harsh, like everything truly loved, the farmer needs robust health impervious to the heat of the sun and the puddles of rain, a health achievable only by getting used to both sun and rain.

With manual labor in school, the farmer gradually learns to do what he has to do afterwards upon his own farm; with his discoveries of the land's obstinacy and eccentricities, he becomes fond of it the way a father is fond of his children. He fancies the land he cares for, knows it, permits it to lie fallow, feeds and treats it much the same as a physician treats his patients. And because he sees that in order to work the fields intelligently he needs a varied and not a simple knowledge—at times even profound—he loses all disdain for work that permits him to be, along with being a creator—and this rejoices and uplifts the spirit—a cultivated man who is fond of books and worthy of his time. The secret of well-being lies in avoiding all conflict between aspirations and occupations.

Pages could be filled with the advantages of this manual work in the schools of agriculture, the report shows.

To make the agricultural students' work doubly useful, the schools do not apply it only to work methods already known, but to the testing of all the reforms which experiments or invention are suggesting; therefore, the agricultural schools are greatly benefiting the country people to whom they are giving reforms already proved, and are avoiding the risk of money and loss of time it might have cost them if they had had to experiment on their own account. And furthermore, the student's mind is kept active by this policy, and so it acquires the healthful habit of desiring, examining, and putting into practice what is new. Today, with the colossal affluence of intelligent and eager men in all walks of life, whoever wants to live cannot sit down to rest and let the pilgrim's staff of his voyage remain idle for a single hour: for when he wants to get up and set out again, the staff will have become a rock. Never, never was the world greater or more picturesque. It is merely difficult to understand and put at one's own level. As a consequence, many would rather speak ill of it and vanish into resentment. It is better to work and try to understand the marvel, and aid in perfecting it.

In one school, that of North Carolina, they have analyzed fertilizers, minerals, mineral waters, potable waters, the germinating power of seeds, the action different chemical substances have upon them, and the action of insects upon plants.

In general, the schools' practical efforts are directed toward the study and improvement of grains and tubers used for food; toward the application of various and better methods of preparing the soil, planting, and harvesting; toward comparing different fertilizers and manufacturing others; toward feeding animals and plants well, and irrigating and preserving the forests.

In addition to this they have courses that teach the students mechanical skills, not in an imperfect and isolated manner by which, in an offhand way and by chance, the attentive and able farmer comes to know a little of them, but with a plan and a system, so that some skills begin perfecting others, and so that they are taught how the latter emerges from the former. Minds are like wagon wheels and words: they light up with use and run more swiftly. When one studies under a good plan, it is a joy to see how the most diverse facts resemble each other and band together, and how the same ideas emerge from the most varied subjects, tending toward one common, lofty, and central concept. If man had time to study all that he saw and coveted, he would arrive at the knowledge of one single and supreme idea, would smile and then rest.

This direct and healthy kind of education; this application of an inquiring intelligence to a responsive nature; this serene and unconcerned employment of the mind in the investigation of all that occurs to it, stimulates it, and gives it a way of life; this full and balanced use of man so that he may be as he himself can be, and not as others were; this natural training— is something we should want for all the new countries of America.

And behind every school an agricultural laboratory, open to rain and sun, where each student could plant his own tree.

The fruits of life do not spring from dry and merely lineal tests, no, indeed.

La América (New York), February 1883

Living Languages
and Dead Languages

New England is famous for its colleges, customs, and learned people. The satirists still represent Massachusetts with skullcap and spectacles, as if to indicate that the historic state of Bunker Hill[1] and Concord[2] is still enamored of the old. But it is true that because of the natural and simple pride given by the legitimate superiority of the intelligence, and because of the improvement that comes to the spirit through its contact with ideas and the people who enjoy them, a Bostonian can be distinguished from the rest of the nation's inhabitants without great difficulty. From Massachusetts came Motley,[3] the profound and picturesque historian whose unforgettable writings must have enriched every good bookstore; from Massachusetts—Emerson,[4] an amorous Dante who lived above the earth rather than upon it, for he saw it fully and with certainty, and he wrote a human Bible. From

1. Bunker Hill is the hill in Charlestown, Massachusetts, near which the first major battle of the American Revolution was fought (June 17, 1775).

2. Concord is a town in eastern Massachusetts, the site of the battle, April 19, 1775, of the Revolutionary War where (with Lexington) the shot was fired "heard round the world."

3. John Lothrop Motley (1814–77), diplomat and historian, author of *The Rise of the Dutch Republic* (1856).

4. Ralph Waldo Emerson (1803–87), lecturer, poet, essayist, and leading exponent of New England Transcendentalism. For Martí's essay on Emerson, see the next volume, on Martí's literary criticism.

Massachusetts—Longfellow, the serene and melodious poet who forged a solid English upon new anvils, and removed it from them rounded and singing so that he could write his sensitive, melancholic, and pithy thoughts in clear, bright stanzas. From Massachusetts—Ripley,[5] the critic; Dana,[6] the journalist; Lowell,[7] the poet of the Yankee tongue, who is now United States ambassador to England, where he was elected, in an obsolete show of affection, rector of St. Andrews University. The best "divines," as priests are called here, are from Massachusetts, and they are a class worth noticing in this land for being cultured, generous, and useful, as if from a virtuous race in which the faculty of meditation has been undergoing purification and submitting itself to close scrutiny. And so are the wise and sensitive novelists such as Howells,[8] whose fame is beginning; the elegant versi-

5. George Ripley (1802–80), journalist, literary critic, and reformer, who became the leading promoter and director of Brook Farm, the famous utopian community at West Roxbury, Massachusetts, based on the utopian socialist ideas of the French social reformer, Charles Fourier.

6. Charles A. Dana (1819–97), noted journalist who lived at Brook Farm community from 1841 to 1846, also worked with Horace Greeley on the New York *Tribune,* where he published the articles of Karl Marx and Frederick Engels, and became a conservative editor and part owner of the New York *Sun,* and held that position from 1868 to his death.

7. James Russell Lowell (1819–91), poet, critic, and diplomat, famous for his antislavery poems; author of the *Bigelow Papers,* in which he satirized the Mexican War as a war of aggression in the interests of slavery. He later served as minister to Spain and ambassador to England.

8. William Dean Howells (1837–1920), novelist and critic and viewed as the dean of nineteenth-century American letters; long-time editor of *The Atlantic Monthly* and author of such novels as *The Rise of Silas Lapham* (1885), and the strongly pro-labor novels *Annie Kilburn* (1888) and *A Hazard of New Fortunes* (1890). Howells vigorously supported the defense movement on behalf of the anarchists in the Haymarket Affair.

fiers—but they are not poets because, although Whittier,[9] the Quaker, Holmes,[10] king of the anthology, and Lowell, the ambassador, are living, there are no poets in the United States now since the death of poor Sidney Lanier,[11] with the exception of Walt Whitman,[12] an academic rebel who breaks off a branch in the forest and finds poetry in it rather than in wrinkled books and gilded academic chains. Walt Whitman is a member of an academy whose president sits in the heavens.

And since the masters live around Boston and for centuries past have been living there, the most important universities, here known as colleges, are near Boston. Harvard and Yale are there, the Oxford and Cambridge of the United States. As numerous as those flocks of little black birds pecking away joyfully and bathing in the snow, good colleges under qualified chancellors abound here, these colleges until now the homes of the classic mind, unfortunately like those the world over. So then, to teach men who must live in these times the languages, feelings, passions, duties, concerns, and cults of long ago, and with courtly prudery—is this not infamy? Is this not slightly less criminal than leading soldiers armed with crooked leather shields and heavy, insecure helmets to fight against adversaries preceded by rumbling war machines and carrying cartridge-belt rifles—the ammunition pouches hang-

9. John Greenleaf Whittier (1807–92), Quaker author and militant abolitionist; wrote antislavery and prolabor poems and edited abolitionist journals.

10. Oliver Wendell Holmes (1809–94), physician, poet, humorist, and author of the "Breakfast Table" series of essays.

11. Sidney Lanier (1842–81), poet and music critic, reared in tradition of the Old South; his poetry reflected the social change of the post–Civil War South.

12. Walt Whitman (1819–92), journalist, essayist, and poet, whose *Leaves of Grass* (1855), made him a revolutionary figure in American literature. For Martí's essays on Whitman, see next volume, on Martí's literary criticism.

ing from the triggers—which they are now exposing to the weather, or equipped with the keen-edged Solinger saber?

This month the cancellors of all Massachusetts colleges have met to see, as Charles Francis Adams[13] wishes, whether less Greek and Latin are being taught in the colleges; or—as the chancellor of ancient Amherst College, noted for language study, and the chancellor of Dartmouth maintain—it is to be recognized that in order to live the impetuous, luxurious, and directly individual life of these days, Greek and Latin are the most necessary subjects. Directly individual, we say, and not a caste system as before; because before, when there were patron kings, and when by virtue of being parasites of the antechamber and greeter of the royal favorite, men were assured of a career; or as they were always figuring in some war, by going into the militia they were well on the way to earning money and honors; or by becoming a friar, for the Church looks out for friars. But today, these old power systems having vanished in some places and being poorly enforced in others, a man cannot seek the protection of their shade, and like a parasite upon the wall live in it. A man must wrest his livelihood from himself. Education, then, is this alone: men's ability to comfortably and honorably obtain the absolutely essential means of livelihood in their lifetimes, without thereby diminishing the subtle, spiritual, and superior aspirations of the best part of the human being.

This question of Greek and Latin is being much discussed now. The various systems of education revolve around it and are combined in it. Furthermore, two epochs are being brought together: that which is dying and that which is

13. Charles Francis Adams (1835–1915), railroad expert, civic leader, and historian, son of Charles Francis Adams, who was for twenty-four years, from 1882, a member of the Board of Overseers at Harvard University. His ideas on the education to be given by colleges and universities were developed in *A College Fetich* (1883), a protest against the study of dead languages.

dawning. The ornamental and flowery education that sufficed in centuries of established aristocracies for men whose
existence was provided for by the nations' unjust and imperfect organization; the literary and metaphysical education,
last stronghold of those who believe in the need to erect
(with an impenetrable and ultralearned class) a barricade
against humanity's new and impetuous currents which are
triumphing and offering challenges everywhere; the ancient
education of Greek poetry and Latin books or the histories
of Livy[14] and Suetonius[15]—all these systems of education are
now engaging in their final battles against a budding system
which is imposing its authority, a legitimate daughter of the
impatience of men who are now free to learn and work and
who need to know how it is done. And the land they must
improve, and from which they must extract with their own
hands the means of universal welfare and their own mainte-
nance, is stirring and being transformed.

We should like to have a review to deal with this situation,
using the breadth and variety of means which reviews permit
and the subject demands. But we must manage by merely
pointing it out.

Some maintain that Greek and Latin are useless from top
to bottom. Those who say this have never smacked their lips
over either Greek or Latin; nor over those chapters in Homer
that seem to be like the world's first forest, with monstrous
tree trunks; nor over the aromatic and discreet epistles of
Maecenas's friend. But this is a gala and joyous kind of
learning for the mind given to literature and born for it; this
is a certain aristocratic and leisurely kind of learning which
will be inevitable for anyone predisposed to acquire it, be-

14. Titus Livius (Livy) (59 B.C.–17 A.D.), one of the three great
Roman historians, the others being Sallust and Tacitus.

15. Caius Suetonius Tranquillus (69–122 A.D.), Roman biographer
and antiquarian, author of the famous *Concerning Illustrious Men*,
divided into books on poets, orators, historians, and teachers.

cause it will be desired; and people with no natural liking for it will remain unimpressed, for the tumultuous modern inclinations will remove it from their memory where it lies unwillingly.

The problem is this: must the greater and most useful part of one's college years be employed in learning two languages which merely influence—and that is what they do at best—the determination of a language's roots?

Is knowledge of language the principal need of modern man?

Must men be educated in opposition to their needs, or so that they may satisfy them?

Will the admirable and never contradictory order of Nature, as a mental exercise and discipline, not be of greater benefit to the mind than capricious, inverted Latin syntax or contrasting the several Greek dialects?

If the essential nucleus, substance, scientific residue, and definitive utility of the study of Greek and Latin—mental gymnastics aside, because in this the more applicable physical sciences are preferable—become the real and undeniably useful knowledge of the roots of language, and the channels through which this knowledge flows, and the axis upon which it turns—then why not give briefly, in a compendium, in essence, in results, this clear and already acquired knowledge? And why make every student lose very precious time in acquiring directly the jumbles and labyrinths of useless rules which will carry him no further than to investigate what is already known? Such a system is like having at hand a basket of ripe apricots and putting the fruit aside uneaten, waiting for the tree to finish strewing its bounty!

Grapes come in a bunch: no more than arguments against this prevalence of a study that gives minimal results in a teaching system of an age that requires maximum and essentially different results than the minimal ones given by the kind of study prevailing today.

Education has an inescapable duty toward man; failing to

comply with it is a crime; it must enable him to conform to his time without dissuading him from the grandiose and ultimate human tendency. Let man live in accord with the universe and with his time; for this, Greek and Latin are of no use to him.

That is why the heads of the most important colleges in the United States have met to see how the study of Greek and Latin can be gradually deemphasized in their programs.

La América (New York), January 1884

The Distribution of Diplomas
in One United States College

We are in a renowned United States college on academic-degree day. The select students number thirty, and their diplomas, tied with green, blue, and red ribbons, glow in their hands. They hold them with pleasure, as if clutching the keys to life. From here they will go out to shed light, to improve the ignorant, to pacify, uplift, and lead; the French word *élever* is a grand one: it means to educate. Those who have lived look sadly upon those who are beginning to live; and to hurl college students into life seems like clipping the wings of birds. The floor is filled with white wings. But life consumes strength, so, in order to restore the level, it demands that new forces periodically enter its tired veins. The students' energy and candor, even when they are not felt, encourage the people's honesty and faith, just as the bounteous waters of the new rains, laden with flowers and fragrant grasses, come down from the virgin hills to enrich with their abundance the impoverished flow of the rivers. A Protestant pastor opens the session: in the United States all public or private ceremonies, whether sad or happy, whether a college festivity or a congress of delegates of a political party, begin with a prayer. The pastor, dressed in black, lifts his eyes to Heaven and implores its blessings. The audience, seated in their pews, cover their faces with their hands, which they lean on the backs of the pews in front of them. And that spontaneous prayer of free men vibrates. Later, with Church quarrels, the prayer's virtue becomes unworthy. A Church without a dogmatic creed, but with that great, firm creed which the majesty of the universe and of the good and immortal soul inspires—what a great Church that would be! And how it would ennoble discredited religion! And how it would contribute to keeping the spirit aflame in these anxious and money-conscious times! And how it would bring together all men who are enamored of the marvelous and need to deal with it, but who cannot conceive of an all-harmonious nature being able to create inharmonious facilities in man, and who do not wish to pay for dealing with the marvelous at the cost of their reason and freedom!

We are in the famous college. The prayer over, one of the graduates mounts the rostrum. And another follows. They talk on deep subjects in certain language. They do not repeat from memory the proofs that the earth is round; nor discourse in detail about the capacity and qualifications of knowledge. Nor do they recite in chorus the ancient names of the coves, backwaters, and river bends of Greek history, as we were made to do in our times, to the great satisfaction of parents and teachers (who in truth derived scant satisfaction from it). The plumage takes on colors with all these extremely useful bits of knowledge, but the brain profits nothing, nor does the life in which it must struggle in an educated way, nor the manner of steering through life and guarding against its afflictions. In some colleges one hardly opens the book which should always be open there: the book of life.

The students in the college where we are do not talk about those specious things; they enter their speeches through the most exacting questions of the moment and through others of constant physical and psychological importance. Their speeches do not fly like the leaves, or like so many conversations, but are weighty like a well-fruited branch. And this, bearing in mind that we are not among doctors, only mere holders of the bachelor's degree. One graduate reads a study on imagination in mathematics, saying that the former plays as much of a part in the constructions of the latter as in the painful and luminous concepts of poetry, and that in order to write *Paradise Lost,*[1] no more power of imagination was needed than to establish the fundamental principles of conic sections. Another examines the reasons for the damaging influence of the ignorant Irish immigration into the cities, where its many people are strangling the vote and taking possession of it, without—because of their habit of congregating only with those from their own native soil, and because idealism is not a singular element of their nature— having their culture rise on a par with their influence and authority in the voting booth among the people who receive them as their sons. In suburban fields the Irish raise geese, ducks, goats, and barefoot children who cannot use their beer-ridden fathers and bedraggled mothers and sordid parish priests as models for a better life. Instead, they come out of their rooted wooden shacks as paupers. And since the Irish immigration to New York is so large, it happens that the great city is truly seriously threatened with mental and moral misery. The Germans would remedy the situation if they were not so given over to their own pleasures and so unmindful of the welfare of others. One can see that brutishness and self-interest make a bad foundation for a formidable city. Certainly there are schools; but what training the schools provide for the children of the Irish, the goat eats up.[2] The German child, because his father is accustomed to making his

1. *Paradise Lost,* the epic poem by John Milton (1608–74) was first published in 1667. The sequel, *Paradise Regained,* was published in 1671.

2. These charges are too sweeping against an entire population, even though aspects of the situation Martí describes did exist. For a more appreciative view of the Irish, see Martí's article, "The Schism of the Catholics in New York," in *Inside the Monster: Writings on the United States and American Imperialism by José Martí,* edited by Philip S. Foner (New York, 1975), pp. 270-87.

own way and does not live in such a squalid community, benefits from his books; besides which, the German is home-loving and industrious, and gives his children good habits without any effort. The graduate's speech did not say all this, but said other excellent things.

Another young bachelor assaults the rostrum and reads. ... But what is it that everyone applauds? Well, nothing less than a study defending the right and capability of the Egyptians to govern their own land, and charges as being only a mask of English ambition that indecent pretext by which it has for years been coiling itself around Egypt the way the boa constrictor coils itself around a dove; the pretext that some ambitious men who know Latin have a natural right to rob some Arabic-speaking Africans of their land; the pretext that civilization, which is the common name by which the present state of European man is known, has a natural right to take possession of foreign territory belonging to barbarity—the name that those who desire foreign territory give to the present state of every man not from Europe or European America, as if, head for head and heart for heart, a subjugator of the Irish or a shooter of Sepoys[3] were worth more than one of those prudent, loving, and impartial Arabs who, without heeding the warning of defeat or quailing before their enemy's number, defend their native land with hope in Allah, a lance in every hand and a pistol between the teeth. But since liberty lives from respect, and reason is nourished on controversy, the youth here are educated in the virile and redemptive practice of saying fearlessly what they think, and to hearing without anger or evil suspicions what others think, so that no sooner does the applause with which all of us receive the upholder of human decency cease, than there is already upon the rostrum a bachelor defending the perfect right of England to definitively place her hands upon

3. Sepoys were native Indian soldiers who fought unsuccessfully against British seizure of India.

the forsaken people of Egypt, and to seize that country, armful by armful,[4] the way the United States seized Indian territory.

Another graduate praises the North American system of public education, and says that the homogeneity of the new citizens proves that this manner of teaching is worthy of a strong people. But the neighboring graduate stands up, deprecates the system in use, and claims that there is no greater failure, because the schools teach for the children of the rich who are to live from their inheritance and not their labors, and because there are hardly any nations where children at the age of fifteen have a more deficient and rudimentary education on leaving school: they know how to spell, write, and count, but their thirst for knowledge has not been awakened, and they are not possessed of that human ingredient and that congeniality without which men are transformed into this empty, destructive, and horrendous creature, the egoist.

A very young bachelor, who carries off all the glances, is the one who immediately, and not without historic style and competent criticism, recounts the life of the two Elizabeths: the odious one of England and the great one of Spain.[5] The following speech seems to show the speaker to be a master of science, for with some ingenious arguments and picturesque turns of phrase this graduate denies that the vital and physical forces are equal, and that these may never attain the original creative power which resides only in the colossal unknown will. "Chemistry," says the graduate, "has been able to fabri-

---

4. The British occupied Egypt in 1882 and established a protectorate over it for forty years. Complete independence was not gained until the victory of the forces led by Gamal Nasser in 1953.

5. Elizabeth I of England (1533–1603), the "Virgin Queen" and dominant force in Europe of the period. The Spanish Elizabeth is undoubtedly a reference to Queen Isabella I (1451–1504), who with her husband Ferdinand V, founded the modern Spanish state.

cate eggs, but not make chicks hatch from them." And the graduate who brings these animated exercises to a close delivers an oration of exquisite tenderness, with concise language and profound vision, about the sound and sad philosophy of George Eliot,[6] the noble and unfortunate English novelist, a new stoic for whom life is put entire—as always for sublime souls—into a bitter glass which she drinks down to the dregs so there would be nothing left for the others to drink, without the mists of bitterness itself, which cloud the eyes of so many, causing them confusion when they see how many elements of solid risk there are in the well-educated consciousness and in Nature. Every living thing liberates a definitive and universal justice which assures a proximate compensation for the world's inequalities and injustices. The valiant consciousness, as outstanding among men as an unconquered giant among Lilliputians, encourages and cherishes.

And still we have not said, and we kept silent purposely, that these bachelor's degree recipients—so graceful and walking through the entrails of a character and repainting past empires so masterfully, and holding high the banner of free men, and balancing the body and soul of Nature—are women. Girls of eighteen to twenty are this year's graduates in Vassar College.

Oh, the day when woman will cease to be frivolous; how fortunate for man! How, from merely a dish of enticing flesh, she will become an urn of the spirit to which men will ever press their eager lips! Oh, the day when reason need not be divorced from the natural love of beauty! The day when, from the pain of seeing empty the glass it imagined to be filled with soul, it need not go—feverish and despairing—from glass to glass in search of a beautiful soul! Oh, the day when what is loved need not be disdained! For this, women do not

6. George Eliot (1819–80), the pen name of Mary Ann Evans, famous English woman novelist.

have to be withered bluestockings; like men who know, by the mere fact of knowing, that they are not pedants. Make instruction so common among women that the knowledge they possess will go unnoticed. Even they themselves will not notice it, and then the languor of love will stay at home. For when a man needs somebody to understand his misery, admire his virtue, or stimulate his wisdom, he will not have to go away from home to seek her, as happens now. Let not compassion, duty, or habit be responsible for keeping a couple together, but rather an ineffable amalgam of spirit, which does not mean a servile respect of one marriage partner for the opinions of the other; on the contrary, it is that delightful closeness of souls in which their opinions, capabilities, and incentives are similar even when their appearances are distinct.

The husband grows because of his wife's merits; with them she thrusts roots into him. This is good: the only pleasure that avoids a painful life and perfumes, uplifts, and fortifies it is that, like a tree in the ground, roots have been thrust into a warm and loving soul.

Furthermore, nations, like waters, seek their own level. Each nation, if it is to be saved, requires a certain portion of intellectuality and the feminine elements, and even as no child is born without a father and mother, so no nation is born without the fortunate communion of the virile and feminine elements of spirit. Nations die of a hypertrophy of strength, making them proud, confused, and intoxicated, and causing them pain and countless upheavals because of their own excess, just as from a hypertrophy of sentiment and art, which debilitates and feminizes them. Spiritual conditions have their hygiene as do physical ones, and from one condition a person will rest in another, which moderates and modifies it. From strength one will rest in tenderness. In addition to this need of femininity in a nation's life, in nations given to fatigue there is a nervous kind of labor and a desire for wealth, a great urgency to balance woman's education—which takes sensitivity and a kernel of intellect to the life of the nation—with the shortage in which these conditions naturally remain because of the almost exclusive consecration of the national majority to battles, emotions, and the pleasures of possessing fortunes. To shed a soft light and illuminate the gloom, like wayfaring stars, those holders of the bachelor's degree, with shapely forms and beautiful long hair, scatter through the country every year; ashamed of not being like them, those earners of wealth who woo and desire them to improve themselves. Their contact, example, and teaching sweeten and spiritualize the existence around them. And just as one takes more enjoyment in good wine in finely wrought goblets or in slender, clear crystal, so one receives the spiritual influence of a cultured and beautiful woman with greater gentleness, pleasure, and profit.

La América (New York), June 1884

Chautauqua:
The University of the Poor[1]

If the patriot is genuinely fond of his country, he will not start reading a newspaper with the editorials that print what is surmised, but with the news items that print what has happened. Seeing everybody work is more beautiful than seeing one person think. There is only one spectacle more imposing than that of men's minds swept by the words of a righteous and fair-minded speaker, and that is an evening in the city when the workers are returning to their homes. "What is the most beautiful sight you've seen in the mountains? " was asked of a poor sham mountaineer who went to set his mind where it would again pay compliments, and where he could reach out to touch the sky. "Well, no storms or waterfalls or pine trees have made an impression on my

1. The so-called Chautauqua movement, a system of popular education, began in 1874 as a Sunday-school teachers' assembly, which met for two weeks in August at Fair Point on Lake Chautauqua in western New York. It was organized by John Heyl Vincent (1832–1920), bishop of the Methodist Episcopal Church and educational leader. Beginning as a tent school for the Sunday-school teachers, the assembly developed rapidly into a summer resort for study and lectures. In 1878 Vincent presented a plan for a course of prescribed readings, with examinations and diploma, which became the Chautauqua Literary and Scientific Circle, and local "circles" sprang up in hundreds of places. It marked the beginning of home-study and correspondence schools in America, while the summer classes at Chautauqua brought immense audiences to hear the most eminent scholars and lecturers.

soul like that last cart in the wagon train where the laborer, his face turned to the theater of hills, is sitting in the fading light among the tools and provisions he is taking home, till he reaches his valley and the little white house nestled at the bottom, and with a 'Good-Bye! ' unhitches his cart by the light of the stars." It is the news item which tells us about people's lives and the welfare and individuality of everyone— the basis of each of us—because there is no pleasure except when it is shared by all, for each person is the creator and joint owner of himself and sees his productivity increase in abundance and order. The only happiness comes from continuous and varied work, without which all else is tiresome or ceases to resemble it, for work is the salt of all the other pleasures. Everyone's freedom has but a single root: everyone's work.

The monthly magazines here are a veritable feast in summer, because, together with the usual advertisements, such as those of water paints instead of oil paints for houses; steel wool to plug up holes and cracks against the cold and heat; quick-acting cameras that take portraits and landscapes in a jiffy and without any preparation; advertisements for boats, heaters, perfumes, and velocipedes—there are the advertisements of schools which in these summer months move about from mountains to seashore, learning the truths of Nature out in the open. One page is for books, the facing page for schools. "A woman bound for the country should take with her Howells' new novel, *The Shadow of a Dream,* in which one is gently taught, in a choice collection of thoughts, that it is not good for a friend who stays out until all hours to live with a married couple," according to a resident of Buenos Aires touring through Germany. "When you go to the country, if there are squirrels about, take along the books of Thoreau; Thomson's,[2] if you go where there are

_____

2. There are several naturalists by the name of Thomson to whom this could apply, such as Sir Charles Wyville Thomson (1830–82) and Sir John Arthur Thomson (1861–1933).

rivers; Burroughs',[3] if you go where there are flowers; Lubbock's,[4] if you want to know about micro-souls and study the universal aspect of small life forms by examining scarabs and spiders." "If you have children and take them to the mountains for an airing, buy them the best novel: Arabella Buckley's book, in which the new science is both sparkling and entertaining, and where one can learn all that is truly known, in 'the short history of natural science' or in 'tales of the magic of science.' " And on the front pages of those magazines are invitations to studious scholars to attend the Curtis School, because "character formation is paramount"; the Home School, a "truly secure haven"; the Friends' Institute, where "each student may worship God as he pleases"; the School for Retarded Children, which "strengthens congenitally weak minds"; Cayuga College, where the students dress in "gray uniforms with gold buttons"; and Greenwich Academy, with "steam heat and electric light."

But there is one school that has no advertisements in the periodicals, wastes no buttons, has no walls or fences, and does not teach present-day Yankee men, or Yankee women, to live as in the days when there were quack doctors and bewigged barristers. On the contrary, at lakeside and upon mountain slopes, from when the laurel blooms in June until the acorns wither in October, this school explains in the bright sunshine how light rays spread rapidly in waves, and how they paint or photograph. It studies the skies in the stars themselves, and in the meteor that fell a month ago from one of the burnt-out stars, and tells about the clouds below these stars.

The school teaches how to cook by cooking, how to hike by hiking, teaches photography by taking photographs. It

3. John Burroughs (1837–1921), essayist and naturalist, who wrote many books on nature.

4. John Lubbock (1834–1913), British banker, politician, and naturalist, famous for his work *Pre-Historic Times* (1865).

offers instruction on how to roast potatoes and measure light waves. It is the free school of Chautauqua, which in the summer throws open its public walks, its temple of philosophy, its ambulant classes, its lake and rustic amphitheater, to all who want to come and go in those picturesque buildings and to study, remember, and teach—calisthenics or commerce or household skills or painting and music—merely for the pennies that can fit into a woman's fist. There, the only matriculation fee is one's will and one's strong desire to learn, the only obligation good manners. It is a university of the people, open upon the bosom of nature. Many men, and many women, when they mean "mother," say "Chautauqua."

The country town of that name has ten thousand residents during these hot months, and its Institution is for all the people; those who do not attend its classes have study courses in their own homes. The thousand daily transients wander wherever their fancy leads—to see the steamboat on the lake, where the meteorology class is held, or to Palestine Avenue, where the hundred botany students forgather to describe leaves. Women teachers go to the retreat for women professors to learn how to subdue the obstreperous students. Speech devotees attend the speech class, where there is one teacher for the humorous speakers and another for the political ones. At the end of the afternoon everyone goes to the amphitheater, nestled in a natural glen, where a philologist who does not believe in Müller[5] talks about the origin of languages, or where an evolutionist of the Mivart[6] school explains the species as a preconceived work of a divine plan for the universe, or where an entomologist demonstrates with

5. Max (Friedrich) Müller (1823–1900), orientalist and language scholar whose works stimulated widespread interest in the study of linguistics.

6. St. George Jackson Mivart (1827–1900), British biologist who became a leading critic of Charles Darwin's theory of natural selection, author of *Genesis of Species* (1871).

his person the truth of Emerson's theory that he who lives by bottling up insects ends by bottling up himself, for what he maintains sheds no light upon, or gives no precise facts about, the formation of new species even if the entomologist knows his approximately one hundred and fifty thousand insects. But what counts in the craftiness of these speakers, in the boredom itself, is that it arouses as much interest as the most amusing story, and the men in the audience put down their pencils, and the women stop knitting, as they wonder if the professor is talking about insects or men and women.

"Thank you, sir," says a big, bald, and bony man from high up in the gallery, "I've always felt that in my town poets can see the truth before anyone else, and this conversation proves it because we men are only grown-up worms, which is what Emerson said before Darwin, when he said that in a worm's struggle to be a man, it climbs from one form to another till it's a bald and bony man like me, or else it spends its life like you, bottling up other worms." And at this point, amid the tumult of birds in the doorway, another man stands up and recites all of Emerson's poetry. Then the volunteer chorus on the platform breaks out into a hymn joined by the audience of five thousand, their heads bared. The amphitheater, with its cedar branches placed in semicircular tiers in the hollow of the hard ground, gradually empties, row by row. And when the man hiding in the entryway sees the people leaving, how misty his eyes become! They are the newly married couples, the honest ones who worked before setting up housekeeping together, and together are learning what they do not know, so that their love will not come to an end because of ignorance or poverty. They are the sons and daughters of farmers, stoop-shouldered and wearing spectacles, come to learn about Horace and Virgil, and about when they were considered magi in Italy, before the moon rises double, the moon that joins the sun in harvest week. They are big men with few clothes and deep-set eyes, coming with a few fifty-cent pieces to study mechanics, bookkeeping, politics, speech, style in writing, photography. They are hotel employees who are reading Goethe[7] or carrying a yellowed volume of Ibsen[8] or a Hebrew grammar. It is a crowd of women of all ages—mothers on holiday, persevering aunts, women professors on leave from their teaching, elegant townspeople, born coquettes, ugly ladies with spectacles. They carry notebooks, workbags of embroidery, summer novels, boxes of watercolors. One sees a German proverb, a French term, a line from Homer, a Latin quotation.

A completely contented husband kisses his sparkling-eyed wife on the cheek: "Woman, we're worth more than we used to be! " Their clothes are of percale or a poor grade of wool. Their hands are weather-beaten.

After eating, they go to the lake, because for the seventy-five cents they pay upon arrival in the town, they may sail in the beautiful steamboat along the green-girdled coves of calm Chautauqua Lake. Or they go to the Temple of Philosophy, where a tutor in architecture is teaching a few gray-haired students about Doric columns; it is open to the public to show some reliefs of Grecian life. Or, taking advantage of the full moon, they go to see the College of Liberal Arts, an impressive place with more Byzantine domes than can fit into the four corners of a Flemish roof, and with a cloistered shelter above another built like a kiosk. Bishop Vincent's son happens to pass by, his wife by the hand. He has been directing this entire enterprise as if it were a game ever since his father assumed the episcopate, and it is a pleasure to see him wandering about, his wife nearby, entering into the affairs of this or that resident, greeting a newly arrived professor, picking a daisy, driving a fence post deep into the ground with a thrust of his arm. The street is like a family, and there is whispering and a shifting of groups. No saloons, no pool halls. The men are men and the women are women—

7. Johann Wolfgang von Goethe (1749–1832), one of the giants of world literature, most famous for *Faust* (Part I, 1808; Part II, 1832).

8. Henrik Ibsen (1828–1906), Norwegian poet and playwright, one of the greatest dramatists of all time, creator of modern realistic drama.

even more so. Some of the women gossip, others discuss Tolstoy,[9] and one of them who "neither wants nor needs any intimacy with gross and despotic males" disclaims him. Another talks softly with her male companion about physics. Still another stands in a group giving recipes for pies. Some boys race down the street hawking an "extra" of the town's daily newspaper. "Extree, extree, read all about the arrival of the professors of natural philosophy, read all about the celebration in the children's church! Buy the *Assembly Herald!* "

And everyone pays for the newspaper out of his own pocket, like any consumer who buys things for his own use and pleasure, though there are few temptations here for spending money, because the community that owns and administers the town does not want any of the "healthy competition" that gives rise to bickering among the shop-keepers and factions and among the buyers, nor does it admit any more stores than necessary, and only one of a kind. The community obviously has money, because the steamboat runs, the highways are not covered with dead leaves, and the streets are like those of a city. Water and gas are not free, and neither is all the music. It costs no small sum to hire pro-fessors or the well-known speakers who come from far and wide to lecture. But only those who put their heart to work know what it can do. An impulse of the heart is worth a million. Chautauqua is made for the good of all, and it helps everybody. Anyone living in a house here for the summer pays rent. Anyone attending classes pays a small fee for each. What is lacking, even covering all the expenses, comes from the students one cannot see—from the ubiquitous university which holds its classes at the sickbed and at the worker's night table—the "fifty thousand" affiliated with Chau-tauqua's literary and scientific circle and with the circle in the homes. A person can write to John Vincent, Buffalo,

9. Count Leo Tolstoy (1828–1910), Russian poet, novelist, and dramatist, social thinker and reformer, whose most famous novel, *War and Peace,* was published 1865–69.

N.Y., Box 194; he then takes his place like any other student among those enrolled in the circle. From Buffalo the circle directs the studies which each one pursues in his own home, and the course takes four years: scientific subjects, history, mathematics, literature. Each student buys the required textbooks wherever he pleases. At the end of the course, the circle sends out its examination questions, which the student answers to see whether or not he is approved. The circle takes the student by the hand and advises him what to read, offers opinions on the new books, answers his questions and resolves his doubts without delay, and sends him the *Chautauqua,* whose monthly index of important events parallels the general reading matter recommended by the circle for that month. And to enter the University of the People—the home study courses—costs fifty cents a year.

There is one motive behind all this good work which, with the subtle and incisive power of dogma, deprives the courses of the greatest benefit that could accrue to the students, that of studying hand in hand with those who had no "axe to grind" or stairs to climb in the world's palaces, but who could teach unselfishly, neither adding to nor subtracting from all that is known of the world's substance—without sinking to the level of the ant who stupidly declares itself healer of the forest: something that men bent upon taking care of God on the earth do. The Methodist Church, dying elsewhere, is flourishing in Chautauqua because there it has stood with the common people, and opened its mind to the times. These days people do not desire a dominical yoke or a closed door, nor are they in favor of underground warfare, of more creed or less creed, but they are demanding of Nature her secret. These times find more worthwhile and incisive pleasure in the liberal and intelligent community—more human and religious than that which, whether the church has one steeple or three, men are about to hate and destroy. Here, the church marches abreast of the world in order not to perish in it. Before, the most intolerant Church prospered; now, only the tolerant one prospers. Each church quietly sends forth its vanguard and tries to win the new town, the empty cathedral, or the dying millionaire away from its rivals, but all the churches know in their hearts that they will die if they fail to unite. All of them are like lawyers who argue among themselves in court and then, in the hotel dining room, sit down at the same table and end by drinking champagne together. Consequently, the people who go to Chautauqua are not required to be Methodists like Bishop Vincent, but every denomination has its own church, all united in a common belief in revelation. On Sundays, when everything in the town shuts down—no stores are open but the divine, no theater but the clergy with their canticles and conclaves, their public and domestic oratories—a rigid clergy, bound to the letter of its appearance, does not preach in the crowded, rustic amphitheater with its open-air roof. On the contrary, a wise and well-known speaker lectures there, a man whose spirit is anything but dull, who moves the assembly by the friendliness of his words, and does not offend it—in these days when a natural religion is dawning—by talking about anything less free and beautiful than Nature, and which might deform, diminish, or contradict it. But Chautauqua Day, an event that people come to see from the most far-flung places—the day of a supreme religion when men seem to be the illegitimate sons of the surrounding mountains—is a day of diploma "recognition" when from every frontier of the republic the home-study students come to shake hands with those who brought the enlightenment of books from the sacred lake to the invalid's wheelchair, the village desk, the pulpit of the poor clergyman, the sewing basket of the hard-working woman, the blacksmith's bench, the hut of the Southern Negro, and the prison cell in classes that would not harm the eyes. And on the day of "recognition" in that open-air amphitheater, all of them, in tears, receive their diplomas.

José Martí

La Nación (Buenos Aires), October 22, 1890

A University Without Metaphysics

Now it is Clark University, in the puritanical heart of Massachusetts, that opens its doors to teach how the new world rules without imposing one kind of metaphysics in place of another, or substituting the infallibility of denominations for scientific infalliability, or wrapping the student's spirit in the preoccupations and hatreds of religious sects. "We want men who recognize the forces of the earth and know how to move them; we do not want living mummies, but four-thousand-dollar professors who never walk the halls of learning with curates, doing work worth four hundred dollars, but those who transmit what they know with the sweat of their brow, and give results rather than methods—a true education deserving of those four thousand dollars."

"This is not an ancient tomb," says another speaker, "where one goes about on tiptoe in order not to awaken ideas; this must be an orderly voyage over the earth, changeable and industrious." Nobody with a discerning mind will accuse us of being immoral or irreligious; the Church has changed, and the church of these days is Nature, where the trees sing and act as a thurible with their exhalations and fragrances when light officiates as a priest in the heavens. The Church has expanded because the new religion, which embraces and unites everyone, cannot fit into a church of only one religion; now religion is more than a creed, for it is a hymn and morality. What is greater in life than order, gently imposed upon free men by the pleasure of working well, and by knowing the order of the world? If a wise man meditates for half an hour, he will weep over a flower. The hummingbirds of knowledge and the flocks of sheep, those who roam the world distorted, are echoes in judicial robes cut from the bookstores' latest novels, their Lilliputian heads peeking out from between two viscera. It is not necessary, a wise man says as he walks through the obscurity of detail, to be absorbed into the marvel—only when, with the keys he takes out of it, he goes forth into the bright and religious sunlight to disclose life. One scholastic world has been cast aside, and will we establish another? The principal freedom, basis of all freedoms, is the mind; a professor must not be a mold into which students pour their character and intelligence to have them come out with tumors and humps, but an honest guide who teaches in good faith what must be examined, and who explains his worth as well as that of his enemies for the purpose of strengthening the manly character of the student, who is a flower that must not wither in the herbarium of the universities. The world in its order, life in its fullness, and science in its applications. These things, and others, are said in the heart of Massachusetts, where colleges are being shot down with arrows, and where young people are refusing to believe that the sky falls at night, as in the days of Troy, to incite the Episcopalians and Presbyterians to battle. "As much as we know," said a graduate student, "we cannot tell our children how a steam engine runs! Gas and steam have been teaching us how to live from the earth! " White-haired people from the old universities were at the festivities of Clark University, the university of physics in which no metaphysics is to be taught—neither that of ideology nor that of science.

La Nación (Buenos Aires), November 21, 1889

An Education Consistent with Life

We now turn to "the battle of presidents," for that is the title of the book which sets forth the reasons why Harvard— repeating, and not without some risk, Thomas More's[1] heroic deed in scholastic times—is gradually replacing mere literary education, useful only when it is exclusive. We turn to the teachers of the liberal arts for that other more efficient and sensible art which, as it polishes the rough tendencies of the student's nature with a knowledge of the finest works of the spirit, also prepares him, as he studies current forces and how to profit from them, to live by his own right and not by the grace of tradition and in its shadow. And it does this in countries where tradition does not matter, or matters less than in any other country, and where everyone is accepted, and where people who fail to be accepted stay under the heel of the rest or rise up behind them confused and covered with dust. Priests no longer have secure employment; lawyers plead their cases before juries which do not recognize Latin phrases, only facts. If a journalist wants to keep his good name now, he must embrace not only those scholastic truisms that are hammered upon the Latin anvil and prepared

1. Thomas More (1477–1535), British humanist and statesman, who was put to death for refusing to accept King Henry VIII as head of the Church of England. He is recognized as a saint by the Roman Catholic Church.

with a provincial personification, which before, with some smattering of foreign things, sufficed to give a writer a reputation for brilliance in the press; but he must also embrace a multiple modern life in all its forms as it roars upon the forge, as it travels and is transformed in commerce, as it gives birth to ideas in literature and politics, and as it is exalted and given credence in the arts. The journalist must be familiar with everything from clouds to microbes, from Omar Khayyam[2] to Pasteur.[3] He must know the literature of the spirit and of matter. He must teach both if the modern college seeks to turn out good men with ideas, or give a good foundation to men of action.

The mind has to be disciplined and exercised, but not by repeating dead rules for languages not in use; it has to be disciplined only by meticulous study of natural organisms, which are no less logical than those of languages, and resemble them. Studying these present-day languages (which together serve as a gymnasium for the intelligence and teach it self-restraint, to group, to be dependent, and to follow channels—all things which the human intelligence greatly needs), leaves the intelligence able to assimilate the current important results of men's work—an advantage not held by the people who acquire imperfectly and reluctantly a language in which men have long ago ceased to live and work, since they have no other stimulus but the enjoyment of literary beauty, something given to very few.

This decision of Harvard gradually to bring a university education close to life has been a welcome one, then, and it deserves to be. It puts the regular student in closer touch

2. Omar Khayyam (1048? –1122), Persian poet, mathematician, and astronomer, known to English-speaking readers for his *Rubáiyát,* in the version published in 1859 by Edward FitzGerald.

3. Louis Pasteur (1822–95), French chemist and microbiologist who proved that microorganisms caused fermentation and disease. He is especially famous for having originated the process known as pasteurization.

with French and German than with Latin and Greek without thereby shutting the lecture halls of ancient languages and literature—for that must never be done—to those students who are irrevocably drawn to letters, or who seek to know more firmly the origins of their native tongue. In these halls of learning one plucks, as it were, the flower of the spirit, blooming upon silver platters under the warmth of an azure sky.

That brilliant ancient tongue sounds like a new sickle on newly ripened wheat. It is like nucleus and substance, with the fragrance of freshly sprouted grass. To peer into an ancient poem is like peering into Paradise. Adam naked, the serpent hissing, Eve awakening. All is roots, tree trunks, flowers. A penetrating perfumed air circulates. Cloaks seem to be falling away from one's body. It is like a radiant Spring. Such pleasures are very sweet to the soul, especially to the privileged, but aside from those few persons who are irrevocably strong in a literary sense, and whom that education provides with the great and solid form that must clothe them in order that their thoughts endure and exert influence—such a spirit in a college, just as it takes the mind away from the usual spheres to other higher and more delightful ones, not only removes it from the possibility of battling successfully in spheres where its education has kept it in ignorance (although that education must enable the mind to battle in those spheres suddenly and fully—but it predisposes the soul to the sharp suffering caused by the incessant clash of a purified mind, exalted by the loving treatment of great ideologues, with the impassioned interests and egoistic, insuperable forces whose permanent and apparently odious battle constitutes the true life.

From now on Harvard College, always disposed to accept the new slightly ahead of Yale, is opening its doors to modern life with greater generosity. It leaves its students the option of studying extensively the ancient languages and literature which are demanded only for an exclusively literary career; its general system establishes the principle of a student's freedom of choice, within the plan and order of the establishment, for those courses whose tendencies most attract him, or for the projects which his future occupations most need. In this way, upon leaping into the struggle for existence, an unyielding struggle of the avaricious and implacable animal spirit, the Harvard student will never be seen rubbing shoulders in daily labor with the sons of Nature and work, like those plebeians compelled in the ordeal of olden times to fight with a stick and on foot against an armed lord on an armored horse—with every weapon.

La Nación (Buenos Aires), June 14, 1885

Education and Nationality

Surrounded by mountains, above whose gentle slopes or sudden heights spreads the sky, is a fertile valley at the gates of New York. Hand-cultivated by prosperous Quakers and the sons of Germans, it is the place where a constructive Cuban is raising with a heavy hand—like raising one's sons—the pupils who come to him from the nations of America to prepare for the study of useful professions. That man, so tenderly loved by the students, who can see his virtues at close range; that companion, every instant of whose conversation shapes and purifies and strengthens their spirits for life's truths; that watchtower, who knows where he is and what each of his students is doing at all times, and who abolishes their wrongful acts at the very outset with either a gentle or a firm hand, according to which may be indicated; that teacher, who seizes the occasion from life's every detail to uproot the defects of pride and disorder which generally deform our peoples' childhood, and who creates a love for work and the constant pleasure in it in the reasonable inclinations of life; that educator, who considers memory as nothing but a fan to the flames of understanding, and does not put it in place of the understanding, as do so many tutors, but who teaches totally, relating some things to others and taking from every opinion all of its origins, uses, and derivations, and from every subject all of its lessons in humanity; that gentlemanly and austere republican, who puts into the sons

166

of America the basic virtues of the North, the virtues of personal work and methods, without stifling the student's reverent love for the country of his birth—the only country where he can live a happy life, and where he could not apply those virtues successfully if he had lost the love and knowledge of his native land; that guide, at once loving and energetic, whose paternal effort, in the example and kindness of that wholesome and majestic valley, soon changes the spoiled child from the city, or the neglected child from the village, or the pampered Cuban, or the frenchified child from Buenos Aires, or the Mexican rebel, or the calm child from Honduras, into a boy who speaks a pure English (different from that vile jargon learned in many of the pompous schools where uniforms are worn), who thinks for himself, loves to read, and rests from his studies by playing games, who composes his ideas correctly in Spanish, English, and French, studies algebra, and knows how to measure fields and plant them; that Cuban of sprightly years and exemplary order, punctilious and firm, who yesterday governed a republic and today governs his celebrated school with all the teachings and practices needed for the independent well-being of working man in republican dignity—that man is the patriot who at the behest of his country left the sovereignty of his estate and the affection of an adored mother for the battle and danger of revolution. He is the prisoner president who refuses to be counted among his country's riches because its masters demand that he purchase his own with the pain of passing under the banner of capitulation. He is the Creole founder, adrift in exile, who a few years ago left a castle in Spain with his only wealth the health of his mind and the strength of his heart, and today is buying a noble edifice, with a lake and woods, for his happy family and the families of his students—a man who, in the heart of the Yankee hills, boasts a Cuban name: Tomás Estrada Palma.[1]

1. Tomás Estrada Palma (1835–1908), Cuban revolutionist who was captured by the Spaniards in 1877 and, upon his release, moved to

The danger of educating children away from their country is almost as great as the need, in the underdeveloped or unhappy nations, of educating them where they may acquire the knowledge necessary to expand their developing country, or where their character will not be poisoned by the educational habits in education and the troubled morality into which nations suffering in slavery fall because of the unwillingness and idleness of their servitude. The danger of educating children away from their homeland is great, because only their parents show the continuous tenderness with which the young flower must be watered and that constant mixture of authority and affection which are ineffective (because of the very justice and arrogance of our nature) except when both come from the same person. The danger is great because one must not grow oranges by planting them in Norway, or apples to bear fruit in Ecuador; the deported tree will have to keep its native sap so that upon returning to its own part of the world it may take root. Man's nature is identical throughout the world, and those who suppose that a man from the North is incapable of the virtues of a man from the South are just as wrong as the sickly-minded who believe that the Southerner lacks even one of the essential qualities of the Northerner. Habits will have to be formed, because the Spaniard did not rear us to be of use to ourselves, but to serve him; and our anguish at finding ourselves changing race, with the ungoverned heroism and visible progress of even the most unhappy of our peoples, will only be thrown in our faces by the ignorant and inconsiderate foreigner or the apostate brother. We do not lack habits in all cases, for in personal habits we are much more progressive than in political ones, and we need no lessons in honesty, activity, and

Orange County, New York, to become the principal of the Central Valley School for Boys. Estrada Palma headed the Cuban Junta in the United States in the 1890s, and became the first president of the Republic of Cuba in 1902.

intelligence in the use of our persons; but prolonged habits create in men and nations such modification in the expression and functions of nature that, without changing in the essentials, they come to make it impossible for a man of one region, with certain concepts of life and engaging in certain practices, to have the happiness of contentment and the success in his work characterized by a man of another region where concepts and life styles are different. The foreign language itself, which is mistakenly viewed as a new source of wealth, is an obstacle to the child's natural development, because language is the product and verbal form of the nation that slowly coins and assembles it, and by means of it the ideas and customs of the people who created it are gradually entering the student's flexible spirit. A cold and densely populated country, where bitter necessity stimulates and provokes rivalry among men, establishes that these necessarily selfish customs not be purified by frankness and unselfishness, qualities which are both proper and indispensable in abundant lands where a sparse population still permits the rapprochement and the pleasant obligations of family life. The purpose of education is not to make a man worthless because of scorn or his own uselessness to the country in which he must live, but to prepare him to live well and usefully in it. The purpose of education is not to make a man unhappy because of the difficult and confused use of his alien soul in the country where he lives, and from which he lives, but to make him happy without robbing him—as his dissimilarity to the country would rob him—of the conditions of equality in the daily struggle with those who preserve the country's soul. A lamentable spectacle is that of a wandering and useless man who never assimilates the spirit and methods of a foreign country enough to compete with the natives, who always view him as a foreigner, but who has adapted to them sufficiently to make his life impossible or disagreeable in a country where he is recognized as being different, or where everything offends his proud and higher nature. They are men without a compass, split in two, worthless to others and to themselves, who are of no benefit to the country in which they must live and who do not know how to receive any benefits from it. In the arduous commerce of living, they are broken merchants.

And this danger of education away from one's country, especially in the tender years, is greater in the United States for the children of our nations because, without being essentially at all preferable to our nations, the United States has created an anxious and uneasy national character, which is excessively and inevitably devoted to personal advancement and security, needing a violent stimulation of the senses, and wealth, to balance life's constant tensions and zeal. A people creates its character by dint of the race from which it proceeds, from the region it inhabits, from the needs and resources of its existence, and from its religious and political customs. The differences among peoples give rise to opposition and scorn. Superiority in number and size, in consequence of antecedents and opportunities, creates in the prosperous nations a scorn for the nations which battle in unequal struggle with lesser or diverse elements. Educating a son of these lesser peoples in a nation of opposite character and greater wealth might lead the student to a fatal opposition to his native land, where he must make use of his education—or to the worst and most shameful of human miseries, the scorn of his people—if, while nourishing him with skills and practices which are unknown or poorly developed in the country of his birth, he was not taught with continuous kindness what relates to him and maintains him in the love and respect of the country in which he must live. Let the water one drinks not be poisoned. Why acquire a language if it is to confuse the mind and rob the heart of its roots? Why learn English to return to one's country as a pedant, and to one's house as a stranger, or to one's nation as an enemy? And that is Estrada Palma's school: a family home where, under the care of a father, the skills and practices of the North are acquired without the loss of our own virtues, character, and nature. That is Estrada Palma's school: a continuation of the fatherland and native home in education abroad. There, the heart is not exchanged for an English heart, and the students enter the new life of the North through the virtues that maintain it, and not, as in so many other schools, through the vices that corrode it. There, they perfect their native culture with our language and history while they learn the good and applicable aspects of Northern culture. There, with the benefit of a fatherly education and a thoughtful way of teaching, they prepare to study special careers in schools where the student, ripe for a decent and industrious freedom, does not fall into the temptation of a careless and excessive freedom. There, perhaps, is the only corner of mountain country to which our parents can safely send their children. And this is the truth, and it must be said.

On June 28, Estrada Palma's school closed for the summer, and in its examinations, of rare truth and simplicity, those Cubans, Mexicans, Hondurans, Yankees, and natives of Buenos Aires, showed the stability, freedom, and practical wisdom of students whom an impartial teacher is training to be men. A general examination is not a correct test of the student's knowledge, even if he is skillfully trained for this or that answer, because improvisation is difficult. In examinations, as in everything else, a strong and most intelligent pupil can sin out of shyness. But the system cannot pretend, and by examinations it can be seen whether or not the teacher leads his pupils by the halter or is a martinet who leads the poor creatures by the nose, or whether or not he is a father of men who enjoys spreading the wings of the soul for flight.

Since morning, which started out overcast, just as freedom begins, the school's assembly hall has been a delight. There is no pedantic prefect there, no crafty doorman, only an air of pleasure as in an affectionate family. The algebra instructor, who tends to his Ayrshire cattle and is the owner of some extremely honorary diplomas, is airing his best suit of clothes. The drawing instructor, who has the schoolhouse full of her books and is an excellent linguist, is arranging her drawings of bridges and roads, flowers and fruit. The teacher of the little ones was rehearsing a childish hymn with a chorus of children who pronounced their *Z*s like the Germans and their *A*s like the Hondurans. The sons of the school were returning from the mountain with armfuls of flowers. Loyal graduates of other years, arrived for the festivities from agriculture at Cornell, commerce in Peekskill, medicine and engineering and mining at Columbia University, were putting flowers into vases and hanging the walls with banners. And the mother of everyone, the woman who watches over her flock with the gentleness of a dove, adored for the health and happiness of that vast home, the Honduran lady who has bound her most exemplary life to that of the teaching profession, was placing upon the breasts of her sons the three colors of liberty.

At examination time, all the town's important people applauded those unaccustomed exercises; that sensitive reading by which the student's unrestricted judgment is seen; that desk without flowers as is appropriate in times engaged in forming loyal character; that geography related to all erudition, in which place names provide the occasion to explain, with their geology and biography and history, the life of the world; that history of causes and results rather than of mute events; that changeable grammar in which words are added and taken away as on a chessboard, and mounted like bones upon a skeleton; that lively and effective arithmetic, like the colonels of long ago, and the algebra and geometry and surveying which, when analyzed upon a blackboard, are as amusing as a novel; that English and French, not with mere words but with the construction and understanding enabling the student to speak the foreign tongue as if he were a native; and that spirit of order, repose, and freedom that makes of simple exercises a veritable human feast. What of the stability and swiftness of those results? The Quirós boys who left Honduras some three years ago, do they not know all the preparatory work in English, French, and Castilian, and have they not kept upon foreign soil their love of homeland and their purity of soul? Irabien, recently arrived from Mérida, excelled in the foreign tongue. The sons of José Jujol, the Havana industrialist, went over maps and problems as if running through their own house, in a language they did not know yesterday. A son of that generous Manuel Barranco, genteel as a page in a court of love, and only nine years old, brought forth resounding applause for his lively geography. Another Barranco, yesterday shy because of sheer goodness, managed his numbers as if they were well-bred puppets. Estrada's two sons, little fellows though they are, and already endowed with a military spirit, demonstrated in their analysis of language, of a country's painting, in their reciting of an ode, that enterprise with which the enthusiastic and disciplined man rules the world. And when the chorus sang the farewell song—in English, like all the school's exercises—it was so that all generous and thinking people, beneath the canopy of free flags, could see the group singing of virtue and glory—Americans from the North and from Mexico, from Yucatan and Central America, free Hondurans and Cubans learning to be free. The reverend of the place stood up in the name of the people, and in the name of the people hailed the school which is honoring him and the virtuous man who is educating his pupils as if they were his sons, who is "undertaking the education of his sons to be good, useful, and free men"—Tomás Estrada Palma.

Patria (New York), July 2, 1892

Education and Freedom

Nicaragua has just heartily celebrated the anniversary of its independence; a school of arts and crafts opened there. Guatemala already has its school. El Salvador is about to have one. Chile is looking for a model for one. Montevideo's school makes those of Europe jealous.

Arts and crafts schools aid in solving the human problem, which is now established with new data, since there has been an increasing lack of those ancient trees—Church and Monarchy—under whose boughs so many men used to live a comfortable life. Now there are neither courtesans nor friars. These are restless times; men are awake, and every one of them has to make with his own hands the chair upon which he sits at the feast of Fortune. No longer are there those stable and ready-made classes through which people entered as if through open channels; no longer are there legions of shoeless beggars or apiaries of office seekers—although some of these still exist—or regiments of knights who kill, rob ladies, and serve; and there are no more flocks of lackeys.

Now, when every man is born, he can see a crown floating above his head; it is up to him to make it fit. It is up to farseeing nations to put the means of coronation within reach of these new armies of kings.

A craft or an art—in addition to bringing to a country the honored skills of those who excel in them; in addition to giving to those who study them the practical abilities of most especial usefulness in semidiscovered, almost virginal peoples; in addition to assuring a leisurely existence to those who possess that art or craft, by means of a constant consumption of what they produce—is an extremely solid support, as common dignity and personal independence assert.

The general happiness of a nation rests upon the individual independence of its inhabitants.

A free nation is the result of its free settlers.

Honorable and durable nations are not made out of men who cannot live for themselves but are attached to a leader who favors, uses, or abuses them.

Whoever desires an enduring nation aids in establishing his country's affairs so that each man may work in active labor applicable to a personal and independent situation.

Let every man learn to make something which others need.

La América (New York), November 1883

The Annual Assembly
of the American Association
for the Advancement of Science

New York, August 17, 1887

To the editor of *El Partido Liberal:*

The New York colleges are deserted in summer. Where the students are studying now is in the country, be it languages at Amherst, or agriculture on the scientific walks at Bryant College in Roslyn, or philosophy, religion, or oratory in classes that have been gathering good teachers since May, and where they and their students have gone into the mountains to protect from the summer heat a liberal school in a pleasant retreat.

The students learn by conversing, rowing, or running along the roads, and by resting from these studies under the august pines, the energetic oaks, or the religious elms. They learn mineralogy among the boulders; botany by making their own herbarium; physics by climbing up and down the mountains; meteorology by watching the mist vanish, or appear from its clouds, or return to dew upon the fallen leaf, or collect in droplets upon the placid leaf. In New York, not even City College[1]—which gives free education for university careers, and is opening its now-gloomy library to its numerous stu-

1. City College, originally named the Free Academy, and now called City University, ceased to provide tuition-free education in 1976, the year of the nation's bicentennial, as New York City faced bankruptcy.

dents, most of them sons of Germans—has anyone living in it, and hundred-year-old Columbia College has no one except a sullen caretaker who, with few words, guides the summer visitors through those halls that comprise everything possessed by the learned man today. In its six special schools they teach the arts and literature and a general knowledge of the world, from lithology to the history of religions and their languages, from Sanskrit to French; mining, with all the engineering tasks, and metallurgy, chemistry, architecture, and paleontology; political science, with all that leads to the understanding and practicing of good government, and how to wisely read what is written about it; library science, a study essential for every nation ruled by the will of the people, a study where one learns to assemble a library, preserving and enriching it; as well as medicine and law. "South Americans? " asks the beadle guide: "We have a South American here, Don Daniel de Leon,[2] who teaches international law and took the award to Blaine's son; he is pale from learning, they say."

What is happening, then, when, in the middle of August, Columbia is opening its doors, refurbishing its examination hall, decorating its doctoral rostrum with banners, dusting off the portraits of its rectors, some robed in black, the rest in red? Everything announces animation and the students' gathering together. Many classrooms are quickly being made ready, as if they were all to be used at one time. A German who never lets go of *The Natural History of the Soul* from time to time looks lovingly at the cardboard insects which he

2. Daniel De Leon (1852–1914), born on the island of Curaçao, of Jewish parents, was educated in Germany and emigrated to the United States in 1874, and in 1883 won a prize lectureship in Latin American diplomacy at Columbia University, which he held for six years. After supporting the Henry George candidacy for mayor of New York in 1886, he joined first the Knights of Labor and then in 1890 the Socialist Labor Party, became editor of the SLP organ, *The People,* in 1892. He held that position and leadership of the party until his death.

has distributed, according to species, in a little improvised store beside the atrium. A pale and sad young girl nearby arranges another table; she is going to sell agate chips, lined up in boxes. There inside, as if Bostonians were coming, a restauranteur prepares something like Catalonian *munyetas*—white beans boiled in salt water and lightly fried with a generous slab of pork, a favorite dish in Boston.

All is because at this time the American Association for the Advancement of Science is holding its annual assembly at Columbia College.

This year about five hundred teachers attended the assembly, among them many ladies of science and others who went for reasons of ostentation or inclination, although it is fair to say that when a teacher of political economy was collecting a mass of numbers in learned columns to prove human progress by means of a census, or when an entomologist was revealing the antecedents of an obscure species, or when a botanist was attempting to demonstrate that the unicellular protococcus, in selecting from itself the best and rejecting the worst, changing by its own efforts into the palest and most perfect *chytridiales,* following the law of nature as a whole—many elderly ladies took out of their cases a pair of gold-rimmed spectacles and out of their reticules the knitting they had begun.

Gathered there were Barnard,[3] Columbia's spirited rector, fonder of laboratories than of pedantic Latin phrases; the historian Martha Lamb,[4] who, with the vividness of Motley

3. Henry Barnard (1811–1900), leading American educator, chancellor of the University of Wisconsin, sponsor of the *American Journal of Education,* and publisher of the *Library of Education* in fifty-two volumes.

4. Martha Joanna Reade Nash Lamb (1829–93), author and historian, author of the *History of the City of New York: Its Origin, Rise and Progress* (two volumes, 1877–81), editor of the *Magazine of American History.*

and the amenity of McMaster,[5] has written about events in New York and manages an excellent magazine; Morse,[6] for whom the world is only a sluggish physical mass that is gradually improving at its own urging; the botanist Britton,[7] who sees nothing in the similarity of plants to prevent people from reverently praising God on Sundays; Newton,[8] the astronomer of the happy and benevolent eyes; Miss Winifred Edgerton, who, in competition with many bearded rivals, won a double prize this past year for her unusual knowledge of higher mathematics. She was wearing a small-sized man's hat, the kind that ladies use this summer, and a tailor-made suit that failed to hide the grace of her body, and was carrying a parasol trimmed with opulent lace.

Many famous scientists were there: Langley,[9] the man who, for his general knowledge, was made president of the Smithsonian Institute, center of all Americans, now that the patient Baird[10] has died, leaving complete his work on fishes; Anthony,[11] the champion of direct and scientific teaching in the public schools out of which the new man will go;

5. John Bach McMaster (1852–1930), author of an eight-volume *History of the People of the United States from the Revolution to the Civil War* (1883–1913).

6. Martí is referring to either Albert Pitts Morse (1863–1936), American entomologist, or Edward Sylvester Morse (1838–1925), American zoologist.

7. Wilton Everett Britton (1868–1939), entomologist and authority on trees.

8. Herbert Anson Newton (1830–1896), American mathematician and astronomer, noted for his work on meteors.

9. Samuel Pierpont Langley (1834–1906), pioneer in research concerning solar radiation and human flight in heavier-than-air machines and third secretary of the Smithsonian Institution.

10. Spencer Fullerton Baird (1823–77), noted zoologist, authority on birds and fishes, and head of the U.S. Commission on Fish and Fisheries.

11. William Arnold Anthony (1835–1908), author of works on physics and teacher of science at Cooper Institute.

Alvord,[12] respected by everyone for his singular skill in the highest or humblest kinds of agriculture; Britton, who is publishing all that could be found of aboriginal poetry and drama, and has published an exact index of the most important books about our America; and Marberry, scarcely out of the classrooms and already a great chemist.

The Protestant Bishop Potter[13] opened the assembly with his pruned and prim language, visibly constrained as if the gathering had too little time in which to communicate its year's successes, inventions, and failures. After the usual prayer, everyone came out of the examination hall and each person went to the classroom of his own branch of science, nine in all: astronomy, chemistry, physics, mechanics, biology, geology, geography, anthropology, and statistics. There, among those interested in their own subject, each one read the most detailed and specific study—this one on transoceanic telephone lines; that one on the heart of snakes, which he finds the same as the heart of frogs; another one on the sense of taste, which seems less acute in women than in men; another on "the morphology of the legs of the hymenopterous insect," which, availing itself of the brushes given to it by nature, incessantly cleans its legs and antennae, with a feline sense of neatness. But when Morse,[14] an enemy of the subterfuge and fastidiousness in scientific truths, starts reading, with sectarian ardor, his aggressive study on the palpable truth of the Theory of Evolution; or when Major Taylor, with a few others, starts defending the short and sensible route of the Nicaraguan canal, leaving aside Tehuantepec and

12. Henry Elijah Alvord (1844–1904), educator and specialist in dairy husbandry and chief of the Dairy Division of the Bureau of Animal Industry of the U.S. Department of Agriculture.

13. Henry Codman Potter (1835–1908), Protestant Episcopal bishop and civil leader who exposed police corruption in New York City.

14. See note 6.

Panama; or when James[15] prepares to discourse on the urgency of teaching children industrial tasks in the schools; or when Brinton,[16] loaded with facts, discusses the appearance of man on the American continent—all of the teachers interrupt their private classroom work and forgather to hear these colleagues who have something serious to say.

What Rabelais[17] said centuries ago about the bad teachers imposed upon Gargantua—for whom it would have been better not to have had such teachers, because their knowledge was only a lack of culture, and their mastery mere froth which debased the noble talents and corrupted the entire bloom of youth—was the same thing that James said when he recommended the efficacy of teaching industrial tasks in school. And it was what Anthony so vigorously affirmed, maintaining the national importance and true urgency of teaching physical sciences in the public schools. When the American leaves school at the age of fifteen, where will he go with his reading, writing and arithmetic, his grammar which he neither understands nor applies, his geography committed to memory? He disdains real work, or does not know, for lack of rudiments, how to approach it. He is a shamefaced gentleman, worthless to himself and to others, who ends as a poor writer, a puny lawyer, or a sterile clergyman. What the child loses in learning useless literature which is prejudicial to his country, says James, as he gains in learning—on a par with the useful aspects of literature—those general fundamentals of all the arts, which in themselves are accumulated knowledge. And he gains in that skill with his hands which will give

15. William James (1842–1910), noted philosopher and psychologist, famous also as an educator.

16. Daniel Garrison Brinton (1837–99), anthropologist, author of *The American Race* (1891), the first systematic classification of the aboriginal languages of both North and South America.

17. François Rabelais (1495–1553), French author of the satirical masterpiece, *Gargantua and Pantagruel*.

him self-confidence, a disposition for the occupation he will choose later, as well as character and orderliness for the tasks to which he will devote himself, even if they are not a job. He gains in a liking rather than a disdain for the industries which today even the sons of workers consider inferior and contemptible. Anthony agrees: "It makes the blood boil to see a handsome boy—who might have learned, instead of the pluperfect, what heat is and how man can make use of it—mumbling verbs, which in the street he will conjugate in a barbarous offhand manner. Until we teach science in the schools we shall not have saved the Republic."

No sooner had Atwater[18] recommended that one should not eat more than the human body requires, which is at most a quarter of a pound of protein in lean meat, milk, wheat gluten, or egg white, another quarter-pound of fat in the fat part of the meat or in butter or meal oil, and about a pound of carbohydrate in finely milled corn flour and sugar; and no sooner had Leeds finished explaining that for every baby dying from among those nursed at the maternal breast, three bottle-fed babies die and eight from those fed upon other substances (counter to what will hardly be a help in imitating mother's milk, such as adding more water and cream to cow's milk and boiling it for five minutes with some peptogen), than the entire assembly's attention centered upon the speech of Brinton, who maintained that man in America lived in the glacial age. Everything proves it: tools for human use discovered in glacial deposits; other tools and potsherds found in shell mounds along the coast; paleolithic remains dug up from the sand pits of Trenton; the extent of maize cultivation, of which extremely out-of-the-way traces have been found from the Hudson all the way down to Chubut in Patagonia. The varied and contrary aspects of the American languages, coming from a common trunk as the similarity of American skulls demonstrates, fell apart in such a manner

18. Wilbur Olin Atwater (1844–1907), famous pioneer in agricultural chemistry.

that only the remoteness of their origins can explain their critical moments and final divergence. Everything, in a word, proves to him that man commenced to live in America thirty-five thousand years ago. But he does not believe that man originated in America itself, "because he could not have developed," he says, "from any of the American mammals found up to now." He believes that he came from Asia and Europe via glacial bridges, as if it were not proved—in the likeness or similarity of man's actions, aspirations, and skills in countries unrelated and with no knowledge of each other, which today we can see with our own eyes—that man could have come into being at the same time over the whole face of the earth!

His very similarities are proof of his variety of origin, on a par with the similarity of his nature. What is the geologist Kunze[19] exhibiting among so many curious people? It is a gigantic jade axe brought from Mexico: on one of its surfaces a face is carved; notches are carved on both sides, "one for every dead chief," says Kunze. And what is it that catches the eye of every teacher? It is a description of the pyromagnet, Edison's new invention:[20] a coil of thin iron tubing is inside of a magnetic circle, and when warm air is precipitated onto the coil, an electric current develops in it. Conducted by the wire wound round the tubing, it travels from ordinary oven or kitchen fire acting upon the pyromagnet to the lamp in the form of light, or to the moving wheel in the form of energy.

Then Drummond[21] spoke about Africa. These mystics whose eyes are turned inward insanely want to adjust the world to fit their own concept of it. Denying the spiritual,

19. Richard Ernest Kunze (1838–1919), physician and naturalist, student of the cactus plant in Arizona and Mexico.

20. Thomas Alva Edison (1847–1931), genius of technological inventions, held over a thousand patents, including the incandescent electric lamp, phonograph, and motion-picture projector.

21. Henry Drummond (1851–97), Scottish writer and lecturer, who reported on exploration of tropical Africa (1888).

which pains and enlightens, guides and comforts, heals or kills, is like denying that the sun sheds light, or that the splendor of a son touches the heart of a father. Such it is to deny that, in the parched desert as in the Scottish cathedral, man's virtues and iniquities are equal. For Drummond, the opposite of what other travelers write, going to Africa is like seeing the dawning of the human animal. By his very own statements, he considers what is observed to be local diversity as a perversion of the intelligence. "In the heart of Africa the human being is half animal and half man." And, failing to see that in the order and relationship of creation, the beings of the different kingdoms inhabiting it are closely bound together with parallel degrees of development, he then recounts that there are valleys extending into the shade of wooded hills where gigantic orchids burst into blue and carmine blossoms, and the verdure sings, and the earth is covered not with grass but with marvelous flowers. And he found no monkeys in these beautiful valleys or in the lonely muddy stretches with their stunted trees through which he descended from the plateau to the rivers.

But what general idea, what logical explanation of the origins, what concept of the world seemed to predominate in the assembly's affirmations? Before, with the secretive Agassiz,[22] friend of Humboldt,[23] it set the whole of American science against the new English discoveries, to a man. Afterward, with the Canadian Dawson,[24] friend of Lyell,[25] it

22. Louis Agassiz (1807–73), naturalist, geologist, and educator who, as a professor at Harvard University and a prolific author, influenced the study of natural history in the United States for many years.

23. Alexander von Humboldt (1769–1859), German explorer and scientist, who achieved international fame as the chief propagator in his time of the study of earth sciences and as the originator of ecology.

24. Sir John William Dawson (1820–79), Canadian geologist who made numerous contributions to paleobotany and extended the knowledge of Canadian biology.

25. Sir Charles Lyell (1797–1875), leading geologist of the Vic-

denied, until that book of Draper,[26] that there was any reason for conflict between biblical history and what the stones tell. Now, before the clearly attentive crowd, Morse said that nobody has removed science from where Darwin placed it, and that his doctrine is unimpeachable, like that of the conservation of energy; that men would be less unhappy if they knew the scientific laws of their reproduction and growth, and that man's contrition because of original sin was felt by him only when he stood upon two feet—when he arose from a quadruped to a two-legged creature.

However, since the morning following Morse's speech was a Sunday, in the same examination hall where he delivered it, almost all of the teachers, with Drummond at their head, gathered together to declare, on the pretext of divine work, that "they found no arguments against the existence and kindliness of the Creator in the scientific procedure by which the world was undoubtedly constructed."

Some forget that in the enchanting universal harmony any theory about the body will be proved by a corresponding one about the spirit; others, boastful and proud, disregard the relation of soul to body, which is not unlike that of sublime music to the feelings it expresses, and with whose perishable strains the music is never silenced! All perfects and purifies itself, and grows.

José Martí

El Partido Liberal (Mexico), 1887
La Nación (Buenos Aires), October 6, 1887

---

torian era in England, author of *The Geological Evidence of the Antiquity of Man* (1863).

26. John William Draper (1811–82), chemist, historian, and natural philosopher, famous for his work on radiant energy, author of *Human Physiology, Statistical and Dynamical* (1856).

Mondays at "The League"[1]

"The League" in New York is a house of education and affection, although anyone who says education says love. After the day's tiring work, there gather at The League those who know that true happiness can exist only in friendship

---

1. In 1889, Martí, along with Rafael Serra, a Cuban Negro exile, established *La Liga de Instrucción* (The League) to act as a kind of training school for revolutionaries. Serra had been born in Havana of poor parents, but by the age of thirteen had become a skilled cigar maker and had determined to get an education. When he was just twenty-one he opened his own free school for poor children in Matanzas. In 1880 he fled to Key West and thence on to New York. Together, Serra and Martí opened an institute for night instruction for Cuban emigrés. The two men found an old building located at 72 East Third Street near Washington Square, and, recruiting two or three other interested Cubans, they began holding night classes. There were lectures for Cuban exiles, chiefly Negro workers, and The League became an integral part of the revolutionary movement after the formation of the Cuban Revolutionary Party.

The idea behind The League—to teach the poor the purposes of the Cuban revolution—led to its adoption in other areas of Cuban revolutionary activity. The "reading room" system of worker education in the tobacco factories in Tampa and Key West was quickly supplemented by the establishment of a league of education in those cities.

For a discussion of the formation of The League in New York, see *Our America,* pp. 17-18, 29.

and culture; those who feel within themselves, or see of their own accord, that being of one color or another never diminishes man's sublime aspirations; those who do not believe that earning one's bread in one occupation gives a man less rights and obligations than earning it in another; those who have heard the inner voice that orders the kindling of one's native light, and heart, as a warm home for man. It is a meeting place for the sons of the two islands which, in the secrecy of creation, are maturing the new character by means of whose justice and steadfast skill the country will assert itself. Conquering that country will be less than maintaining her, and together with the gun that is to rescue her one must take her a republican spirit and the habitual management of unhampered skills, which over and above all her sources of discord will be her salvation. And if The League might have made some special imprint upon our country's affairs, it would be of the presence there—without distrust and without arguments about fame or bread—of those who come from the oppressed country, and of those abroad who welcome them with open arms. And it would be that of gathering there—all traces of the day's weariness erased by their desire for knowledge—people who, instead of knowing merely the pedantic and literal meanings in books, would rather extract their spirit, by means of the fires and clashes of conversation, or teach those who know less than they do, or learn more than they themselves know. It would be that of gathering there—without the flattery of some or the humiliation of others, but with all eyes at the same level—the sons of the unjust and those who have suffered injustice.

With their elbows resting upon The League's tables, love is being spun and books are revealing the truth. Eloquence is laid aside and a sober way of saying things is bred where music itself, useful to truth, does not come on loan as in literature, from a swaggering use of words without foundation, or from the sonorous scale of resounding voices, but from wisely composed thinking, and from the inflexible habit of putting one's own unique voice where it belongs. Some persons learn to read and write at one table, and others, studying and correcting each other's essays, wrestle in the very depths of the human heart, and for the enlightenment of judgment and the good of the country seek the occult and the true which can scarcely be suspected from the pages of history. It is not a house of professional believers or of rebels by trade, but a house one enters with modesty and leaves with truth. It is a place where, instead of submitting to a gnashing of teeth because of their jobs, men throw them off to be able to learn more freely, or purposely take on the more difficult jobs where their daily savings go neither to gambling—the typical pleasure of incapable and egoistic people—nor to an excessive desire to behave like a coxcomb— all roses and patent leather—nor to those many frivolous chores that are more tiring and costly than those of the affections and understanding. No, their savings go to keeping the hearth of aspiration ablaze, to reserving some pleasant and honored corner where minds, not useless hands, begin to warm themselves around the fire, and to buying wines and sweets for their lady companions on reception days.

The League sets aside one Monday of each month to welcome the families of its members; and those good men, healthier and more cheerful than those who live less virtuously, attend to their duties as gentlemen-servants with exemplary courtesy.

Rafael Serra is there; he presides everywhere. And Juan Bonilla, important in everything; and his brother Jerónimo, whose judgment is superlative. Manuel González is there, a man born with a privileged heart and mind. Miguel González, with his flowery verse and courageous youth and sterling affections, is there; Arturo Beneche, the enthusiast from Baracoa who sees with his eyes and detests the vain and uncertain, is there. Worthy of every festivity at The League is Pedro Calderón, a man who is a true leader and knows how to live, because to him life is not lacking in excellence and continued betterment, and a man makes his own happiness in life and contributes to that of others. And Justo Castillo is there; a short while ago he was a person with more years than literary ability, and now, through his work at The League, his writings touch the emotions. Enrique Sandoval is there; he learned from the good Father Germán the virtue of work and of using in the cultivation of men the savings and leisure derived from it. There, always enthusiastic, are Francisco Padrón and Ruperto Bravo, Magín Courduneau and Martín Cárdenas and Joaquín Gorozabe.

On other days, presently to be described in *Patria,* The League is a school of necessary letters, both excellent and infamous, and not only of pleasant social evenings as on Mondays. Someone teaches a lively arithmetic and breaks down the numbers so his students may see how they work, a better method than using mere rules. Another, with a hand that has attained great glory, guides the fully matured man who comes to ask for handwriting instruction. Another, in a shifting conversation dealing with early accomplishments, maintains the thread of each and inspires the beginner with the greatest curiosity. Another sits down at the question table, which is heaped with unsigned queries, and talks about each of them, answering the point at issue, noting the writer's merits, correcting his mistakes, and preaching honesty of form—which exalts its character as well as vitiating it— without considering the form insincere. Another is a grammarian who arranges and disarranges the artifice of language before one's eyes so that no matter how the phrase may deviate from the right path, it remains standing. And he searches for the history and relationship of words, the best training for anyone who longs to think clearly. Behind the teacher and available to all is the book collection in its light-colored shelves.

On Mondays the school is devoted to the social arts, and The League gathers to hear good music, read enriching poetry, and keep the conversation moving. Hearts should not be embittered by the world's pettiness, their only shade being that of the nose itself. Life debases and must be lifted up. Friendship is a certain cure for every sorrow. With a friend, the world is friendly. The weasel lives well upon gossip; the integrated man can live away from it. And The League, on its second Monday, was just that: a family night when the daughter sings, the young girl recites, and her young man shows off his new speech.

The program does not paralyze the pleasant festivities, but sets the will on its feet. A girl sheds her fear, another recites a ballad, another defends herself in an elegant manner, another parodies a well-known speaker. This last Monday, with the simplicity of whoever was chatting, a happy evening party was being concocted. Like a bird having its wings sharpened, Federico Sánchez's daughter, whom he has taught to read in the name of the heroes, recited their story in rhyme.

One child played some native music in exile, as it were: the plaintive immortal melody of the *muzhik,* who gazes, up to the elbows in his servitude, over the vast and dismal steppes. "La Bayamesa," from the lips of Mariana Calderón, showed how all sad peoples, from Russian cold to tropical sun, are brothers.

Fornaris was the poet of the night because Benech carried all of him in his memory with a passion that justly or not sees him as the filial Creole painter of Cuba's essence. At times with a raised voice, and at other times with a sensitive one, Benech's lady companion recited "The Beauties of Cuba"; América Fernández provided songs and poetry; Serra read in a way that reflected his instruction; Gonzalo, timid as are all strong men, recited in a manner that gives the interpreter an author's prerogative in the work; Bonilla read a few paragraphs of his own, in which his admiration for good models, because of the strength of the one who loves them, is now approaching the power of equaling them; Manuel Barranco, whose teaching spirit knows no tepidity, gave some ardent, heartfelt prose, and studded his useful and informal discourse with vigorous ten-line stanzas; José Martí spoke of life's most powerful boon—good friends. And with ice cream and Creole sweets, talking about country and home and poetry, the hours passed quickly.

Patria (New York), March 26, 1892

A Beautiful Night
at "The League"

"The League" in New York, house of affection and education, where, in the warmth of a stove paid for by the poor, a determined group of sincere men come together, held a beautiful meeting on Thursday. The men returned to their classes and the hall was filled. Women went there, old women recently arrived from Cuba, and patriarchs from towns in Oriente, and youths whose proud brows sparkled with freedom. Work in the factories stops at six, and here in New York people live very far from where they work; but at eight those disciplined souls were already at that house of affection. The League—does no one know how many souls its heart embraces? —is a home of ideas which for years has been subsidized by a few Cuban workers—colored workers—by sacrificing their hard-earned salaries, and by those workers of ours who, although it may seem ridiculous to some useless soul, have lying open upon their desks copies of Spencer's *Education*,[1] or Jung's *Bonaparte*, or Plutarch's *Lives*;[2] and he who is not afraid of dark stairways, let him roll up his

1. Herbert Spencer (1820–1903), English social philosopher, formulator of "social Darwinism," whose popular work *Education*, a small volume, was published in 1861.

2. Plutarch (46–119 A.D.), Greek biographer whose works strongly influenced the evolution of the essay, biography, and historical writings in Europe from the sixteenth to nineteenth centuries.

192

shirtsleeves and go to see for himself. There is no more courteous hall of learning than The League's, nor are there more sincere and splendid people.

The house really does creep into one's heart. From the plaque upon the door on the poor street facing Washington Arch (72 East Third Street) to the plaque saying *Reason,* it plays the part of a temple in that friendly corner. One enters and the world seems to be left behind—the evil world, that is. Friendship, culture, sincerity—are they not life's only pleasures and strengths? The rest is nightmare, soap bubbles, and nausea. A corner for the affections is the glory of the world, the sanctuary and workshop of freedom, the smile of life. Infamous or hoodwinked people compare and measure each other and separate into compartments according to their degrees of wealth, something that amounts to splitting hairs, or according to their ancestry, unaware that mundane honors come more commonly from villainy than from virtue, or according to those degrees of color that gave Confucius to China, Falucho to Buenos Aires, and Juárez to Mexico. Infamous people put themselves into compartments and show their heads above the barnyard gate like unhappy horses that do not know what to do with themselves when the storm breaks, and gallop alone and disconsolate, or knock against each other. They cause grief, the overproud. The world never stops. Let it move on as it should, in an orderly way and well, in the healthy, turbulent, and ever-youthful order of freedom. But as the world goes forward, he who puts himself into compartments is left behind, or else the world drags him along in its destined progress. One must set out upon the road, and drink *bejuco* juice, and wear sandals. Nature is good! —and that is the charm of The League, for it is both good and natural.

A piano to the left, new light-colored chairs in the background, at the end of the room a bookshelf of books, along the walls portraits of friends in gratitude for their aid to The League. Burning brightly in an alien land, the stove paid for by the poor! There is never a sign of dust or iniquity in that house so filled with paintings and self-sacrifice; in its difficult week, a week when the house itself was frugally maintained, those good men faithfully deferred putting their beloved home up for rent.

And in the classes themselves, as well as in what is said and written by the sons of the house, the strength and reality of those generous people is easily seen. They stand for the useful and not the ornamental, for results and not pedagogy, for asking heartfelt questions and receiving heartfelt answers. As soon as there is someone to learn, there are teachers to spare. Students assemble, and they have teachers. Year upon year, a sickly businessman has gone there to teach a lively grammar, and one like an anatomy of the language, on the rawest of winter nights. A busy but very kindly physician has taught English there, deep into the night. A friend of the house would go there to tell the students things they wanted to know; the students would leave upon that gracious table their anonymous questions directed to him—questions about the composition of peoples, or about physics or history or human hates or the dark hours of the soul; and that friend would read those writings aloud, writings whose form he would trim and set right as he went along, so that by strong and simple expression the lucid idea could be easily seen. And then, to the sweep of thought and with the central idea of the world's goodness and individuality, he would answer the questions—very deep and subtle at times—harmonizing apparent differences and basing his opinions upon the methodical and visible evidence in the details. A student would like to know about the senate and its function in republics; another, who is reading Marcus Aurelius, or considers him adequate, inquires about the religious yearnings of the human spirit; another asks the reason for those red, bare bushes in the Atacama desert; another, suffering from love or friendship and under the pretense of common doubt, proposes some punishment for his soul; others, merely for correction, take him essays they have written, on his advice, about writings that have interested or moved them. And from this practice the house is gradually creating a mode of expression which, although still confusing because of the sudden mass of new ideas and the stubborn search for their substance and reason, is concise and powerful and bathed in a tender love for men and nature.

So Thursday was a beautiful night: questions upon the table, a hymn on the piano, and the women, after their inhuman drudgery in an often poor and gloomy house, going to hear ideas and genial words and poetry, or to express these themselves with gracious modesty and Antillean passion. But before beginning the class there were visitors, and the first thing was to thank them. There was a distinguished one-armed Venezuelan who did not lose his hand in robbing men of their freedom, like so many vile soldiers, but in fighting to secure it; he was General Julio Sarría, famed and romantic hero who moments later, while giving thanks for The League's greeting, tremulously and with moving eloquence raised his voice, which had not trembled often upon the field of battle or in the councils of his country. And the other visitor, also from Venezuela, was Andrés Alfonso, brave as his island of Margarita—land of women who gave up all their pearls for their country's war and in support of Bolívar in one of his unfortunate trials. Andrés Alfonso once again showed his generous spirit that cheered so tirelessly the people of October Tenth.[3] He also gave thanks as a son of Cuba, as a brother of The League. Because some men are not made to be brothers, and others are. Then there was a class like the previous ones: in a row before the friend lay the questions and compositions, and the friend examined them by the light of his affection, and gave answers from the truth of life and of his heart. *Patria* is publishing three of these

3. October 10, 1868, was the date of the *Grito de Yara,* opening the Ten Years' War for Cuban independence from Spain.

compositions taken from that table on Thursday—compositions written by Cuban laborers, some of them extremely young; compositions that have been showing the rapid progress, with very high purpose and great capability, of those exemplary men's resilient and orderly minds. The dignity and enthusiasm of that night kindled in one brave Baracoan heart the words he seldom speaks, the words that come, proud and perfected, from the enlightened nobility of the soul, and with their skill and power Severiano Urgellez, a man of the new times, spoke out of sudden impulse and in a manly fashion: "Not long ago I heard a strong, young white Cuban say that today's youth would emulate the youth of '68; the Negro youth of '93 will never desert the white youth in the fight for their country! " And Francisco Marín, obedient to the mandates of affection, "Caesar who cannot be disobeyed," spoke with true warmth of feeling about "the house where a seat is denied only to enmity, intrigue, and hatred," and then recited some of his mysteriously doleful poetry, with flying sparks from his martial verse. Following this some piano playing by América Fernández, the piano teacher, and by Juan Bonilla, who played the "Hymn of Bayamo"[4] for those loving hearts that were silent with friendship and hope.

Patria (New York), November 4, 1893

4. The "Hymn of Bayamo," written by Pedro Figueredo following the capture of Bayamo by the Cuban Revolutionaries at the end of the month of October 1868, afterwards became the Cuban national anthem. Its words are:

> To the battle, Bayameses!
> Let the fatherland proudly observe you!
> Do not fear a glorious death,
> To die for the fatherland is to live!

II

For Children
Selections from The Age of Gold
(La Edad de Oro)

To the Children Who Read
The Age of Gold

This magazine is for boys, and of course for girls too. Without girls it would be impossible to live, just the way the earth could not live without light. Boys have to work, travel about, study, be strong and handsome. A boy can become handsome even if he is ugly; a boy who is good, intelligent, and neat in appearance is always handsome. But he is never more handsome than when he takes a flower in his strong little manly hands and gives it to a little girl whom he likes, or when he takes his sister by the arm to protect her from insults. These are the times when boys grow and seem to be giants. Boys are born to be gentlemen, girls to be mothers. This magazine is published once a month to talk like a good friend to the gentlemen of tomorrow and the mothers of tomorrow; to tell little girls some wonderful stories, which they in turn can tell to their friends and their dolls; to tell boys what they must know to be truly men. We are going to tell them everything they want to know, in plain language and with fine pictures, in such a way that they will clearly understand. We are going to tell them how the world is made, and all that men have done till now.

That is why *The Age of Gold* is being published—so American boys and girls can know how people lived before and how they live now, in both America and other lands; how they make so many things out of iron and glass, how steam engines are made, and suspension bridges and electric lights, so that when a child sees a colored stone he knows why it is colored and what each color means; so the child becomes familiar with the famous books that tell about the battles and the religions of ancient peoples. We will explain to them everything that is made in factories and laboratories where things happen that are stranger and more interesting than in tales of magic—and they really are magic, more wonderful than the other kind. And we will tell them what is known about the sky and the depths of the sea and the earth. And we will print funny stories and children's stories, for those times when the children have studied too much or played too hard and want to rest. We are working for the children because they are the ones who know how to love, because they are the hope of the world. And we want them to love us and to look upon us as close to their hearts.

When a child wants to know something which is not in *The Age of Gold,* he should write to us as though he had always known us; we will answer. It makes no difference if the letter comes with spelling mistakes. What matters is that the child is eager to learn. And if the letter is well written, we will print it in our letter columns, with the signature, so everyone will know that here is a child who amounts to something. Children know more than it seems, and if they were to write what they knew, they would write some very good things. This is why *The Age of Gold* is going to hold a contest every six months, and the child who submits the best work— provided it is really his—will receive a fine prize of books, together with ten copies of the issue of *The Age of Gold* in which his piece appears. What he submits must be in keeping with his age, because to write well on a subject he has to be very well informed about it. This is what we want American boys to be when they grow up: men who say what they think, and say it well; men who are eloquent and sincere.

Girls should be as informed as boys, to be able to talk with them as friend to friend while they are growing up. It is a shame for a man to have to leave his house to find someone to talk to because the women of the house can talk about nothing but fashions and amusements. But there are some things of a tenderer and more delicate nature which are understood better by girls than by boys, and so for the girls we will write in a style that appeals to them. Because *The Age of Gold* has its own magician in the house, and he says that in girls' souls something happens like what the hummingbird sees as it goes from flower to flower. We will tell the girls about such things—things that the hummingbird might read if it knew how to read. We will tell the girls how a fiber of thread is made, how a violet is born, how they make a needle, how the nice old Italian ladies make lace. The girls also may write to us and ask us what they would like to know, and send us their compositions for our twice-yearly contest. The girls will surely win!

We want children to be happy—happy as the young brothers and sisters in our illustration. And if a boy from America should happen to meet us somewhere in the world one day, we want him to squeeze our hands hard as if he had known us for a long time, and say so that all may hear:

"This man from *The Age of Gold* is my friend!"

Three Heroes

There is a story about a traveler who came to Caracas one day as night was beginning to fall, and even before brushing off the dust of the road, or asking where he could eat and sleep, he wanted to know the way to the statue of Bolívar. And the story goes on to tell how, when the traveler was alone with the tall and fragrant trees of the square, he wept in front of the statue, which seemed to be moving, like a father at the approach of a son. The traveler did well, for every American should love Bolívar as a father—Bolívar and all the soldiers who fought as he did so that America would belong to Americans. He should love them all: the famous hero as well as the very last soldier, who is an unknown hero. Men who fight to see their country free even become handsome.

Freedom is everyone's right to be honest and to think and speak honestly. In America a man could not be honest or think or speak his mind. A man who hides what he thinks, or dares not say what he thinks, is not an honest man. Anyone who obeys a bad government, without working to make that government good, is not an honest man. Anyone who is willing to obey unjust laws, and who allows men who mistreat him to tread the land of his birth, is not an honest man. From the moment a child is able to think, he must think about everything he sees, must suffer for all who cannot live in honor, must work to enable all men to be honest, and must himself be honest. The child who is heedless of what happens around him, and who is content merely to live, not caring if he lives honestly, is like a man who lives from the work of a scoundrel. There are men who are worse than animals, because animals need freedom to live happily. The elephant does not want to bear young while in a cage at the zoo; the Peruvian llama throws itself to the ground and dies when the Indian speaks harshly to it or puts too big a load on its back. Man must be at least as decent as an elephant or a llama. Before America was free, man lived like an overloaded llama. He had to throw off his burden or die.

There are men who can live contentedly even if they do live indecent lives. There are others who suffer agonies when they see the men around them living indecently. There must be a certain amount of decency in the world, just as there must be a certain amount of light. When there are many indecent men, there are always others who have within them the decency of many men. These are the ones who rebel ferociously against those who rob nations of their decency, which is robbing men of their decency. Those good men contain thousands of men, an entire nation, human dignity itself. Those men are sacred. These three men are sacred: Venezuela's Bolívar, San Martín from the Río de la Plata, and Mexico's Hidalgo.[1] Their mistakes should be forgiven,

1. Miguel Hidalgo y Costilla (1753–1811), the "father of Mexican independence," was ordained a priest in 1789, and joined secret societies in Dolores to oppose Spanish domination over Mexico. When he was threatened with arrest, instead of fleeing, on September 16, 1810, he rang the church bell in Dolores to call his parishioners to an announcement of the revolution against the Spanish. Thousands of the poor, including Indians, flocked to Hidalgo's banner of the Virgin of Guadalupe. But in time the movement was crushed, and Father Hidalgo himself was caught, degraded from the priesthood, and shot. Father Hidalgo became the symbol of the Mexican Revolution, and September

because the good they did outweighed their faults. Men cannot be more perfect than the sun. The sun burns and warms with the same light. The sun has sunspots. The ungrateful talk only about the spots. The grateful talk about the light.

Bolívar was a short man. His eyes flashed fire and the words poured out of his mouth. He seemed always to be waiting to mount his horse. It was his country, his oppressed country, that hung heavily on his heart, and it would not let him live in peace. All America seemed to be awakening. One man alone is never worth more than an entire nation, but there are men who never tire when their nation tires, men who decide upon war before their nation decides, for they have nobody to consult but themselves, and nations are composed of many men and cannot be consulted so quickly. That was Bolívar's merit: he never tired of fighting for Venezuela's freedom when Venezuela seemed to be tiring. The Spaniards had defeated him, had thrown him out of the country. He went away to an island, seeing his country nearby and thinking about it.

When nobody wanted to help him any more, a generous Negro came to his aid. One day Bolívar returned to fight, with three hundred heroes, three hundred liberators. He liberated Venezuela. He liberated New Granada. He liberated Ecuador. He liberated Peru. He founded a new nation, the nation of Bolivia. He won sublime battles with the help of soldiers who were half naked and had no shoes. Everything around him shimmered and was filled with light. Generals fought beside him with supernatural bravery. It was an army of the young. Never on earth had there been so much

---

16, the anniversary of the "Grito de Dolores" (Cry of Dolores), is celebrated as Mexico's Independence Day.

Martí's piece in "Three Heroes" on Father Hidalgo is the only extended one on Hidalgo that he wrote. It has also been excerpted and published separately as part of *Our America,* pp. 95-97.

fighting, or better fighting, for freedom. Bolívar did not defend men's right to govern themselves as fiercely as he did America's right to be free. The envious exaggerated his faults. Bolívar died of a heavy heart, rather than of any sickness, in the house of a Spaniard in Santa Marta. He died poor, but he left a family of nations.

Mexico had some courageous men and women of humble origin but who were very valuable: half a dozen men and one woman prepared the way for making their country free. They were a few brave youths, the husband of a liberal woman, and a village priest of sixty who was extremely fond of the Indians. Ever since childhood Father Hidalgo had belonged to the *good race,* those who love knowledge. People who do not love knowledge belong to the *bad race.* Hidalgo knew French, which was then something to be admired because few people knew it. He read books of the eighteenth-century philosophers, books that explained man's right to be honest and to think and speak without hypocrisy. The sight of Negro slaves filled him with horror. He saw the Indians mistreated—such gentle and generous souls—and felt like an older brother among them, teaching them skills which the Indians learned so well: music, which is comforting; raising worms that produce silk; raising bees that give honey. He was filled with enthusiasm and enjoyed making such things as kilns for drying bricks. Now and then his green eyes were seen to sparkle. Everyone said that he talked very well, knew much that was new, and that the priest from the town of Sonora was very charitable. They said he used to go to the city of Querétaro occasionally to talk with a few of the brave and with the husband of a good lady. A traitor told a Spanish *comandante* that some friends in Querétaro were trying to set Mexico free. The priest mounted his horse, followed by all his people who loved him dearly. He set about gathering together the *vaqueros* and servants of the ranchers, men who would compose the cavalry; the Indians went on foot, carrying sticks and arrows and slings and lances. A regiment was

vaquero said. Hidalgo declared the Negroes free. He returned
to the Indians their land. He published a journal which he
called *El Despertador American* [*The American Awakener*].
He won and lost battles. One day seven thousand Indians
equipped with arrows joined him, and the next day they
deserted him. The bad people wanted to go with him so they
could steal in the towns, and also take revenge upon the
Spaniards. He informed the Spanish commanders that if he
won the battle about to be fought, he would receive them in
his house as friends. That is a great man! He dared to be
magnanimous, without fear of the deserters who wanted him
to be cruel. His companion Allende was jealous of him and so
he surrendered the command to Allende. Both men in their
defeat went to seek shelter when the Spaniards fell upon
them. As if to offend Father Hidalgo, the Spanish stripped
him of his vestments one by one. They took him behind a
wall and fired fatal shots into his head. He fell while still
alive, writhing in his blood, and on the ground they finished
him off. They decapitated him and hung his head in a cage in
the very same public granary where his government used to
be. The headless body was buried. But Mexico is free.

San Martín was the liberator of the South, the father of
the Argentine Republic, the father of Chile. His parents were
Spaniards and they sent him to Spain to be a soldier under
the king. When Napoleon took his army into Spain to rob the
Spaniards of their freedom, all the Spaniards fought against
Napoleon, even the old men and the women and children.
One night a brave Catalonian boy routed an entire company,
shooting at its soldiers again and again from his hiding place in
the mountains. They found the boy frozen and starved to
death, but his face was bathed in light and smiling as if he
were happy. San Martín fought very well in the battle of
Bailén, and was made lieutenant colonel. He seldom spoke,
seemed to be made of steel, and had the look of an eagle.
Nobody disobeyed him; his horse raced all over the battlefield like a streak of lightning. As soon as he learned that

formed and it took a convoy of gunpowder which was meant
for the Spaniards. Hidalgo entered Celaya in triumph, with
music and cheering. On the following day the municipal
government met, named him general, and a nation was in
process of being born. He made lances and grenades by hand.
He gave talks that warmed the heart and threw sparks, as one
America was fighting for its freedom, he came to America;
what did he care if he had to give up his career as long as he
could fulfill his duty? He arrived in Buenos Aires, wasted no
time on speeches, raised a squadron of cavalry, and fought his
first battle in San Lorenzo.   Sword in hand, San Martín
marched behind the Spaniards, who were very self-confident
and beating their drums; they lost their drums, their cannon,
and their flag. In other nations of America the Spaniards
were winning: Morillo the Cruel had thrown Bolívar out of
Venezuela, Hidalgo was dead, O'Higgins[2] had fled Chile. But
wherever San Martín was, America continued being free.
There are men who cannot bear to see slavery. San Martín
was one of them, and so he went on to liberate Chile and
Peru. In eighteen days he and his men crossed the bitter cold
and very high Andes; the hungry and thirsty soldiers marched
as if in the sky. Below, far below, the trees looked like weeds
and the waterfalls roared like lions. Then San Martín found
himself facing the Spanish army, and he shattered it in the
Battle of Maipú, defeating it for good and all in the Battle of
Chacabuco. He liberated Chile. Then he and his troops
boarded their ships and sailed on to liberate Peru. But Bolívar
was already there, and so San Martín gave him the glory. San
Martín went sadly back to Europe, and died in the arms of
his daughter Mercedes. He wrote his will on a little sheet of
paper, as if it were a battle order. They had given him the flag

2. Bernardo O'Higgins (1780–1846) served against the royalists, and
is credited with the victories over Spain at Chacabuco (1817) and
Maipú (1818). When the independence of Chile was established he was
made dictator; he resigned in 1823.

that the conqueror Pizarro had brought four centuries before, and San Martín in turn bequeathed it to Peru. A sculptor is admirable because he can make a figure emerge out of rough stone, but these men who make nations are in a sense more than men. At times they try to achieve something they have no right to desire, but for what will a son refuse to forgive his father? The heart fills with tenderness when one thinks of those gigantic founders of nations. They are heroes, the men who fight to give their people their freedom, or who suffer in poverty and affliction to defend a great truth. If men fight for their own ambitions, or to enslave other peoples, or to gain more power than they already have, or to rob another nation of its lands—those men are not heroes, they are criminals.

Homer's Iliad

Twenty-five hundred years ago the poem of the *Iliad* was already famous in Greece. Some say that it was composed by Homer, the blind poet with the curly beard, who went from town to town singing his verses to the accompaniment of the lyre like the bards of those days. Others say that there was no Homer but that the poem was composed by various singers. It seems unlikely, however, that a poem in which the language, thought, and verse structure is so unified, and in which from beginning to end the character of each protagonist is so clearly delineated by what he or she says or does that the reader need not know his or her name, could have been the work of many. Nor is it probable that a single people could have many poets who composed verses with as much sense and lyricism as those of the *Iliad*, with neither too many words nor too few. And it is not likely that different singers could have had the wisdom and greatness of Homer's songs in which the teller of the tale is like a father.

The *Iliad* does not recount the entire thirty years' war of Greece against Ilion, the former name of Troy, merely what occurred in that war when the Greeks were still upon the plain assaulting the walled city, and when the two famous Greeks, Agamemnon and Achilles, were fighting because of jealousy. Agamemnon was called King of Men and he was indeed like a great king who had more command and power than all the others who came from Greece to fight against

Troy when the son of the King of Troy, of old Priam, stole the wife of Menelaos,[1] who served as king in one of the Grecian towns and was Agamemnon's brother. Achilles was the bravest of all the Greek kings, an amiable and cultured man who sang the stories of heroes with his lyre and became loved by the very slave girls who fell to him as spoils when the prisoners were distributed after his victories. The kings' dispute arose over the female prisoner Chryseis, whom Agamemnon refused to return to her father, Apollo's priest, when the Greek priest Calchas said she should be returned in order to calm the fury of the sun god Apollo in Olympus, the heaven of those times. Apollo, god of the sun, was angry with the Greeks because Agamemnon held captive the daughter of a priest, and Achilles, who was not afraid of Agamemnon, rose up from among all the rest and said that he must do what Calchas wanted him to do to end the plague of heat which was killing the Greeks in such great numbers that the sky was never clear of smoke from the pyres upon which their bodies were being burned. Agamemnon promised to return Chryseis if Achilles would give him, Briseis, the captive he held in his tent. And Achilles called Agamemnon "a drunken lout with the eyes of a dog and the heart of a deer," and withdrew his silver-handled sword to kill him before the kings. But the goddess Minerva, invisible at his side, stayed his hand as the sword was midway out of its sheath. And Achilles threw his golden scepter to the ground, sat down, and said that he and his fearless Myrmidons would fight no more on behalf of the Greeks, and that he was going back to his tent.

Thus began the fury of Achilles, which is what the *Iliad* recounts, from when he was angered in that dispute until his heart became enraged when the Trojans killed his friend Patroclus and he went out to again give battle to Troy, which

1. The wife of Menelaos was Helen, who traditionally was the most beautiful woman of Greece and the indirect cause of the Trojan War.

was burning the ships of the Greeks and had almost defeated them. The Trojan army was thrown back merely by the voice of Achilles shouting from the walls, like a wave encountering an opposing wind, and the knees of the Trojan horses trembled. The entire poem is an account of what happened to the Greeks after Achilles considered himself offended—the dispute between the kings; the council of the gods of Olympus in which they decided that the Trojans should defeat the Greeks in punishment for Agamemnon's offense against Achilles; the contest between Paris, son of Priam, and Menelaos, Husband of Helen; the truce between the two armies, and how the Trojan archer Pandarus broke the truce by shooting Menelaos with his arrow; the first day's battle, in which the most courageous Diomedes nearly killed Aeneas with a stone; the visit of Hector, hero of Troy, to his wife Andromache, who watched them fight from the walls; the second day's battle, in which Diomedes fled in his war chariot pursued by the victorious Hector; the legation sent to Achilles by the Greeks asking him to again aid them in battle because since he was not fighting, the Trojans were winning; the sea battle in which not even Ajax himself could defend the Greek vessels from attack until Achilles consented to allow Patroclus to fight with his armor; the death of Patroclus; Achilles' return to combat with new armor made for him by the god Vulcan; the struggle between Achilles and Hector; Hector's death; and the entreaties with which Hector's father Priam succeeded in making Achilles return the body in order to burn it in Troy upon a pyre of honor and preserve the whitened bones in a golden casket. Thus did Achilles become furious, and these were the events of the war until his fury subsided.

The poem does not depict Achilles as the son of a man but of the sea goddess Thetis. And this is not strange because even today kings say that the right of command over peoples comes from God, which is what is called "the divine right of kings," and so it is only an old idea of those times of struggle in which nations were new and did not know how to live in peace the way the stars in the heavens do, for they all shed light even if they are many, and each one shines regardless of having another beside it. The Greeks, like the Hebrews and many other peoples, believed that they were the nation favored by the creator of the world, the only sons of heaven upon earth. And since men are arrogant and unwilling to confess that another man is stronger or more intelligent than they, when there was a strong or intelligent man who became king through his own power, they said that he was a son of the gods. And the kings were glad that the people believed this. The priests claimed that it was true in order to make the kings help and be grateful to them. And thus both kings and priests ruled together.

Each king had his relatives on Olympus and was a son or nephew or grandson of a god who could descend from the heavens to protect or punish him according to whether he took many or few gifts to the priests of his temple, and the priest would say that the god was angered when the gift was a poor one, or that he was happy when he had been given a large quantity of honey or many sheep. So it is in the *Iliad,* which tells us two stories, one on earth and the other in the heavens, and tells us that the gods of Olympus are one family, as it were, except that they do not talk as well-bred people do, but quarrel and insult each other just like men in the world. Jupiter, king of the gods, never knew what to do; his son Apollo wanted to protect the Trojans and his wife Juno the Greeks, the same as his other daughter, Minerva. There were great quarrels at mealtimes in the heavens, and Jupiter told Juno that it would go hard with her if she refused to hold her tongue immediately; and Vulcan the lame, the sage of Olympus, would laugh at the jokes and curses of Apollo the redheaded, who was the mischievous god. And the gods used to ascend and descend to take and bring the messages of both Trojans and Greeks. Or they would fight invisibly in the chariots of the heroes they befriended. Or they would carry their hero through the clouds to prevent the victor from killing him with the aid of the enemy god. Minerva takes on the form of old Nestor of the honey-sweet voice and advises Agamemnon to attack Troy. Venus unfastens Paris's helmet while the enemy Menelaos is dragging him along the ground by it, and carries off Paris through the air. Venus also carries off Aeneas, defeated by Diomedes, in her white arms. In one skirmish Minerva is driving the war chariot of the Greek and Apollo confronts her, driving the Trojan chariot. Again, when, because of a trick of Minerva's, Pandarus pulls his bow against Menelaos, the terrible arrow wounds him only slightly because Minerva turns it aside in midflight, the way a mother chases a fly off of her child's face. In the *Iliad* gods and men are always together, like fathers and sons. And the same things happen in the heavens as upon earth; for it is men who invent gods in their likenesses, and every people imagines a different heaven, with divinities who live and think the same as do those who have created them and worship them in their temples. Because man considers himself small in the face of the Nature which creates and kills him, and feels the need to believe in something powerful which he can implore to treat him well in the world and not take his life. The heaven of the Greeks resembles Greece so closely that Jupiter himself is like a king of kings, a kind of Agamemnon more powerful than the others. He does not do everything he desires, however, but has to listen to the kings and make them happy, as Agamemnon has to do with Achilles. There is much philosophy in the *Iliad,* although it may not seem so, and much science and much politics, and men are taught, in spite of themselves, that the gods are really only a poetry of the imagination, and that countries cannot be governed by the whim of a tyrant, but by the accord and respect of the illustrious men whom the people choose to explain to them how they want to be governed.

The beauty of the *Iliad* is the way it depicts the world, as if man saw it for the first time and ran from one end to the other crying with love, arms upraised, asking the heavens who can be so powerful and where the creator is and how he made and preserved so many marvels. Another beauty of the *Iliad* is how things are said without those swaggering words that poets use because they have a pleasant sound, but with very few and very powerful words, as when Jupiter consents to having the Greeks lose some battles until they repent of their offense against Achilles, and "when he said yes, Olympus trembled." Homer looks for no comparisons in things that cannot be seen, only in things seen, so that one does not forget what he tells, for it is as if he holds the incidents of his narrative there before the eyes. Those were times of struggle, when every man became a soldier to defend his country and went forth motivated by ambition or jealousy to attack his neighbors. And since there were no books or theaters then, diversion consisted in listening to the epic poet sing with his lyre the sruggles of the gods and the battles of men; and the bard had to cause laughter with the evil deeds of Apollo and Vulcan so the people would not tire from serious song; and he dealt with what the people would be interested in hearing, which were tales of heroes and accounts of battles in which the bard introduced medical and political subjects so that the people would find pleasure and profit in them and give fame and high pay to the singer whose verses taught them how to govern and heal themselves. Something else much enjoyed by the Greeks was oratory, and he who spoke well or brought tears to the eyes, or gave the people understanding, was considered the son of a god. That is why the *Iliad* contains so many descriptions of fights and so much curing of wounds and so many speeches.

Everything known about the early Greeks is in the *Iliad*. In Greece the singers who went from town to town singing the *Iliad* and the *Odyssey*—another poem apparently composed by Homer and telling about the return of Ulysses—were called rhapsodic. Some say that Homer composed more poems, but others are of the opinion that those are not his, even if the Greek Herodotus, who gathered together all the history of his time, brought news of them, as well as of a number of unclassified verses, in his life of Homer—the best of the eight in print, although it is not known for certain whether Herodotus actually wrote it or told it in great haste and without thinking, as he was in the habit of writing.

One feels like a giant or as if on the crest of a mountain with an endless sea at one's feet when reading those lines of the *Iliad* which resemble words of stone. There are many good translations in English, and readers of that language must read the *Iliad* of Chapman,[2] or Dodsley,[3] or Landor[4] who captures more of Homer than does Pope,[5] who is the most elegant. Let the reader of German read the Wolff translation, which is like reading the Greek itself. Anyone not acquainted with French, let him learn it immediately so that he may enjoy all the beauty of those times in the translation of Lecompte de Lisle, whose lines were set in the ancient style as if they were made of marble. In Castilian it is better not to read the existing translation, which is by Hermosilla; the words of the *Iliad* are there but not the fire or movement or majesty or at times the divinity of Homer's poem, in which it seems that one can see the world dawning—where men fall like oak trees or like pines; where the warrior Ajax defends his ship from the most courageous Trojans with his lance; where Hector tears down the fortress gates with a stone; where the two immortal horses, Xanthus and Balius, weep in sorrow when they see their owner Patroclus die; and

2. George Chapman (1591–1634), British poet and dramatist, whose translation of Homer remained the standard English version until modern times.

3. Robert Dodsley (1703–64), London author, bookseller, publisher, playwright, and editor.

4. Walter Savage Landor (1775–1864), British writer.

5. Alexander Pope (1688–1744), outstanding poet and satirist in England.

the goddess friends, Juno and Minerva, come from the heavens in a chariot which, with each turn of the wheels, travels across as much space as a man atop a mountain can see from his seat of rock to where sky meets sea.

Every tableau of the *Iliad* is such a scene. When the timorous kings desert Achilles in his dispute with Agamemnon, Achilles goes to weep at the seashore where the ships of the hundred thousand Greeks who attack Troy have been at anchor for ten years, and the goddess Thetis comes forth to hear him like a mist rising from the waves. Thetis ascends to the heavens and Jupiter promises her, although Juno is angered, that the Trojans will win their battles with the Greeks until the time when the kings repent of the insult to Achilles. There are great warriors among the Greeks: Ulysses, who was so tall that he walked among other men like a he-goat among a flock of sheep; Ajax, with his eight-layer shield—seven of leather and one of bronze; Diomedes, who enters the fight in shining armor, devastating as a hungry lion in a flock of sheep. But as long as Achilles still suffers insult, those who win the battles will be the warriors of Troy: Hector, son of Priam; Aeneas, son of the goddess Venus; Sarpedon, bravest of the kings come to the aid of Troy—he who rose to the heavens in the arms of Sleep and Death and who kissed his father Jupiter upon the forehead when he killed Patroclus with a single lance thrust. The two armies meet to engage in combat, the Greeks silently, shield to shield; the Trojans crying out like sheep bleating for their lambs. Paris challenges Menelaos and then retreats; but the most beauteous Helen herself calls him a coward, and Paris, the handsome prince who inspires love in women, consents to battle with Menelaos, chariot to chariot, with spear, sword, and shield. The heralds come and cast lots by means of two stones in a helmet to see who will hurl his spear first. Paris hurls first but Menelaos drags him away, as Venus unfastens the chin strap of his helmet and disappears with Paris into the clouds. Then comes the truce until Minerva, dressed as the son of the Trojan Antenor, treacherously counsels Pandarus to let fly his arrow at Menelaos—the arrow of the enormous bow made of two horns bound together with gold—to make the Trojans appear before the world as traitors, and to facilitate the victory of the Greeks, Minerva's protégés. Pandarus shoots his arrow and Agamemnon goes from tent to tent rousing the kings. Then comes the great battle in which Diomedes wounds the god Mars himself, who ascends to the skies in a cloud of thunder, shouting vociferously as when the wind blows from the south. At this point the beautiful interview between Hector and Andromache takes place when a little boy is unwilling to embrace Hector because he is afraid of his plumed helmet. But later he plays with the helmet while Hector tells Andromache to attend to her household duties as he enters the fray again. On another day, Hector and Ajax fight like wild boars until the sky grows dark; they fight with stones when they no longer have any spears or swords; the heralds come to separate them, and Hector presents his sword with the finely wrought hilt to Ajax, and Ajax presents a purple belt to Hector.

That night the Greeks hold a banquet with honey wines and roast ox. Diomedes and Ulysses enter the enemy camp alone to spy on what Troy is preparing, and return, blood-stained, with the horses and chariot of the Thracian king. At dawn the battle is fought upon the strong wall built by the Greeks on the beach facing their ships. The Trojans have defeated the Greeks on the plain. There have been a hundred battles upon the bodies of dead heroes. Ulysses protects the cadaver of Diomedes with his shield and the Trojans fall upon him like dogs upon a wild boar. From the walls, the Greek kings hurl their spears at victorious Hector who attacks on all sides. The valiant fall, those of Troy and those of Greece, like pines to the axe of a woodcutter. Hector goes from gate to gate like a hungry lion. He picks up by its pointed end a stone which no two men would be able to lift, tears down the main gate, and runs over the dead bodies to attack the ships.

Every Trojan carries a torch to set the Greek ships on fire. Ajax, weary of the slaughter, can no longer oppose the attack from the prow of his ship, so shoots from the stern, from the gunwale; now the sky reddens with the splendor of the flames. And still Achilles fails to come to the assistance of the Greeks, pays no attention to what Agamemnon's ambassadors tell him; does not carry his golden shield, or gird his sword, or leap nimbly into his chariot, or grip the spear which no man can lift—the Battle Spear. But his friend Patroclus entreats him and consents to dress him in his armor and let him go out to fight. Within view of Achilles' weapons, within view of the Myrmidons who enter the battle in close ranks like the stones in a wall, the timorous Trojans are thrown back. Patroclus plunges into their midst and kills nine of their heroes with every turn of his chariot. The great Sarpedon goes forth to meet him on the road and with his spear pierces Patroclus in the temple, for Patroclus forgot Achilles' warning not to come so close to the walls. Invincible Apollo awaits him at the foot of the walls, climbs into his chariot, stuns him with a blow to the head, flings Achilles' helmet down—it has never touched the ground before—breaks Patroclus' spear, opens his suit of armor, all so that Hector can wound him. Patroclus falls and the divine horses weep. When Achilles sees his friend lying dead, he throws himself to the ground, covers his face and head with sand, and tears out the hairs of his yellow beard, bellowing loudly. And when Patroclus is brought to him in a coffin, Achilles weeps. His mother ascends to the skies to have Vulcan make him a new shield engraved with earth and sky, sea and sun, moon and all the stars, a city at peace and another at war, a vineyard when the ripe grapes are being harvested, a child singing and playing a harp, a drove of oxen about to plow, shepherd dancers and musicians, and all around, like a river, the sea. And Vulcan makes him a suit of armor that shines like fire, and a helmet with a golden visor. When Achilles appears upon the wall to shout three times, the Trojans throw themselves against the city in three great surges, the rumps of their frightened horses shattering the chariot, and both men and beasts die in the confusion merely from the sight of Achilles upon the wall, the flame of his helmet shining like an autumn sun. Agamemnon has now repented, the council of kings has sent Achilles precious gifts, Briseis has been returned to him, weeping at the sight of the dead Patroclus because he was amiable and good.

Another day at sunrise the people of Troy, like lobsters escaping the fire, enter the river terrified, fleeing from Achilles who kills as well as the sickle mows, and with one turn of the chariot he carries off twelve captives. He stumbles across Hector but they cannot fight because the gods have cast their spears aside. In the river Achilles is like a great dolphin, and like fishes the Trojans tear themselves to pieces as they flee from him. From the walls Hector's aged father begs him not to fight with Achilles, and so does his mother. Achilles arrives; Hector flees; three times their chariots circle the walls of Troy. All Troy is upon the walls, Hector's father tearing the hairs out of his beard, his mother weeping and beseeching with outstretched arms. Hector stops and talks with Achilles before fighting, asking him not to carry off his dead body if Achilles should win. Achilles wants to burn Hector's corpse at the funeral of his friend Patroclus. They engage in combat. Minerva is with Achilles and directs his blows, brings him the spear unseen, and Hector, now without a spear, attacks Achilles like an eagle swooping out of the sky upon a cadaver, its claws extended. Head lowered, Achilles falls upon Hector, the Battle Spear gleaming in his hand like the evening star. He thrusts his spear into the neck of Hector, who falls dead as he asks Achilles to give his body to Troy. Both father and mother have seen the struggle from the walls. The Greeks come to the dead man, pierce him with their spears, kick him from side to side, and mock him. Achilles orders his ankles run through and threaded with two leather thongs, and he is dragged away by chariot.

Then they build a great pyre of firewood for burning Patroclus's body. He is carried to the pyre in a procession, every warrior cuts off a lock of his own hair to put upon the body, four war-horses and two dogs are sacrificed; with his own hand Achilles kills the twelve prisoners and throws them upon the pyre; Hector's body is pushed aside like that of a dead dog; and they burn Patroclus, cool the ashes with wine, and place them in a golden urn. Earth is thrown upon the urn until it reaches the height of a mountain. And every morning Achilles ties Hector to his chariot by the feet and circles that mountain three times. But Hector's body remains undamaged and its beauty unimpaired, for Venus and Apollo are looking out for him from Olympus.

Then comes the funeral feast, which lasts twelve days: first, a race of war chariots, won by Diomedes; then a fist fight between two men until one of them is left for dead; later a wrestling match between Ulysses and Ajax, both naked; this followed by a foot race won by Ulysses, and a contest with spear and shield; and another with bow and arrow to see who is the best marksman; and another with spears to see who can throw his the farthest.

Suddenly one night, Achilles hears a noise in his tent and sees that it is Priam, father of Hector, who has come unnoticed with the god Mercury—Priam, he of the white beard and white hair; Priam, who kneels at Achilles' feet and kisses his hands many times and tearfully pleads with him for Hector's body. Achilles rises to his feet and lifts Priam from the ground and orders Hector's body bathed with sweet-smelling unguents and clothed in one of the tunics from the great treasure which Priam has brought to Achilles as a gift. And that night Achilles eats meat and drinks wine with Priam, who goes to bed for the first time because his eyes are heavy. But Mercury tells him that he must not sleep among his enemies and carries him off to Troy again, unseen by the Greeks.

There are twelve days of peace then, to enable the Trojans

to celebrate Hector's funeral. The people walk behind the procession as Priam arrives with the body. Priam accuses them of cowardice for having permitted his son to be killed; the women weep and the poets sing until they have entered the house and laid Hector upon his bed to sleep. And Hector's wife Andromache arrives and talks to the corpse. Then comes his mother Hecuba, who calls him handsome and good. Later Helen talks to him and calls him amiable and polite. And all the people weep when Priam approaches his son, his arms held out to the heavens, his chin trembling, and orders firewood brought for the pyre. It takes nine days to bring the wood, until the pyre is taller than the walls of Troy. And they set it ablaze and quench the flames with wine and save Hector's ashes in a golden casket and cover the casket with a mantle of purple and put everything into a coffin and pile so much earth upon it that it resembles a mountain. And then there is a great feast in Priam's palace. So ends the *Iliad* and the tale of the fury of Achilles.

An Excursion
in the Land of the Annamese[1]

There is a tale about four blind Hindus, from faraway
Hindustan in Asia, who were blind from birth and wanted to
know what an elephant looked like. "Let us go to the tame
elephant at the Rajah's house," said one of them, "for the
Rajah is a gracious prince, and he will let us know." And so
they went to the Prince's house in their white robes and
turbans, and on the way they heard the panther roar and the
golden pheasant cackle—the pheasant that looks like a turkey
with two very long tail feathers. After a night's sleep at the
stone ruins of the famous Jehanabad, which in olden days
was the seat of much commerce and power, they crossed a
waterfall, pulling themselves hand over hand by a rope
stretched across and secured on both sides by a stout forked
stick, like a tightrope in a circus. A kindhearted wagon driver
asked them to climb into his wagon, for his humpbacked,
short-horned ox was a good-natured animal who must have
been very like a grandfather in a former life, and would not
be annoyed if the men added to his load; rather, he was used
to looking at wayfarers as if he were inviting them into his
wagon. And that is how the four blind men reached the
Rajah's palace. The outside looked like a castle, and the

1. Situated between Tonkin in the north and Cochin-China in the
South, Annam, an important province for the manufacture of silk, was
a French protectorate after 1884 but later became part of Vietnam.

inside like a casket of precious stones. It was filled with cushions and rich hangings, and its walls and ceilings were embellished with big flower designs of emeralds and sapphires. There were chairs of ivory, and the Rajah's throne was made of ivory and gold. "We have come, Lord Rajah, for you to let us see with our hands, which are the eyes of the unfortunate blind, what a tame elephant looks like." "Blind men are saints," said the Rajah, "and men with a desire for learning are saints. People should learn everything by themselves, and never believe without first inquiring, or speak without first understanding, or slavishly think what others order them to think. You four blind men may go to see with your hands what the tame elephant looks like." The four started running as if their sight had suddenly returned. One tripped on the steps of the Rajah's throne and fell on his nose; another bumped into the wall so hard that he fell down in a sitting position and sat there wondering if the bump had knocked out a piece of his skull. The two others, because their arms were held out, suddenly found themselves embracing. The Rajah's secretary took them to where the tame elephant was eating his ration of thirty-nine rice cakes and fifteen corn cakes out of a silver platter with ebony feet, and when the secretary said "Now!" each blind man threw himself onto the elephant, a chubby little fellow. One hung onto a leg; another grabbed the trunk, going up and down with it and being loath to let go; another clung to the tail; and the fourth held onto a handle of the corn cake and rice cake platter. "I know," said the one clinging to the elephant's leg, "that the elephant is tall and round, like a moving tower." "Not so!" said the one on the trunk. "The elephant is long and ends in a spout, like a funnel made of flesh." "Wrong, all wrong," said the one grabbing the tail. "The elephant is like the clapper of a bell!" "All of you are mistaken, all of you," said the one holding onto the handle of the platter. "The elephant is ring-shaped and never moves." And that is what men are like, for each believes that nothing is the truth but what he thinks and sees. In prose and poetry we are told that we should believe only what these writers themselves believe, just as in the tale of the blind men and the elephant, when what a man should do is to lovingly study the things that men have thought and done, and a very pleasant task it is. By doing this we discover that all men have the same troubles and the same life story and the same love, and that the world is a beautiful temple where all the men on earth can live together in peace, because all of them have wanted to know the truth, and have written in their books that it is useful to be good, and have fought and suffered to be free—free in their countries and free in their thought.

The poor Annamese too have fought, and will fight again, as hard as the bravest—those who live on rice and fish and those who dress in silks in faraway Asia, by the sea below China. To us they do not seem handsome, nor do we to them. They say it is a sin to cut the hair; Nature gave us long hair, and it is a conceited man who thinks he is wiser than Nature. So they wear their hair in a topknot, just like women. They say the hat is meant for giving shade, unless it is worn as a sign of authority in the house of the governor, and then it can be a skullcap without a brim. So the Annamese hat is cone-shaped, with the point on top and the open part very wide. They say that in their hot country one should wear loose, light clothing to let air reach the body; one must not be imprisoned in wools and cashmeres which soak up the sun and are hot and stifling. They say that men have no need for strong backs, for the Cambodians are taller and stronger than the Annamese, but in war the Annamese have always defeated their Cambodian enemies. They say that the eyes should not be blue, for blue deceives and forsakes, like clouds in the sky and water in the sea; that one's color should not be white, for the earth, giver of all beauty, is not white but various shades of the bronze of the Annamese. They say that men should not wear beards, for they are a mark of the wild beast; although the French, who now rule Annam, reply that this idea about beards is only one of envy, because the

Annamese is proud of his wisp of a moustache. And who plays the role of king in their plays but the man with the longest beard? And the Mandarin, does he not appear on the stage with the beard of a tiger? And the generals, do they not have red beards? "Why do we need to have bigger eyes?" ask the Annamese. "And why must they be closer to our noses? With these almond-shaped eyes of ours we have fashioned the Great Buddha of Hanoi, the bronze god whose face seems to be alive; we have built the Angkor pagoda as high as a tower, in a palm grove, with porches two leagues long and lakes in the courtyards, and inside the pagoda a house for every god, and fifteen hundred columns, and avenues lined with statues. On the Saigon road we have built Cholem, the pagoda where under a crown of fretwork towers sleep the poets who sang of love and patriotism, the saints who lived pure and kindly lives among men, the heroes who fought to free us from the Cambodians and Siamese and Chinese, and nothing resembles light itself so much as the colors of our silken robes. We wear topknots and pointed hats and wide trousers and long colored overblouses, and we are yellow, squat, weak-looking, and ugly, but we can work in bronze and silk at the same time. And when the French came to take away our Hanoi, our Hue, our cities and wooden palaces, our seaports filled with bamboo houses and reed boats, our warehouses of fish and rice, yet with our almond-shaped eyes we have known how to die—thousands upon thousands of us—to cut off their path! Now they are our masters; but tomorrow, who knows!"

They move about silently, with a sad and even gait, surprised at nothing and learning what they do not know, their hands in the pockets of their blouses, those blue blouses fastened at the neck with a yellow glass button, and for shoes they wear rope soles tied round the ankle with tape. This is the dress of the fisherman; of the builder of reed houses whose roofs are thatched with rice straw; of the slight-bodied sailor in his double-prowed boat; of the cabinetmaker who manages his tools with both hands and feet, and decorates his chairs and beds of precious woods with inlaid mother-of-pearl; of the weaver who uses threads of silver and gold to embroider his three-headed birds, and his lions with beaks and wings, and his swans with human eyes, and his gods with a thousand arms. This is the dress of the poor coolie who dies young, worn out from hauling the *jinrikisha,* the two-wheeled carriage hauled by the Annamese poor. He trots, trots, like a horse, even more than a horse, and faster, and inside sits a man, comfortable and shameless! Later the poor coolie dies, like the horse, from so much running. And those who let themselves be taken from place to place in the *jinrikisha,* stirring the air with their fans, die red-faced and fat from drinking claret and Burgundy—English military men, French officials, Chinese merchants.

Could it have been that nation of trotting men that built those three-storied pagodas with lakes in their courtyards, and houses for every god, and avenues of statues? Was it they who fashioned those porcelain lions and bronze giants, wove silk so brightly colored that it sparkled in the sun like a cape of brilliants? This is what becomes of men grown weary of defending themselves; they haul their masters' carriages like workhorses while the master sits inside, red-faced and fat. The Annamese are weary now. It takes much effort for little nations to live. The Annamese have always been defending themselves. Their powerful neighbors, the Chinese and Siamese, have tried to conquer them. To defend themselves against Siam, they made friends with the Chinese, who flattered them and received them with processions and fireworks and celebrations on the rivers, and called them "beloved brother." But as soon as they entered the land of Annam, about two thousand years ago, they tried to rule it as if they were already its masters, and for two thousand years the Annamese have been defending themselves against the Chinese! The same thing happened with the French, for under a king's way of ruling, nations can never grow. In faraway places like China, where they say the king is the son of Heaven, and where they believe it is a sin to look him in the face—even if the kings themselves know that they are only men, like other people—they fight one another to win more towns and more riches, and men die without knowing why, defending one king or another. A French bishop was traveling through Annam during one of those battles between kings, and he convinced the defeated king that Louis XVI of France would help him fight the one who took the rule of Annam away from him. The bishop went to France with the king's son, and then returned alone because the revolution in Paris prevented Louis XVI from being able to keep his promise. So the bishop joined the French who were in India, entered Annam, seized the power from the new king, and installed the former king as ruler. But the real rulers were the French, who wanted everything in the country for themselves. So they took away the power of the Annamese and replaced it with their own—until Annam saw how dangerous was that foreign friend, and realized that it was better to have no friend at all, and in a battle they threw him out of their country, which still knew how to fight. The French, however, came back again later, stronger than before and with cannon on their battleships. The Annamese could not defend themselves on the sea in their reed boats that had no cannon, nor could they hold their cities, for it is impossible to fight bullets with spears. And Saigon, the place where the French entered, has little stone to use for building fortifications. The Annamese were not accustomed to that strange kind of fighting; all they knew was man-to-man and horse-to-horse combat with sword and spear. They had been defending themselves from the French for a century, town by town, sometimes fleeing from them, sometimes falling upon them with the full force of their chargers, tearing their army to bits. China sent them her war-horses because she too wanted to keep foreigners out of her land, and throwing them out of Annam was like throwing them out of China. But the French come from another world, and know more about wars and ways of killing. Town by town, and waist-deep in blood, she has been robbing the Annamese of their country.

The Annamese move about silently, with a sad and even gait, their hands in the pockets of their blue blouses. They work. They have the skill of a fine silversmith in everything they do: working in wood and mother-of-pearl, making weapons, weaving textiles, painting, embroidering, fashioning plowshares. They plow with buffalo, not horses or oxen. The cloth for their clothes they paint by hand. With knives and chisels they carve entire towns out of hard wood, with a house in the background and ships sailing the river and people by the thousands in the ships, and trees and lanterns and bridges and fishing boats, all as tiny as if they had been carved with a thorn. Their houses look as if made for dwarfs, and are so well constructed that they seem to be toy houses, all put together out of little pieces. They paint the walls; they carve the wooden roofs in a very painstaking manner, like the outer walls. In every corner there are porcelain vases, and bronze griffons with outspread wings, and screens of embroidered silk framed in bamboo. There is no home without its coffin; in Annam this is a fine piece of furniture decorated with mother-of-pearl. Good sons present their father with the gift of a luxurious coffin, for death there, with its noisy music and its pagoda chants, is like a celebration. They do not feel that life belongs to man, but is merely loaned to him by Nature. Dying is only returning to the Nature from which he came, and where everything is kindly and companionable. That is why the dying usually leave instructions in their wills to have an arm or leg of theirs put where the birds can peck at it, or where the wild animals can devour it, or where the invisible creatures of the air can consume it. Since the Annamese live in slavery, many of them go to their pagodas, because there the priests talk to them about the saints of their country, who are not the saints of the French. Many people go to the theaters where they are not told things that make them laugh, but the history of their kings and generals instead. Squatting there, they listen silently to stories of battles. . . .

Naughty Nené

I wonder if there is another little girl like Nené! A wise old man says that all little girls are like Nené. Nené would rather play house or store, or make sweets with her dolls, than recite the three and four tables for the teacher who comes to give her lessons. Because Nené has no mother; her mother is dead, and that is why Nené has a teacher. Making sweets is what Nené likes to do more than anything else; I wonder why. Who knows? —perhaps because to play making sweets they give her real sugar. Of course the sweets never turn out well the first time—they are very difficult to make— so she always has to ask for sugar twice. Since everyone knows that Nené never likes to make her little friends work hard, when she plays at taking a drive or going shopping or visiting, she always calls them; but when she is going to make sweets, never. And once a very strange thing happened to Nené; she asked her *papá* for two cents to buy a new pencil, but on the way to the store she forgot all about the pencil; what she bought was a strawberry meringue. Her little friends found out about this, of course, and so from then on they called her "Strawberry Meringue" instead of Nené.

Nené's father loved her very much. They say he did poor work if he failed to see his little daughter in the morning. He called her "little daughter," not Nené. When her *papá* returned from work she always went out to greet him with open arms, like a little bird opening its wings to fly; then her *papá* would pluck her from the ground the way you pluck a rose from a rose bush. She would look at him most fondly as if to ask him things, and he would look at her sadly as if he wanted to burst into tears. But he would turn happy right away, lift Nené onto his shoulders, and both would go into the house singing the national anthem. Nené's *papá* always used to bring home some new book and let her see if there were pictures in it; she especially liked some books he brought that had pictures of stars in them, each with its own name and color. The red star and the yellow star and the blue star each had names, and she read that light is made up of seven colors, and that the stars go through the sky the way little girls go through a garden. No, not quite; for little girls go through a garden helter-skelter like a flower petal blown by the wind, while the stars go through the sky always following the same path and not wherever they wish. Who knows, perhaps there is somebody up there taking care of the stars the way *papás* take care of their little girls here upon the earth. Only stars are not little girls, of course, nor are they flowers of light as they appear from down here; they are as big as this world, and they say there are trees and water and people upon them, as there are here; and her *papá* says that in one book they tell about going to live upon a star when you die. "So tell me, *Papá,*" Nené asked him, "why is there such sadness in houses where someone has died? If I die, I don't want to see anybody cry; I want them to play some music for me because I'm going to live upon that blue star." "But just you, you alone, without your poor *papá?*" And Nené replied: "How wrong of you to think so!" That night, instead of going to bed early, Nené wanted to sleep in her *papá's* arms. *Papás* are very sad when the mother of the house dies! Little girls should be very, very fond of their fathers when their mothers are dead.

The night they talked about the stars Nené's *papá* brought home a very big book; oh, how heavy it was! Nené tried to pick it up, but she fell down with the book on top of her; all you could see was a little blond head coming out from one side of it and some little black shoes from the other. Her *papá* came running and pulled her out from underneath the book, and he laughed at her a lot; she was not even six years old and she wanted to carry a book that was a hundred. The book was a hundred years old and had not yet grown a beard! Nené had once seen a little old man who was a hundred, but he had a very long beard that came down to his waist. And the model handwriting sentence says that good books are like old men: "A good book is like an old friend." That is what it says. Nené went to bed very quietly, thinking about the book. What was the book her *papá* refused to let her touch? When she awakened that was the only thing on Nené's mind. She wanted to know what book it was. She wanted to know just how they made a hundred-year-old book that has no beard.

Her *papá* is far, far from home, working so the little girl can have a pretty house and eat delicious sweets on Sundays; working to buy her little white dresses with blue ribbons on them; working to put aside a little money so that if her *papá* should die, his "little daughter" would not be left without a penny. Her poor *papá* is far away from home, working for his "little daughter." The servant is inside, preparing her bath. Nobody can hear or see Nené. When her *papá* goes out of the room, he always leaves his books open. Nené keeps her little chair there, and often sits beside her *papá*'s desk to watch him work. Five, six, seven little steps . . . now Nené is at the door; now she pushes it open; now she goes in. What things happen then! As if expecting her, the old book lies open upon his chair, open at the middle. Step by small step Nené draws near, very serious and as if deep in thought, her hands behind her back. Nené would not touch the book for anything in the world, only look at it—no more than look at it. Her *papá* has told her not to touch it.

The book has no beard; a lot of ribbons and book marks come out of it, but these are not a beard. The giant pictured in the book does have a beard, though. And he is painted with shining, enamel-work colors like the bracelet her *papá* gave her. They do not put that kind of picture in books anymore! The giant is seated upon a mountain top with something swirling over his head like clouds, and only one eye just above his nose. He is wearing a shepherd's smock, a smock as green as the fields, with gold and silver stars painted upon it, and his beard is so long, so very long, that it hangs all the way down to the foot of the mountain. And up each strand of its hair climbs a man, like an acrobat in a circus climbing up the rope to the trapeze. But this cannot be seen from far away! Nené must take the book down from the chair. How heavy is that naughty book. Now it is down on the floor.

The men climbing up the beard are five in number. One is a white man wearing a dress coat and boots, and he too has a beard; that artist is very fond of beards! Another looks like an Indian—yes, an Indian, with a feathered headdress and a quiver of arrows upon his back. Another is a Chinaman, like the cook, but he is wearing a dress with a floral pattern, like a lady. Another looks like the Chinaman, and he is wearing a pear-shaped, pointed hat. Another is black, a very pretty Negro, but naked! That is wrong, going without clothes! That is why her *papá* did not want her to touch the book! No, she would never look at that page again; then her *papá* would not be cross. How pretty is this old book! And Nené is lying almost on top of the book, as if she wanted to talk to it with her eyes.

The page is almost torn! No, not quite. Only half torn. Nené's *papá* has poor sight; no one will notice. This is really a fine book! It is better, much better, than *Noah's Ark*. All the animals in the world are pictured here, and in color like the giant! Yes, see, oh see the giraffe gobbling up the moon; see the elephant, the elephant with that saddle full of little children. Oh, look at those dogs; look how this one runs! Come here, dog; I shall spank you, dog, because you won't come! And Nené, of course, tears the page. And what does our Miss Nené see now? The other picture shows a world of monkeys. Both pages are filled with monkeys—a red monkey is playing with a little green one, a big bearded monkey is nipping the tail of a tremendous monkey that walks upright like a man, and holds a stick. A black monkey is playing in the grass with a yellow one. Those, the ones up in the trees, are the monkey children! How funny! See how they play! They go back and forth from branch to branch like a swing! How well, how well they can leap! One, two, three, five, eight, sixteen, forty-nine monkeys holding on by their tails! They are going to throw themselves into the river! *Wheeee*—there they go! And Nené, full of enthusiasm, tears both pages out of the book. Who is calling to Nené; I wonder who? Her *papá,* her *papá,* watching from the doorway.

Nené neither sees nor hears. Her *papá* seems to be growing, growing very tall, touching the ceiling; he seems bigger than the giant of the mountain. Her *papá* seems like a mountain towering above her. She is quiet, so quiet, her head hanging, her eyes shut, the two torn pages in her limp hands. And her *papá* is talking to her: "Nené, didn't I tell you not to touch this book? Nené, don't you know that this book is not mine, that it is worth a lot of money, a very great amount of money? Nené, don't you know I'll have to work for a whole year to pay for it? " White as a sheet of paper, Nené stands up, her head still hanging, and clasps her *papá* around the knees: "*Papá,*" says Nené, "my darling *Papá!* I made my *papá* angry! I'm a naughty girl! Now when I die I won't be able to go to that blue star!"

The History of Man,
Told by Way of His Houses

People live in big houses now, with doors and windows, paved courtyards, and columned porches, but many thousands of years ago men did not live like this, nor were there countries with sixty millions of inhabitants as there are today. In ancient times there were no books to tell about things; we determine how men used to live by the stones, bones, shells, and tools we find. We call those times the "Stone Age" when men went about almost naked or dressed in animal skins, fighting the wild beasts of the forest, living hidden away in mountain caves, and not knowing—back in "Paleolithic"[1] days—that there was copper or iron in the world. "Paleolithic" is a big word! The men of those days did not even know how to cut stone, although they soon learned how to shape it with axes made of sharp-edged flint, and that was in the new stone age called "Neolithic."[2] *Neo* means new and *lithic* means stone. *Paleo,* of course, means old, ancient. In those days men lived in mountain caves where wild animals could not reach them, or else they dug a hole in the ground

1. Paleolithic was an ancient cultural stage characterized by distinctive tool types that are simple and relatively crude in the Early Paleolithic but become more complex and sophisticated in the later Paleolithic time.

2. Neolithic, a term introduced by the English anthropologist Sir John Lubbock in 1865, designates all archeological inventions that include stone tools shaped by polishing or grinding.

and covered the entrance with a door made out of branches, or they used branches to roof over a cleft in the rock, or they set three tall sticks into the ground and bound their tops together into a point, covering them with hides from the animals they hunted. Animals were large then. Apparently in America the men of those times did not live like that, but gathered in villages instead of in separated families. We can still see the ruins of what are called "earth-builders" because they built thick walls of earth in round or square or triangular shapes, or in four circles, one inside the other. Some Indians lived in stone houses that were like villages and were called *pueblos* because they housed almost a thousand families at one time, and these people, like the present-day Zuni Indians, entered their homes through the roof rather than through the doors as we do. In other places there are stone houses in the crevices of rocks, reached by toeholds cut out by pickaxes, like a staircase. Families got together everywhere to defend themselves and build cities in the rocks or in the middle of lakes—these latter known as lacustrine cities because those houses made out of tree trunks are built upon stilts dug into the lake bottoms, or secured at the base by stones so their weight would keep the houses from floating away. Sometimes the houses were connected by logs and surrounded by stockades to defend the people living in them from their warlike neighbors or from the mountain animals. Their beds were made of dry grass, their bowls of wood, their tables and chairs of tree trunks. Other peoples put three large stones in the middle of a forest and built a flat roof on top where the three slanted stones came together, and put a fence around it; but these constructions were not meant for living, but for burying their dead, or to go to when they listened to their old men and sages at the change of seasons, or when there was a war, or to elect a chief. And to remember where each of these were, they erected a very tall stone like a column, called a menhir in Europe and *katún* by the Mayan Indians, because the Mayans of Yucatán did not know that across the sea lived the Gauls, where France is today, but they did the same things as the Gauls and the Germans, who lived where Germany is now. By studying we learn all this: that man is the same everywhere, and appears and progresses in the same way, and makes and thinks the same things, their only differences being those determined by the lands in which they live. Because a man born in the lands of trees and flowers thinks more about beauty and adornment and has more things to say than a man born in a frigid land, where what he sees most often is a dark sky and his cave in the rock. And there is something else to be learned: where a savage is born, not knowing that there are nations in the world, he lives just like men did thousands of years ago. Next to the city of Zaragoza in Spain there are families living in open holes in the ground in the outlying countryside. In Dakota in the United States, the pioneers going there to settle the country live in shanties with roofs made of branches as in the Neolithic age. On the shores of the Orinoco in South America the Indians live in lacustrine cities just like the Swiss lake dwellers did hundreds of years ago. The North American Indian makes his horse drag the three poles of his tepee, which is an animal-skin tent like the tent the Neolithic men pitched in the deserts. Today the African Negro makes his house with earth walls and roof of branches the same as the Germans did long ago, leaving the door hole high to keep out snakes, also copying the Germans. There was not a Stone Age in which all peoples lived at the same time in the same way, and then a Bronze Age when men began to work metal, and then an Iron Age. There are peoples who live in the most beautiful stage of the Iron Age,[3] as in France today, with their Eiffel Tower that pierces the sky; and other

3. The Iron Age was the final technological and cultural stage in the Stone–Bronze–Iron Age sequence. The date of the Iron Age, in which this metal largely replaced bronze in implements and weapons, varied geographically, beginning about 1200 B.C., but in China not until 600 B.C.

peoples who live in the Stone Age, like the Indian who builds his house in the branches of a tree, and with his flint-tipped spear goes out to kill the birds of the forest and run through in the air the flying fish of the river. But peoples these days advance more quickly, because they join forces with the older peoples and learn from them the things they do not know—not the way it was before, when they had to go little by little, discovering everything by themselves. The Stone Age was when men were beginning to live, for they went from place to place fleeing from animals, and they lived here one day and there another and were unaware that the fruits of the earth were good to eat. Later, men found copper, which was softer than flint, and tin, which was softer than copper, and they saw that metals could be extracted from the rocks with fire, and that by mixing tin and copper a new metal could be made, very good for axes and knives and for cutting stone. When peoples commence to know how to work metal and blend copper with tin, then they are in their Bronze Age. There are people who have arrived at the Iron Age without having passed through the Bronze Age, because iron happened to have been the metal found in their own land, and they began to work with it without knowing that there was any copper or tin in the world. When the Europeans lived in the Bronze Age they were already building better homes, although not as finished and perfect as those of America's Peruvians and Mexicans, among whom the two ages always existed at the same time. Because they continued working with flint when they already had their gold mines and their temples with golden suns like the sun in the sky, and their *huacas*—Peruvian cemeteries—where they buried their dead with the vessels and personal belongings they used while still alive. The Peruvian Indian's house was built of masonry, with two storeys and windows placed very high and doors that were wider at the bottom than at the cornice, which was usually delicately carved stone. The Mexican did not build his house that strong, but with more elaborate decorations, as you would expect in a country where there are many trees and birds. The roofs were built in steps, upon which they placed statues of their saints the way many of them now put figures of children and arms and legs of silver upon their altars. They decorated the walls with carved stone and borders like beads or braided ropes, as if copying Grecian fretwork, and their wives embroidered the hems of their gowns. In the inside halls they carved the ends of the beams with images of their gods, animals, or heroes, and outside they placed gracefully curved drains at the corners, as if modeled after feathers. From a distance those houses shone like the sun, as if made of silver.

You can see the three ages more clearly in the central European peoples, and even better farther to the north, because there men lived in separate villages for centuries and centuries, and since they began to live at the same time, you notice that although they never knew one another, they progressed alike. The earth is beginning to form layers as the centuries go by; the earth is like a puff-paste pie with many layers, one on top of the other, and sometimes a mass of rock from deep inside the world breaks through the flat layers and comes out into the open air and remains on top of the ground like a grumbling giant or like an angry wild animal, spewing smoke and fire through the crater; that is how mountains and volcanoes are made. You can come to know how man has lived by means of those layers, because buried in each are his bones and the remains of the animals and trees of that age, and the pots and jars and axes. By comparing the layers in one place with those in another, you can see that men everywhere live almost alike in every age; but the earth takes a long time in going from one age to another, and in laying down a new layer, and that is why it happens that the Romans in Julius Caesar's time had marble palaces with golden statues and wore clothing of very fine wool, while the Britons of England lived in caves and dressed in the hides of savage animals, and fought with war clubs made of hard wood.

In those ancient peoples you can really see how man was progressing, because on top of the Stone Age layers, where everything you find is made of flint, there are Bronze Age layers with many things made of a mixture of copper and tin. And then come the upper layers, those of later times called the Iron Age, when man learned that iron could be softened in a hot fire and that with softened iron he could make hammers to break up the rocks, and spears for his fighting, and knives and pickaxes for working the soil. It is at this stage that we see houses of stone and wood with courtyards and rooms, always in imitation of the miserable huts of rocks placed one atop another without any mortar at all, or like the animal-skin tents of the plains and deserts. What we do see is that ever since man came into the world he has enjoyed drawing the things he saw, for even in the darkest caves where savage families lived, there are many figures carved or painted on the rock walls, and when the people of today went to live in that region, they discovered in the mountains and along the river banks some strange signs and impressions of hands and animal paintings that have been there for many centuries. And we also note that all peoples have taken a great deal of care in burying their dead most respectfully, and have built tall monuments, as if wanting them to be closer to the sky, the way we do now with our towers. The men who worked with earth made hills in which they buried the bodies. The Mexicans put their temples on the tops of some very tall pyramids; the Peruvians had their stone *chulpa,* a tower wide at the top like the handle of a truncheon. On the island of Sardinia there are some towers known by the name of *nuragh,* and nobody knows to what people they belonged. The Egyptians erected their pyramids with enormous blocks of stone, and with an even harder porphyry they built their famous obelisks, upon which they inscribed their history in signs called hieroglyphics.

The Egyptian ages began to be called "historic times" because their history can be written by what we know of

them. Those other peoples of the early ages are called "pre-
historic peoples"—from before recorded history—or "primitive peoples." But the truth is that in those same historic
peoples there is still much that is prehistoric, because you
have to do a lot of guessing to discover where and how they
lived. Who knows when the Quechuas built their aqueducts
and roads and paved highways in Peru, or when the Chibchas
of Colombia started to make their jewelry and golden
pitchers, or what peoples lived in Yucatán before the Mayans
whom the Spaniards found there, or where the unknown race
came from that built the mud walls and *pueblo* houses in
North America? Almost the same thing came about with the
people of Europe, although there men appeared at the same
time in many different places, as if born of the earth, except
that man lived first where it was less cold and in higher
country. And since men lived there first, that was where the
people came to learn things sooner, and to discover metals,
and to make things, and—with wars and floods and a desire to
see the world—man commenced to travel from there by land
and sea. Man across the Atlantic became civilized first in the
highest and most fertile part of the continent. The same thing
happened in our America. The American Indian had his best
villages upon the high plains of Mexico and Peru, in the high
valleys with good soil. Apparently Egypt was the oldest
nation of the continent across the Atlantic, and it was from
there that men gradually went to what is now called Persia
and Asia Minor, and went to Greece in search of freedom and
change, and in Greece they constructed the most perfect
buildings in the world, and wrote the most beautiful and
well-composed books. Peoples originated in all those countries, but those who came from the oldest knew more and
defeated the others in war, or taught them what they knew,
and joined them. Other stronger men, made to fight wild
animals and live in cold climates, came from the north of
Europe. And the mountain peoples, after a great war, fled
from what is now called Hindustan and joined the Europeans

of the cold lands who then came down from the north to fight the Romans, because the Romans had been robbing them of their freedom, and because they were poor but ferocious people who envied Rome for being wise and rich and a daughter of Greece. That is how peoples began to travel over the world, like currents through the sea and winds through the air.

Egypt is like a father-nation of the transatlantic continents: the oldest nation of all those "classical" countries. And the Egyptian house is like its people were: pleasing and elegant. Egypt was a very rich country because the great river Nile used to rise every year, and with the silt it left behind when it fell, the crops flourished. That is why the houses were built upon high ground, for fear of floods. Since there are many palm groves in Egypt, the columns of the houses are tall and slender like the palm trees. And on top of the second floor there was another, without walls but with a flat roof, where the people spent the afternoon in the fresh air, watching the Nile and its many barges sailing back and forth with their passengers and cargoes, and looking at the gold and saffron-colored evening sky. The walls and roofs are filled with paintings of their history and religion, and they were so fond of color that even the matting that covered their floors was woven of different-colored fibers.

For a long time the Hebrews lived in Egypt as slaves, and they were the best brick-makers. Later, when they were set free, they built their houses with crude bricks like our adobe, and the roof was made of the trunks of the sycamore, their beloved tree. The flat roof had a low wall at the edge; people went up there to sleep because of the heat, and the law made them build their roofs with low walls to keep them from falling off. They usually patterned their houses after the temple of their great King Solomon—a square building with wide doorways below and narrow windows along the cornice, and with a column at each side of the door.

In those lands lived the Assyrians, a warlike people who

added towers to their houses as if to catch sight of the enemy while he was still far away, and the towers had merlons so they could shoot their arrows from safe positions. Their houses had no windows, but light came in through the roof. Over the doors they sometimes put stones carved with mysterious figures, such as a bull with the head of a man, or a head with wings.

The Phoenicians built their houses and monuments out of uncarved stones, one on top of another like the Etruscans; but since they were seafaring men who lived from commerce, they soon began to imitate the houses of the peoples they saw most often—the Hebrews and Egyptians—and then the Persians who conquered Phoenicia in a war. And so their houses had a Hebrew entrance with the upper part like the houses of Egypt or Persia.

The Persians were very powerful, since there was a time when all those people around them lived as their slaves. Persia was a land of jewels: clothing, horse blankets, the hilts of swords, everything there was covered with jewels. They used a lot of green, red, and yellow. All Persians were very fond of color, very bright and shiny. They liked fountains and gardens and enamelware and veils woven of silver threads and finely wrought jewelry. The Persians are still like that today, and already in those times their houses were made of colored brick—not with a flat roof like that of the Egyptians and Hebrews, but with a round cupola, as if copying the vault of heaven. Their baths were out in the courtyard, and the water was delicately scented. The wealthy houses had square courtyards flanked by many columns, and a fountain in the center among urns of flowers. The columns were made of many colorfully painted little pieces, with grooves and bands of color, and the capitals were made in the shape of animals with green bodies and gold dog collars.

Beside Persia lies Hindustan, the oldest nation in the world, and it has golden temples wrought the way silversmiths made filigree, and other temples dug out of rock, and statues of its god Buddha carved out of the sides of mountains. Its temples, tombs, palaces, and houses are like poetry written in color upon ivory, saying things as if among the leaves and flowers. There is a temple in Hindustan which had fourteen storeys like the Lahore pagoda, and all of it is carved, from the foundation to the cupola. And the houses of the ancient Hindus were like the pagodas of Lahore or Kashmir, with highly decorated ceilings and balconies and many vaults, and at the entrance a stairway without a railing. Other houses had fortified towers at the corners and terraces like the Egyptian ones, unbroken and without towers. But the beauty of the Hindu houses was their fantastic embellishments, a never-ending braid of feathers and flowers.

Greece was not at all like this; it was all white and simple, with no brightly colored splendor. Greek houses had no windows, because for the Greeks a house was always a sacred place, not to be looked into by strangers. The houses were small, like their monuments, but very pretty and cheerful, with their rose bush and statue beside the front door, and with a columned corridor inside where the family spent the day, for only at night did they go to their small, dark rooms. Only the corridor and dining room were furnished, and these sparingly. They put their beautiful jars in niches in the walls. The chairs had carved borders like those they were accustomed to put around the doors, which were wide at the bottom and had cornices decorated with paintings of palms and honeysuckle. The Parthenon is said to be the most beautiful building in the world, for it has no adornments simply for the pleasure of adorning—which is what ignorant people do with their houses and clothes—but its beauty comes from a kind of music you feel rather than hear, because the size is determined on the basis of how well it goes with the color, and there is nothing there that is unnecessary, nor any decoration that might be in the way. Greek stones seem to have souls. They are modest and as if friends of the person looking at them. They enter your heart like friends. They seem to be talking.

The Etruscans lived in the north of Italy in their twelve famous cities, and were an original people who had their own government and religion and an art like that of the Greeks, although they were fonder of jests and extravagance and used lots of color. They painted everything, like the Persians, and the walls of their tombs have pictures of horses with yellow heads and blue tails. As long as Etruria was a free republic the Etruscans lived a happy life, with very good teachers of medicine and astronomy and with men who talked well about life's responsibilities and about how the world was made. Etruria was famous for its wise men, and for its jars made of black clay with figures in relief, and for its statues and tombs of fired earth, and for its wall paintings and wrought metal. But with slavery the Etruscans became vicious and rich, like their masters, the Romans. They lived in palaces and not in their houses as before, and their chief pleasure was eating—hour after hour while reclining upon a couch. Before this, the Etruscan house was of one storey with a railed terrace and a roof of sloping eaves. On the walls they painted their celebrations and ceremonies with portraits and caricatures, and they knew how to draw their figures as if in motion.

At first the Roman house was like the Etruscan, but later the Romans came to know about Greece and copied not only the Grecian houses but everything else that was Greek. At first the atrium was the entire house, but later it was only the porch, from which you went through a corridor to the inner courtyard, surrounded by columns, onto which opened the rich quarters of the owner, who had a different room for every use. The dining room faced the corridor and so did the hall and family room, whose opposite sides looked out into a garden. The walls were decorated with drawings of figures in brilliant colors, and in the corners there were many niches with jars and statues. If the house was on a street where many people passed by, those Romans built rooms with doors to the street and rented them out for shops. When the doors were open you could see as far as the back of the garden. In many houses the garden and courtyard and atrium had a series of arches around them. Afterward, Rome owned all the countries around it, until it had so many people that it was unable to govern them, and every nation was becoming free and appointing its own king, who was the most powerful of all the warriors in the country, and lived in a stone castle with towers and drawbridges, like all those who were called "lords" in those warlike days. And the workers lived around the castle in miserable little shacks. But the power of Rome had been very great, and everywhere there were bridges and arches and aqueducts and temples like those of the Romans. Only around France, where there were many castles, they were building new structures, especially churches, as if they were fortresses and churches at the same time, and their architecture was called Romanesque. And around Persia and the Arabs, where Turkey is now, the buildings were so lavishly and colorfully decorated that the churches looked like caverns of gold because of their grandeur and splendor, so that when the new nations around France began to have cities, their houses had dark porches and many peaked roofs like those on the Romanesque churches. And around Turkey the houses were like palaces, with columns of costly stone and floors of many small pieces of colored stone, and wall paintings with gold backgrounds, and golden windows. The Byzantine houses had banisters made out of an alloy of all the metals, and they shone like fire. Houses with so much ugly and offensive decoration look like the tombs of conceited men—now that the houses are empty.

The Romans also ruled Spain, but then the Moors overran the country and built those churches of theirs called mosques, and those palaces that seem like something out of a dream—as if one no longer lived in this world, but in another world of lace and flowers. The doors were small, but with so many arches they seemed big. Slender columns supported horseshoe arches topped by a point as if opening a pathway to the sky. The ceiling was made of fine woods covered all over with carvings of Moorish letters and horses' heads; the walls were covered with designs, like a rug; in the marble courtyards there were laurel bushes and fountains, and those balconies looked as if they wore woven veils.

Both wars and friendships brought those different nations together, and when the king became more powerful than the lords of the castles, and when everyone believed in the new heaven of the Christians, they commenced to build those Gothic cathedrals, with their pointed arches and their towers like needles piercing the clouds and their finely carved porticos and their stained glass windows of many colors. And the towers reached higher and higher, because every church wanted its tower to be taller than the others, and that is how they made houses too, and their furnishings. But the decorations were becoming too fancy, and the Christians stopped believing in Heaven as much as before. There was much discussion about the grandeur that was Rome; Greek art was praised for its simplicity; people said there were plenty of churches already but looked for new ways to build palaces, and from a combination of these feelings came a mode of construction resembling the Greek, which is called Renaissance architecture. But because the Gothic pointed arch—the *ojiva*—was so beautiful, houses no longer returned to that Greek simplicity but were decorated with graceful corners, high windows, and elegant balconies built in the Gothic style. Those were the days of art and riches and great conquests, so there were many lords and merchants living in palaces. Never had men lived—nor have they lived again—in such beautiful houses. The nations of other races, who knew little about the Europeans, fought on their own account or became friends and learned each other's special art, so that you see something of the Hindu pagoda all over Asia, and the Japanese houses have spires like the palaces of Lahore—pinnacles that seem to be made of air and enchantment—or little houses of recreation with their delicately railed porches and their walls of willow or rice straw. Even in the Slavic or Russian houses you can see the restless curves and pointed roofs of the Hindu peoples. Our American houses have something of the Roman and the Moor because the Spaniards who ruled in America had Roman and Moorish blood, and they tore down the Indians' houses. They demolished them right down to the foundations, tore down their temples, their observatories, their signal towers, the houses in which they lived. The Spanish conquerors burned and destroyed everything that was Indian except the highways, because they were unable to carry away the huge stones which the Indians knew how to bring there, and the aqueducts that brought the Spaniards water to drink.

Today all the peoples of the world know one another better and visit back and forth. And every nation has its own method of building according to whether its climate is hot or cold, or is composed of one race or another. But what seems to be new in the cities is not their way of building houses, but the fact that every city has Moorish, Grecian, Gothic, Byzantine, and Japanese houses, as if a happy time were to come in which men treat each other like friends and are coming together.

A New Game
and Some Other Old Ones

There is a most curious game in the United States today, known as "pin the tail on the donkey." In summer, when you hear a lot of laughter in the house, it is because the children are playing "pin the tail on the donkey." Not only do children play the game, but adults as well. And it is very easy to make. Upon a large sheet of paper, or a piece of white cloth, you draw a donkey about the size of a dog. It should be done with charcoal because regular coal does not work—only charcoal made out of burnt wood. Or the donkey can be drawn with a paintbrush dipped in ink; because you do not have to put in the shadings, merely the outline. You paint the whole donkey, all except the tail. The tail must be drawn separately on a piece of paper or cloth, and then cut out along the outlines so that it really looks like a tail. And there you have the game—pinning the tail on the donkey where it should go. What is not as easy as you think is that when you play, your eyes are bandaged and you are turned around three times before being allowed to walk toward the donkey. And you walk every which way, and the onlookers try to control their laughter. Some of the players pin the tail on the hoof or the side or the forehead. And other players pin it on a door, thinking the door is the donkey.

In the United States they say that this game is new and that nobody ever played it before; but it is not new, merely another way of playing blindman's buff. It is very curious;

children these days play the same games as children did before; children of peoples who have never seen each other play the same games. There is much talk about the Greeks and Romans who lived two thousand years ago, but Roman children played just the way we do, and Greek children had dolls with real hair just like the children of today. There is a picture showing some Greek girls putting their dolls in front of a statue of Diana, who in those days was like a saint; because the Greeks also believed that there were saints in heaven, and little girls prayed to this Diana to give them long life and always keep them beautiful. It was not only dolls that the children took to Diana, because the little gentleman in the picture, who looks at the goddess with the face of an emperor, takes her his little wooden chariot so that Diana will mount her own chariot when she goes out to hunt, as they say she does every morning. There was no Diana, of course, nor any of the other gods to whom the Greeks prayed in beautiful words and processions and songs. The Greeks were like all new nations that believe they are masters of the world, just as children do. And because they see that both sun and rain come from the sky, and corn and wheat from the earth, and that there are birds and animals good to eat in the forest, they pray to the earth and the rain, to the forest and the sun, and give them the names of men and women, and picture them with human bodies, for they believe they have thoughts and desires the same as themselves and therefore must look like humans. Diana was the goddess of the forest and the hunt. In the Louvre Museum in Paris there is a very lovely statue of Diana; it shows her going hunting with her dog and is modeled so well that she seems to be in motion. Her legs are like a man's legs, so you can see she is a goddess who does a lot of walking. And Greek girls loved their dolls so dearly that when they died, their dolls were buried with them.

All games are not as old as bowling or dolls or cricket or ball or swings or jumping. Blindman's buff is not so old, although it was played in France about a thousand years ago. And children do not know, when their eyes are bandaged, that this game was played by a very brave French knight who was blinded one day in a fight and refused to give up his sword or be healed, but kept on fighting until he died. His name was Colin-Maillard. So then the king ordered that in sports contests, called tourneys, one knight always had to go out to fight with his eyes bandaged so the people of France would never forget the knight's great courage. And that is how the game got started.

What really does not seem to be a manly thing is how the friends of Henry III[1] amused themselves. This man was also king of France, but not as brave and generous as Henry IV of Navarre, who came later; he was a ridiculous little man like those who think of nothing but how to comb their hair and powder themselves like women, and how to trim their beards into a point. That is how the friends of Henry III spent their lives: playing and fighting, because of jealousy, with the court jesters who hated them for their laziness and told them so to their faces. Poor France was in a wretched condition, and the hard-working people paid a great part of their wages so the king and his friends could have gold-hilted swords and clothes of silk. There were no newspapers then to publish the truth. In those days jesters were somewhat like newspapers, and kings did not keep them in their palaces merely to make them laugh, but to find out what was happening and to be told the truth, which the jesters told to the courtiers and the kings themselves in the form of jokes. Those jesters were nearly always very ugly or skinny or fat or humpbacked. One of the saddest paintings in the world is the one by the Spaniard Zamacois; all those unhappy men are waiting for

---

1. Henry III of France (1551–89), who ruled France after 1574, and whose reign was featured by the prolonged crisis of the Wars of Religion and by dynastic rivalries.

the king to summon them to make him laugh with their brightly colored suits and little bells.

Those Negroes in the other picture, naked as they are, are happier doing their pole dance than are the jesters. Nations, like children, from time to time need something such as running a lot, laughing a lot, shouting and jumping. The truth is that you cannot do everything you want to do in this life, and what is going to be left undone sometimes turns into a sort of madness. The Moors hold a kind of horse fair they call "fantasy." Poor Fortuny, another Spanish artist, has painted it very well. His painting depicts the Moors entering the city at full gallop, their horses as crazy as themselves, the riders stretched out over the necks of their steeds—kissing them, biting them, firing their long Moorish shotguns into the air, dismounting while still racing at top speed and then mounting again. They shout as if their chests were bursting, and the air is dark with gunpowder. Men of all countries—white men or black, Japanese or Indian—need to do something beautiful and daring, dangerous and full of movement, like that pole dance of the New Zealand aborigines. New Zealand is very hot, and its inhabitants have proud bodies like those who do a lot of walking, and they are brave people who fight upon the ground as well as they dance in the air, swinging from their poles. They rise and fall and go round and round till the ropes go straight out from the pole, and then they gradually come down to the ground. They let the ropes fly like a swing, hold on by a hand, by their teeth, by a foot or a knee. They bounce against the pole as if they were balls. They shout at each other and embrace.

When the Spaniards came to Mexico, they found that the Indians there had that same pole dance. Those Indians had some very beautiful games. They were very fine men and hard workers and had no knowledge of either gunpowder or bullets, like the soldiers of the Spaniard Cortés; but their city was as if made of silver, and the silver itself wrought like lace as delicately as the finest jewelry. They were as nimble and original in their games as in their work. For the Indians that pole dance was a most agile and daring amusement; they hurled themselves from the height of the top of the pole, about fifty feet above the ground, and flew through the air whirling and tumbling and doing acrobatic feats, being held by nothing but a very strong and slender rope woven by themselves. It made a person shudder to see such daring; and one old book tells how "horrible and terrifying it is to see them," and how it "fills one with anguish and fright."

The English believe that the pole game is their own invention, and that all they have to do in their fairs is to display their skill with the club, which they grab at one end and by the middle; or their skill with the billy club, which they also handle very well. The Canary Islanders, who are very strong men, believe they invented the pole acrobatics, not the English; and an islander going through his paces in the air and swinging round and round is indeed something to see. It is the same with wrestling, which in the Canary Islands is taught to children in the schools. And the dance on the ground with ribbons tied to the top of a pole is a very difficult performance, in which each man holds a ribbon of a different color and goes around the pole crisscrossing those ribbons and braiding and unbraiding them in pleasing knots and patterns, never making a mistake. But the Mexican Indians did their stunts from the pole as well as the fairer-skinned English or the broader-shouldered Canary Islanders. And they did not use what they knew of this merely for self-defense, but to do exercises on the balance bar like those now done by the Japanese and some Moorish tribes. And there are five peoples who have done the same thing as the Indians: the New Zealanders, English, Canary Islanders, Japanese, and Moors. All peoples play ball, but among the Indians it was a passion because they thought that a good ball player came down from heaven, and that the Mexican gods—different from those of the Greeks—would come down to tell them how to throw and catch it. The ball games, very curious things, will be left for another day.

Now, we told you about the bar and the balancing acts the Indians did on it—tremendously difficult feats. They also lie down upon the floor as the Japanese do in the circuses when they are going to do tricks with a ball or stunts with a barrel. On a bar placed across the soles of their feet they can support up to four men, which is more than the Moors can do, because the strongest of the Moors can support four men upon their shoulders but not on the soles of their feet. There is another exercise called *tzaá:* first two Indians mount the ends of a bar, then two more climb upon the first two, and without falling, the four do a great many stunts and acrobatics. And the Indians have their chess, their jugglers, and their fire-eaters who exhale the flames through their noses. But this, like ball playing, will be left for another day. Because with stories you have to do what Chichá, the pretty Guatemalan girl, did. Someone asked her:

"Chichá, why do you take so long to eat that olive?" And she replied:

"Because it tastes so good."

The Indian Ruins

There is no more tragic or beautiful poem than that which can be taken from the story of America. We cannot read one of those fine old parchment-covered books without a feeling of tenderness and visions of flowers and feathers in the air, as it were—those books that tell about the America of the Indians, their cities and festivals, the greatness of their arts, and the graciousness of their customs. Some of these Indians lived isolated and simple lives, going naked and lacking the necessities of life, like nations newly born; and they began painting their strange figures upon rocks at the river banks, where the forest is in deeper solitude and man gives more thought to the world's wonders. Others belonged to older nations and lived in tribes in villages of cane or adobe bricks, eating what they hunted and fished and fighting with their neighbors. Still others were nations already formed, with cities of a hundred and forty thousand houses, palaces adorned with gold-leaf paintings, much buying and selling in the streets and plazas, and marble temples with gigantic statues of their gods. Their creations do not resemble those of the rest of the nations, except as one man resembles another. These were innocent, superstitious, and terrible people. Their government, religion, art, warfare, architecture, industry, and poetry came from their imagination. Everything of theirs was interesting, daring, and new. They were an artistic, intelligent, and pure race of men. The stories of the

252

Nahuatls and Mayans of Mexico, the Chibchas of Colombia, the Cumanagotos of Venezuela, the Quechuas of Peru, the Aymarás of Bolivia, the Charruas of Paraguay, and the Araucanians of Chile read like a novel.

The quetzal is the beautiful bird of Guatemala, a bird of brilliant green plumage and long tail feather, which dies of grief when captured or when its tail feather is broken or injured. It is a bird that shines in the light like the iridescent heads of hummingbirds, which resemble precious gems or iridescent jewels—topaz or opal or amethyst, depending upon the angle from which they are seen. And when one reads in the voyages of Le Plongeon the stories about the loves of the Mayan princess Ara, who refused to love Prince Aak because for the love of Ara he murdered his brother Chaak; when in the story of the Indian Ixtlilxochitl one sees how elegantly and lavishly they lived in the royal cities of Mexico, Tenochtitlán and Texcoco; when in Captain Fuentes' *Flowered Memory,* or in the chronicles of Juarros, or in Bernal Díaz del Castillo's[1] *True History of the Conquest of New Spain,* or in the Englishman Thomas Gage's *Voyages,* these Indians come to life as though they were standing before one, dressed in their white clothes, holding their children by the hand, reciting poetry, and erecting buildings—then those wise men of Chichén, those potentates of Uxmal, those merchants of Tulán, those artisans of Tenochtitlán, those priests of Cholula, those loving teachers and docile children of Utatlán, that courteous race of men who lived out in the sun and never shut the doors of their stone houses, seemed not to exist merely between the yellowed pages of a book in which the *S*'s look like *F*'s and words are used with much ceremony. No, we can actually see a quetzal die as it gives its final cry upon finding its tail feather broken. The imagination sees things invisible to the eye.

1. Bernal Díaz del Castillo (1492–1581?), Spanish soldier and author who took part in the conquest of Mexico.

Friends are made by reading those ancient books. There are saints and heroes in them, lovers and poets and apostles. There are descriptions of pyramids larger than those of Egypt; deeds of giants overcoming wild beasts; battles between giants and men; gods flying through the air sowing the seeds of nations over the world; abductions of princesses who compel nations to fight to the death; hand-to-hand combat of superhuman bravery; vice-ridden cities defending themselves against the powerful men of the North; and the varied, friendly, industrious life of their amphitheaters and temples, canals and workshops, courts of justice and marketplaces. There are kings such as the Chichimecan Netzahualpilli who murder their sons for breaking the law, just as the Roman Brutus allowed his son to be murdered. There are orators, such as the Tlascaltecan Xicotencatl, who rose up tearfully to beg his people not to admit the Spaniard, the way Demosthenes rose up to beg the Greeks not to let Philip enter. There are fair-minded monarchs such as Netzahualcoyotl, the great poet-king of the Chichimecans, who knew, like the Hebrew Solomon, how to build magnificent temples to the Creator of the world, and how to administer justice with a fatherly spirit. Beautiful young girls were sacrificed to the invisible gods of the sky, just as in Greece where there were so many sacrifices at times that it was unnecessary to build a new altar for the next ceremony, because the pile of ashes from the last burning was so high that those in charge could lay their victims upon it. There were immolations of men like that of the Hebrew Abraham who bound his son Isaac to the tree to kill him with his own hands, for he thought he heard voices from Heaven commanding him to stab his son to death to appease his God with Isaac's blood. There were mass sacrifices like the ones in the Plaza Mayor, before king and archbishops, when the Spanish Inquisition burned men alive accompanied by much ceremony with the processions and the firewood, witnessed by the ladies of Madrid from their balconies. Ignorance and superstition make barbarians of men in every nation, and the conquering Spaniards have been overzealous in accusing the Indians of these things, exaggerating or inventing the defects of the conquered race so that the cruelty with which they treated them would appear just and appropriate in the eyes of the world. At the same time you should read what the Spanish soldier Bernal Díaz del Castillo says about Indian sacrifices, and what the priest Bartolomé de las Casas[2] says. His is a name to be engraved upon the heart like that of a brother. Bartolomé de las Casas was frail and ugly, with a big nose and an abrupt and confused manner of speech; but his pure and ardent eyes reflected a sublime soul.

Now we will discuss Mexico, because the pictures are of Mexico. This country was first populated by the fierce Toltecs who pursued, with their cane shields held high, the captain who carried a shield overlaid with gold. Then those Toltecs succumbed to luxury, after which the barbarous Chichimecans, clad in their animal skins, came down from the North with terrible force and remained in the country. Their kings, however, possessed great wisdom. Later the free peoples around them banded together, with the wise Aztecs in the lead, and won the government from the Chichimecans who were now living slovenly and licentious lives. The Aztecs ruled like merchants, amassing wealth and oppressing the country; and when Cortés arrived with his Spaniards, he conquered the Aztecs, aided by the hundred thousand Indian warriors who joined him along the way as he passed among the oppressed peoples.

The Spanish guns and suits of armor failed to intimidate the Indian heroes; but the fanatical people no longer wished to obey their heroes, for they believed that those Spanish

2. Bartolomé de las Casas (1474–1566), early Spanish historian and missionary in the Americas, who was the first to expose the oppression of the Indian by the European and to call for the abolition of Indian slavery. To his later regret, he suggested replacing it with African slavery.

men were the soldiers of the god Quetzalcoatl, who, according to the priests, would return from heaven to free them from tyranny. Knowing the Indian rivalries, Cortés treated the jealous parties badly, gradually removed the chiefs from their cowardly people, conquered the weak with gifts or terrified them with threats, imprisoned or killed the wise and the brave; and the priests, who came from Spain after the soldiers, demolished the temple of the Indian god and built upon its ruins a church to their own god.

What a handsome city was Tenochtitlán, the Aztec capital, when Cortés arrived in Mexico! It was like morning all day long, and the city seemed to be in a constant state of celebration. Some of the streets were canals, others dry land; there were many spacious plazas, and the environs were covered with great groves of trees. Canoes plied the canals as swiftly and skillfully as if they had understanding, and at times there were so many of them that one could walk upon them as upon terra firma. Some were loaded with fruit, others with flowers, still others with pitchers and cups and other pottery objects. The marketplaces seethed with people exchanging affectionate greetings, going from stall to stall, praising the king or speaking ill of him, prying about and selling things. The houses were built of adobe, a sun-dried brick, or of stone masonry if the owner were rich. And standing upon its five-terraced pyramid, overlooking the entire city with its forty lesser temples at its feet, stood the great temple of Huitzilopochtli, built of ebony and jasper and cloud-white marble and fragrant cedar columns, with the sacred flames in their six hundred braziers at the summit never extinguished. On the streets below there were people coming and going in their short sleeveless blouses, white or colored or white with embroidery, and their loose footwear that resembled laced sandals reaching halfway to the knee. From around a corner came a group of children shooting fruit seeds from a blowgun, or playing in time upon their clay flutes on the way to school, where they were taught handicrafts, singing and dancing, skills with the lance and archery, and how to plant and cultivate the soil. For every man must learn to work in the fields, to do things with his hands, and to defend himself. An important gentleman passed by wearing a long robe adorned with feathers, and beside him walked his secretary, who was holding open a book freshly painted with all the figures and signs so that when closed the colors would not come off onto the unpainted part. Behind that distinguished gentleman came three warriors in wooden helmets, one shaped like the head of a serpent, another of a wolf, another of a jaguar, all covered with the skins of these animals, but every helmet showing above the ears the three stripes which in those days were a sign of bravery. A servant was carrying in a large reed cage a yellow and gold bird for the king's well-stocked aviary, and the king also had many red and silver fish in marble aquariums hidden among the labyrinths of his gardens. Another servant was coming up the street shouting for people to make way for the ambassadors, appearing with their shields strapped to their left arms and their arrows pointed downward to demand captives from the tributary nations. At the doorway of the gentleman's house a carpenter sang as he very skillfully repaired an eagle-shaped chair whose overlay of silk and gold was coming loose from the deerskin seat. Other men were loaded with painted animal skins, stopping at every door to see if someone wanted to buy the red or the blue, used in those days to decorate their halls, as we now use pictures. A widow was returning from market, her servant lagging behind with not enough hands to carry all her purchases—pitchers from Cholula and Guatemala, a green obsidian knife with a paper-thin blade, a mirror of polished stone that reflected one's face as clearly as glass, a closely woven length of cloth whose color would never fade, a fish with gold and silver scales that seemed to be moving, an enameled copper parrot with moveable beak and wings. Or people would stop in the streets to watch a newly married couple pass by, the husband's tunic sewn to the wife's as if to proclaim to the world that they would be together until death; and behind them ran a little child pulling his toy wagon. Others were standing in groups to hear a traveler tell about what he had seen in the wild land of the Zapotecans, where another king ruled in the temples and in the royal palace itself. This king never appeared on foot, but upon the shoulders of the priests as he heard the pleas of the people, who would ask him to intercede for favors from the one who rules the world from the sky, and from the kings in the palace, and from the other kings who go about upon the shoulders of priests. In a group near at hand, still others were praising a speech in which the priest told the story of the warrior who was buried yesterday with a sumptuous funeral, and the flag commemorating the battles he had won, and the servants who carried upon trays made of eight different metals the dead warrior's favorite foods. Above the conversations in the street one could hear the rustle of leaves from the trees in the plazas, and the sounds of rasps and hammers. Out of all that greatness the museum has only a few gold vessels, a few yoke-shaped stones of polished obsidian, and an occasional hand-wrought ring! Tenochtitlán does not exist. Nor does Tulán, city of the great market. Texcoco, city of palaces, has vanished. When the present-day Indians go past the ruins, they bow their heads, move their lips as if saying something, and do not replace their hats until the ruins are well behind them. From this part of Mexico where all those peoples lived—peoples united by a common language and lineage, who were gaining power throughout the central part of the Pacific coast inhabited by the Nahuatls—not one complete city or temple remained after the conquest.

Of Cholula, that Cholula of the temples so amazing to Cortés, the only thing left is the ruins of the four-terraced pyramid, which is twice the size of the famous pyramid of Cheops. All that stands in Xochicalco, on its hilltop filled with tunnels and arches, is the temple of chiseled granite, its enormous blocks of stone fitted together so perfectly that you cannot see where they join, and so hard that you wonder what kind of instrument was used to cut them, and what contrivance could have dragged them to such a height. In Centla the ancient fortifications lie in disarray upon the ground. In Tula the French Charnay has just excavated a twenty-four-room house with fifteen stairways that is so handsome and fanciful that he calls it "a work of fascinating interest." In La Quemada the Hill of Buildings is covered with columns of colossal blocks of porphyry and the ruins of fortress bastions. The city of the Zapotecans was Mitla, and there in all their beauty stand the walls of the palace where the prince who always traveled upon men's shoulders came to tell the king what the self-created god Pitao-Cozaana ordered from Heaven. Carved wooden columns with neither base nor capital support the roof, and in that solitude the columns that have not yet fallen seem more imposing than the mountains around the luxuriant valley where Mitla lies. Out of the tree-high vegetation loom those magnificent walls that are completely covered with the most delicate fretwork and incised drawings—walls without a single curve but with very graceful and majestic straight lines and angles.

Mexico's most beautiful ruins are not there, however; they are in the land of the Mayans, a very powerful and warlike people who received visits and ambassadors from across the sea. Belonging to the Mayans of Oaxaca is the much celebrated city of Palenque, with its massive palace walls covered with carved stone depicting men with beaklike heads and mouths placed well forward. These men wear profusely decorated clothes and have plumed crests upon their heads. The fourteen doorways and the stone giants between each of them provide the palace with a grandiose entrance. Both inner and outer walls are covered with stucco and filled with red, blue, black and white paintings. The inner courtyard is lined with columns. And there is a Temple of the Cross, so called because one of the blocks of stone bears two others that resemble priests flanking still another of equal height in the shape of a cross. This is not a Christian cross; it is more like that of believers in the religion of Buddha, which also has its cross. But not even Palenque can compare with the ruins of the Mayans of Yucatán, which are still more amazing and beautiful.

Through all of Yucatán spreads the empire of those Mayan princes of broad cheekbones and foreheads like the white man of today. Yucatán has the ruins of Sayil with its three-storeyed Great House and a staircase twenty-eight feet wide. There is Labná, with that curious edifice that has a frieze of stone skulls around the roof, and that other ruin where there are two men bearing a great sphere, one on foot and the other kneeling. In Yucatán is Izamal, where they found that giant head, a stone face over five and a half feet high. And Kabah is there also, that Kabah with its arch still standing, although broken at the top, that cannot be seen without one's feeling filled with nobility and grace, as it were. But the cities praised in the books of the American Stephens, of Brasseur de Bourbourg and Charnay, of Le Plongeon and his fearless wife, of the French Nadaillac, are Uxmal and Chichén Itzá, the cities of painted palaces, of houses whose carvings are delicate as chasing, of deep wells and magnificent monasteries. Uxmal is about five miles from Mérida, the present-day city known for its beautiful sisal fields and for its people who are so kind that they welcome strangers as if they were brothers. Uxmal has many famous ruins, and all of them, as throughout Mexico, are at the top of pyramids as if considered the buildings of greatest importance, for they were left standing long after the habitations of more fragile construction had toppled. These books mention the most famous as the "Governor's House," made entirely of rough stone, more than two hundred eighty feet wide and about thirty-six feet deep, whose wooden door frames contain a wealth of carving. They describe another structure known as the House of Turtles, truly a curious one because of its stone turtle, enclosed as if by a fence, and at regular intervals other turtles in relief. Then there is the very handsome House of Nuns, which is not only one house but four, built atop the pyramid. One of these is called The Serpent, because outside there is an enormous serpent carved out of the enduring stone and coiled around the entire house. On another near the top of the wall is a frieze of idol heads or masks, but each one different and with very expressive faces, arranged in groups, which are a veritable work of art for the very reason that they look as if placed there by chance. Another of the buildings still has four of the seventeen towers it once had, now somewhat resembling the shells of decayed molars. And Uxmal still has its multicolored House of the Soothsayer and its House of the Dwarf, small and as intricately carved as the kind of Chinese wooden box with hundreds of carved figures upon it, and so graceful that one traveler refers to it as "a masterwork of art and elegance," and another says that "the House of the Dwarf is pretty as a jewel."

The entire city of Chichén Itzá is like the House of the Dwarf. It is like a stone book, a broken book, its pages lying upon the ground, buried in the jungle, mud-stained and shattered. The five hundred columns have toppled; headless statues lie at the foot of those half-standing walls; the streets are obliterated and overgrown by the vegetation of many centuries. But of what remains, of all that is visible or touchable, there is nothing without its extremely fine painting with handsome curves, or its noble sculptured figures whose heads have aquiline noses and long beards. The walls tell the famous story of the war between the two mad brothers who fought to see which one would win the Princess Ara. There are processions of priests, warriors, and animals that seem to be watching and aware of what is taking place, of double-prowed ships, black-bearded men, kinky-haired Negroes; and all with solid profiles and color as bright and fresh as if the blood were still coursing through the veins of the artists who left the history of a nation inscribed with hieroglyphics or portrayed in color—the history of a nation that sent its ships up the rivers and along the coasts of all of Central America, and that knew about Asia from the Pacific and about Africa from the Atlantic. There is a block of stone upon which a standing man sends a lightning bolt from his half-open lips to another man who is seated. There are groups of people and symbols that seem to be telling—in a language that cannot be read with the inadequate Indian alphabet of Bishop Landa—the secrets of the nation that built the Amphitheater, the Castle, the Palace of Nuns, the Tower of the Snail, the Well of Sacrifices, filled at the bottom with something like white stone—possibly the hardened ash of the bodies of the beautiful virgins who died smiling and singing as an offering to their god. They were sacrificed much as the Christian virgins used to die in the Roman amphitheaters for the Hebrew God; much as the most beautiful virgin, crowned with flowers, followed by the populace, and immolated in the waters of the River Nile, died for the Egyptian god. Who could have carved those lacelike statues of Chichén Itzá? I wonder where those powerful and accomplished people have gone—those people who conceived the round Tower of the Snail, the little carved House of the Dwarf, the great serpent of the House of Nuns at Uxmal? What a beautiful novel, the story of America!

Musicians, Poets, and Painters

There are more young people than old in this world. Most of humanity is composed of youths and children. Youth is the age of growth and development, activity and liveliness, imagination and impetuosity. When you have failed to take good care of your heart and mind while young, you may well fear that your old age will be desolate and sad. The poet Southey[1] has rightly said that the first twenty years of life are the most influential in forming character. Every human being carries within himself an ideal man, just as every block of marble contains in the rough a statue as handsome as that which the Greek Praxiteles[2] made of the god Apollo. Education begins with life and does not end until death. The body is always the same, although it fails with age; the mind changes unceasingly and becomes richer and more perfect with the years. But the essential qualities of character, the originality and energy of every man, can be seen from childhood in an action, an idea, or a glance.

In the same man a small heart and a great talent usually go together. But everyone is duty-bound to cultivate his intelligence out of respect for himself and for the world. It gen-

1. Robert Southey (1774–1843), British poet and writer of prose and close associate of Coleridge and Wordsworth.
2. Praxiteles (370–330 B.C.), greatest of all the sculptors of Athens of the fourth century and one of the finest of the Greek artists.

erally happens in life that man does not achieve any permanent well-being except after many years of waiting patiently and being good, never tiring. It is fun to be good, and it makes a person strong and happy. "Actually," says the North American Emerson,[3] "the world's real novel is the life of man, and no fable or romance created by the imagination is any better than the story of a brave man who has fulfilled his duty."

The difference in men's ages when they achieve talent is remarkable. "There are some," says the Englishman Bacon,[4] "who mature early and go as they come," which is just what the rhetorical Quintilian[5] says in his polished Latin. You can see this in many precocious children who seem to be prodigies of wisdom in their early years and are lost to sight as soon as they are older.

Heinecken, son of the ancient city of Lübeck, memorized almost the entire Bible by the time he was two; at three he was speaking Latin and French; at four he had studied the history of the Christian Church, and at five he died. We could agree with Bacon about that poor creature: "Phaëthon's chariot ran for only a day."

There are some children who are able to save their intelligence from these exaltations of precocity and expand the glories of their childhood when they are older. We see this frequently in musicians, because the excitement of the art is natural and healthful, and the soul that feels it suffers more by containing it than by releasing it. At the age of ten

3. Ralph Waldo Emerson (1803–82), lecturer, poet, and essayist who made a deep impression on Martí.

4. The reference is to either Roger Bacon (1220–92), British philosopher and educational reformer, noted for his zeal in the pursuit of experimental science, or Francis Bacon (1561–1626), British lawyer, courtier, statesman, and philosopher.

5. Marcus Fabius Quintilianus (Quintilian), Roman writer whose work on rhetoric (*Institutio oratoria*) is a great contribution to educational theory and literary criticism.

Handel[6] had composed a book of sonatas. His father wanted him to be a lawyer and refused to let him play an instrument; but the boy secretly acquired a silent clavichord and spent his nights playing upon the soundless keys in the dark. The Duke of Saxe-Weissefels, by dint of much imploring, succeeded in having Handel's father permit that persevering genius to study music, and at sixteen he had composed his first opera, *Almira.* He composed his masterwork, the *Messiah,* in twenty-three days, and he was still writing operas and oratorios until he died at fifty-seven.

Haydn[7] was almost as precocious as Handel, and at thirteen had already composed a mass; but he wrote his finest composition, the *Creation,* at sixty-five. It was almost as difficult for Johann Sebastian Bach to take his first music lessons as it was for Handel, because his elder brother, the organist Johann Christoph,[8] was jealous of him and hid the book containing the best pieces by masters of the clavichord. But Johann Sebastian[9] found the book in a cupboard, took it to his room, and began to copy it at inconvenient times after sunset, when the light in summer is quite adequate, or by moonlight. His brother discovered this and was cruel enough to take away from him both the book and the copy, but this

6. George Frederick Handel (1685–1759), German-born but English by adoption, one of the greatest composers of the late Baroque era, noted especially for his operas, instrumental compositions, and oratorios, the best known of which is his *Messiah.*

7. Franz Joseph Haydn (1732–1809), Austrian composer who was one of the most important figures in the development of the Classical style in music during the eighteenth century.

8. Johann Christoph Bach (1671–1721), Johann Sebastian Bach's elder brother. But Martí may be in error here since according to historical records, Johann Christoph Bach took his younger brother into his home and became his teacher after their father died in 1695.

9. Johann Sebastian Bach (1685–1750), one of the greatest of all composers, who wrote an enormous amount of sacred choral music as well as music for the organ and harpsichord, concertos, and sonatas.

did not do Christoph any good because at eighteen Johann Sebastian was already the musician at the famous court of Weimar, and his only rival as organist was Handel.

Of all the child prodigies in the art of music, however, the most celebrated is Mozart.[10] Apparently he learned without the aid of teachers. At the age of four, even before he could write, he was already composing tunes; at six he arranged a concerto for piano, and at twelve he had no equal as a pianist and composed *La Finta Semplice,* his first opera. Those serious teachers were unable to understand a child who improvised extremely difficult fugues upon unknown themes, and then immediately started to play "horsie" with his father's walking stick. His father went through Europe's principal cities displaying his son's talent, the boy dressed like a prince with his short, dun-colored jacket, velvet leggings, buckled shoes, and long curled hair tied behind like a wig. Mozart's father disregarded the pygmy pianist's health, which was not of the best, and was interested only in getting out of him all the money he could. But Mozart's salvation was his cheerful personality, for he was a master musician but a child in everything else. At fourteen he composed his opera *Mitridate Re di Ponto,* which was performed twenty nights in succession; at thirty-six, on his deathbed, wasted away by the tempestuous life he had led and his disorganized work, he composed the *Requiem,* one of his most perfect works.

Beethoven's[11] father wanted to make his son a wonder child and taught him so much music, by dint of spankings and penance, that at thirteen the boy was playing in public

10. Wolfgang Amadeus Mozart (1756–91), an extraordinary genius in composing opera, concert music, symphonies, and concertos for various instruments, viewed as one of the greatest musical geniuses of all times.

11. Ludwig van Beethoven (1770–1827), the predominant composer of his time and one of the greatest figures in the history of Western music, composer of nine great symphonies, the ninth of which (the Choral Symphony) is one of the greatest works of music.

and had composed three sonatas. But he did not begin to produce his sublime compositions until he was twenty-one. Weber,[12] a very mischievous boy, published his first six fugues at twelve, composed his opera *Das Waldmädchen* at fourteen, and the very famous *Der Freischütz* at thirty-six. Mendelssohn[13] learned to play before he could talk, and at twelve he had written three quartets for piano, two violins, and cello; he was sixteen when he finished his first opera, *Die Hochzeit des Camacho;* at eighteen he wrote his B-flat sonata; before the age of twenty he composed his *Midsummer Night's Dream,* at twenty-two his *Reformation* symphony, and he continued to write very difficult and profound works until his death at thirty-eight. By the time Meyerbeer[14] had reached his ninth birthday he was already an excellent pianist, and at eighteen his first piece, *Jephthas Gelübde,* was performed in a Munich theater; but his *Robert le Diable* earned him no fame until he was thirty-seven.

The English Carlyle,[15] in his life of the poet Schiller,[16] speaks of one Daniel Schubert who was a poet, musician, and preacher, but in reality was a nobody. He did everything by fits and starts and was bored by it all—his studies, his laziness, and his excesses. But he was a man of much ability, notable as a musician, eloquent as a preacher, and able as a journalist. He died at fifty-two and left his wife and son in misery.

12. Carl Maria von Weber (1786–1826), German composer famous for his operas and an important figure in the transition from Classical to Romantic music in Germany.

13. Felix Mendelssohn (1809–47), German Romantic composer, whose music is noted for its lyricism and vivacity.

14. Giacomo Meyerbeer (1791–1864), German composer of French and Italian opera who established the vogue in Paris for spectacular romantic opera; real name Jacob Liebmann Beer.

15. Thomas Carlyle (1795–1881), British essayist and historian, famous for his theory of the role of the hero in history.

16. Friedrich Schiller (1759–1805), famous German poet, dramatist, and literary theorist.

But Franz Schubert,[17] the wonder child of Vienna, lived differently, though he was no happier. He played the violin when he was no larger than that instrument, as well as both the piano and organ. Reading a song but once, he knew enough about it to put it into an exquisite musical setting that seemed dreamlike and whimsical and gave rise to vari-colored zephyrs, so to speak. He wrote more than five hundred melodies in addition to operas, masses, sonatas, symphonies, and quartets. He died poor at the age of thirty-one.

The same precocity was observed in the Italian musicians. Cimarosa,[18] son of a cobbler, wrote *Le Stravaganze del Conte* at twenty-three. When Paganini[19] was eight he played one of his sonatas on the violin. Rossini's[20] father played the trombone in a company of itinerant actors in which his mother was a singer. At ten Rossini went with his father as assistant, then sang in choruses until his voice changed; and at twenty-one he was the famous composer of the opera *Tancredi*.

Many of the painters' and sculptors' talents were revealed in their childhood. The most glorious of all is Michelangelo.[21] At birth he was sent to the country to be nursed by the wife of a stonecutter, which is why he later said that he had drunk the love of sculpture along with the mother's milk. As soon as he was able to manage a pencil, he filled the stonecutter's

17. Franz Schubert (1797–1828), Austrian composer noted for his songs and chamber music.

18. Domenico Cimarosa (1749–1801), one of the principal Italian composers of comic opera.

19. Nicolò Paganini (1782–1840), composer and principal violin virtuoso of the nineteenth century, who was a popular idol and whose playing revolutionized violin technique.

20. Gioacchino Rossini (1792–1868), Italian composer noted for his operas, the most famous of which is *The Barber of Seville*.

21. Michelangelo (1475–1564), Italian painter, sculptor, and architect, who was one of the greatest and most versatile artists of the Renaissance.

walls with drawings, and when he returned to Florence he covered the floors of his father's house with giants and lions. In school he made little progress with books, nor did his pencil ever leave his hand; and they had to forcibly drag him away from the painters' studios. Painting and sculpture were menial tasks in those days, and his father, who came from a noble family, wasted his slaps and arguments in an effort to convince his son not to be a miserable stonecutter. But a stonecutter he would be, and nothing else. He finally gave in to his father and was made a student in the studio of the painter Ghirlandaio,[22] who found his apprentice so advanced that he agreed to pay him a small monthly stipend. Within a short time the apprentice painted better than his teacher, but he saw the statues in the famous gardens of Lorenzo de' Medici[23] and thereupon enthusiastically exchanged his colors for a chisel. He progressed so rapidly in sculpture that at the age of eighteen he amazed Florence with his bas-relief *Battle of the Centaurs;* at twenty he carved his *Cupid* and soon afterward his colossal *David.* Then, one after another, he painted his terrible and magnificent pictures. Benvenuto Cellini,[24] that creative genius in the art of ornamentation, says that none of Michelangelo's paintings is as fine as the one the master painted when he was twenty-nine, in which some soldiers from Pisa, surprised in the bath by their enemies, leave the water to attack them.

Rafael's[25] precocity was equally amazing, although his

22. Domenico Ghirlandaio or Ghirlandajo (1449–94), early Renaissance painter of the Florentine school, famous for his detailed narrative frescoes.

23. Lorenzo de' Medici (1449–92), member of the Italian family that ruled Florence and later Tuscany during most of the period from 1434 to 1737, who is also known as Lorenzo the Magnificent.

24. Benvenuto Cellini (1500–71), Florentine sculptor, goldsmith, writer, and author of a famous autobiography.

25. Rafael (1483–1520), painter and architect, who was one of the masters of the Italian High Renaissance style.

father did not stand in his way but rejoiced in his passion for art. At seventeen he was already an outstanding painter. They say he was filled with admiration when he saw Michelangelo's great paintings in the Sistine Chapel, and that he thanked God aloud for having been born in the same century as that extraordinary genius. Rafael painted his *School of Athens* at twenty-five and his *Transfiguration* at thirty-seven. He was putting finishing touches to it when he died, and the Romans took the painting to the Pantheon on the day of his funeral. Some people consider Rafael's *Transfiguration,* unfinished as it is, the most beautiful painting in the world.

Ever since Leonardo da Vinci[26] was a child he had excelled in mathematics, music, and drawing. In one of the pictures of his teacher Verrocchio, Leonardo painted such a beautiful angel that the master, grief-stricken at being less accomplished than his pupil, left his art forever. When Leonardo reached his mature years, he was admired by the whole world for his ability as architect and engineer, and as musician and painter. Guercino[27] at ten decorated the facade of his house with a finely drawn Virgin. Tintoretto[28] was such a superior disciple that his master Titian[29] became jealous of him and dismissed him from his service. The rebuff encouraged rather than intimidated him, and he continued to paint in such haste that he was called "The Furious." The sculptor Canova[30] carved a lion out of a lump of butter when he was

26. Leonardo da Vinci (1452–1519), Italian famed for the range of his genius, excelling as a painter, sculptor, architect, and engineer.

27. Guercino (1591–1666), Italian painter whose frescoes made a profound impact on seventeenth-century Baroque decoration.

28. Tintoretto (1518–94), one of the great painters of the Venetian school and one of the most important artists of the late Renaissance.

29. Titian (1477–1576), painter of the Venetian school whose mastery of handling color and the technique of painting have made him one of the greatest artists of the Renaissance.

30. Antonio Canova (1757–1822), Italian sculptor who achieved international fame as one of the greatest exponents of Neoclassicism.

only four. The Danish Thorvaldsen[31] at thirteen carved grotesque masks for ships in the workshop of his father, who was a sculptor in wood, and at fifteen won a medal in Copenhagen for his bas-relief *Love in Repose.*

Poets also usually give early signs of their vocation, especially those with a restless, sensitive, and impassioned nature. Dante[32] at nine wrote poetry to a little girl of eight, of whom he talks in his *La Vita Nuova.* At the age of ten Tasso[33] lamented in verse his separation from his mother and sister, and was compared with the sad Aeneas when he fled from Troy with his aged father upon his back. At thirty-one he added the final eight-line stanzas to his poem *Jerusalem Delivered,* started at twenty-five.

From the age of ten Metastasio[34] used to go through the streets of Rome improvising; and Goldoni,[35] who was very mischievous, composed his first play at eight. Goldoni often escaped from school to follow the roving players. His family succeeded in having him study law, and in a few years he won fame as an excellent lawyer; but his natural vocation prevailed, so he left the legal profession to become the famous poet of the stage.

Alfieri[36] had shown extraordinary qualities ever since his

31. Bertel Thorvaldsen (1770–1844), Danish sculptor prominent in the Neoclassical period and who became the first internationally acclaimed Danish artist.

32. Dante Alighieri (1265–1321), the greatest poet of Italy, world famous for his epic, *The Divine Comedy.*

33. Torquato Tasso (1544–95), greatest Italian poet of the late Renaissance, who is celebrated for his epic poems. His father Bernardo Tasso (1493–1569) was author of romantic epic poems.

34. Pietro Metastasio (1698–1782), poet and most celebrated librettist in Europe during the eighteenth century among those writing for the *opera seria.*

35. Carlo Goldoni (1707–93), dramatist who changed the entire form of the Italian *commedia dell'arte* dramatic form and is considered the founder of Italian realistic comedy.

36. Conte Vittorio Alfieri (1749–1803), Italian playwright and poet;

youth. As a boy he was very frail, like many precocious poets, and extremely pensive and secretive. At eight, in a spell of sadness, he tried to poison himself with an herb he thought was hemlock, but all it did was act as a purgative. They locked him in his room and made him go to church as penance, wearing his nightcap. When he caught his first glimpse of the sea, he felt some mysterious desires and knew he was a poet. His wealthy parents had not seen to it that he received a good education, and he was unable to put into words the ideas that were seething in his mind. He studied, traveled, lived in a dissolute manner, and fell frantically in love. The object of his affection failed to return his love, so he resolved to die, but a servant saved his life. He was cured, fell in love again, was again rejected, shut himself in his room, shaved his head, and in his self-imposed solitude began to write poetry. He was twenty-six when his tragedy *Cleopatra* was performed; in seven years he wrote fourteen tragedies.

Cervantes[37] began to write in verse, and the down had scarcely appeared on his upper lip when he had written his pastorals and lyric poems in the Italianate mode. Wieland,[38] the German poet, read rapidly at the age of three, was translating Cornelius Nepos[39] from the Latin at seven, wrote his first didactic poem, *The Perfect World,* at sixteen. Klopstock,[40] impetuous and impassioned since boyhood, commenced to write his *Messiah* at twenty.

---

a fervent adversary of political tyrany and champion of freedom, he was a hero of the Italian nationalist movement.

37. Miguel de Cervantes (1547–1616), Spanish novelist, playwright, and poet, who, through his novel *Don Quixote,* became the most important figure in Spanish literature.

38. Christoph Martin Wieland (1733–1813), German poet and man of letters whose work is representative of the late Enlightenment.

39. Cornelius Nepos (100–25 B.C.), Roman historian and biographer.

40. Friedrich Gottlieb Klopstock (1724–1803), German epic and lyric poet who made the break with the Rationalism that dominated German literature in the early eighteenth century.

Schiller was born with a passion for poetry. They say that one stormy day he was found high in a tree, where he had climbed "to see where the lightning was coming from, because it was so beautiful!" Schiller read the *Messiah* at fourteen and began to compose a sacred poem about Moses. Goethe[41] is said to have been writing in German, French, Italian, Latin, and Greek before he was eight; his thoughts were so occupied with religious matters that he conceived of a great "God of nature," and lit fires symbolizing his adoration. With the same enthusiasm he studied music and drawing and all kinds of sciences. The brave poet Körner[42] died at the age of twenty-one as he wished to die—defending his country. He was a sickly child, but nothing restrained his love for the noble ideas praised in his poetry. Two hours before he died he wrote *Das Schwertlied.*

Thomas Moore,[43] the poet of *Irish Melodies,* says that almost all good comedies and many of the well-known tragedies have been works of youth. Lope de Vega[44] and Calderón,[45] who have produced so many works for the theater, began very early in life, one at twelve and the other at thirteen. Lope exchanged his verses with his schoolmates for toys and pictures, and at twelve he had written dramas and comedies. At eighteen he published his *Arcadia,* with

41. Johann Wolfgang von Goethe (1749-1832), German poet, novelist, and dramatist, who is one of the giants of world literature, famous for his classic work *Faust,* his greatest drama.

42. Theodor Körner (1791–1813), German poet of the war of liberation against Napoleon whose death in battle made him a popular hero.

43. Thomas Moore (1779-1852), Irish poet, satirist, composer, and musician, whose major work was *Irish Melodies.*

44. Félix Lope de Vega (1562-1635), oustanding dramatist of the Spanish Golden Age.

45. Pedro Calderón de la Barca (1600-81), Spanish dramatist and poet who succeeded Lope de Vega as the greatest Spanish playwright of the Spanish Golden Age.

shepherds for heroes. At twenty-six he sailed in a ship of the Spanish Armada in its attack upon England, and on the voyage he wrote several poems. But the hundreds of comedies that have made him famous he wrote after his return to Spain; by that time he was already a priest. Calderón wrote no less than four hundred plays. At thirteen he composed his first work, *The Chariot of Heaven.* At fifty he became a priest, like Lope, and wrote only religious pieces.

These Spanish poets wrote their principal works before reaching their mature years. Among the poets of the northern lands, intelligence develops much more slowly. Molière[46] had to educate himself, but at thirty-one he had already written *L'Etourdi.* When Voltaire[47] was twelve he was writing satires directed at the Jesuit fathers of the school he attended. His father wanted him to study law and was deeply troubled when he discovered that his son was going about reciting poetry among the carefree people of Paris. At twenty Voltaire was imprisoned in the Bastille[48] because of his comical verses against the vice-ridden king ruling France. While there he corrected his tragedy *Oedipus* and began his poem entitled the *Henriad.*

The German Kotzebue[49] was another precocious genius. At

46. Jean Baptiste Poquelin Molière (1622–73), French dramatist and comic genius, considered to be one of the greatest of all French writers.

47. François Marie Arouet de Voltaire (1694–1778), one of the greatest of eighteenth-century authors, who used his remarkable wit and satire to crusade against tyranny, bigotry, and cruelty.

48. The Bastille was a medieval fortress on the east side of Paris that became, in the seventeenth and eighteenth centuries, a French state prison and a place of detention for important persons charged with miscellaneous offenses. As a symbol of the despotism of the Bourbons, it was stormed by an armed crowd of Parisians in the opening days of the French Revolution.

49. August Friedrich Ferdinand Kotzebue (1761–1819), German dramatist, author of over two hundred plays, many of them popular in England and other European countries.

seven he wrote a one-page comedy in verse. He would sneak into the Weimar theater and when he did not have the money for a ticket, he would hide behind the bass drum until the performance began. His greatest pleasure was going about with the puppet troupe and managing the puppets on stage. At eighteen his first tragedy was performed in a theater belonging to some friends.

Victor Hugo[50] was only fifteen when he wrote his tragedy *Irtamène.* He won three prizes in a row in the floral games; at twenty he wrote *Bug-Jargal* and a year later his novel, *Han d'Islande,* and his first *Odes* and *Ballades.* Almost all the French poets of his time were very young. "In France," said the critic Moreau in fun, "nobody respects a writer any longer if he is older than eighteen."

The English Congreve[51] wrote his novel *Incognita, or Love and Duty Reconciled* at nineteen, and all his comedies before he was twenty-five. Sheridan's[52] teacher called him an "incorrigible ass," but by the time he was twenty-six he had written his *School for Scandal.* Among the English poets of antiquity there were very few prodigies. Little is known about Chaucer,[53] Shakespeare,[54] and Spenser.[55] Shakespeare himself called the poem *Venus and Adonis* "the first-born of my

50. Victor Hugo (1802–85), poet, dramatist, novelist, and most important of the French Romantic writers.

51. William Congreve (1670–1729), Restoration dramatist who shaped the English comedy of manners and whose masterpiece is *The Way of the World.*

52. Richard Brinsley Sheridan (1751–1816), playwright, noted for his comedies of manners, especially *The School for Scandal* (1777), but also an impresario, orator, and politician.

53. Geoffrey Chaucer (1342–1400), outstanding English poet before Shakespeare, famous for his *Canterbury Tales.*

54. William Shakespeare (1564–1616), poet and dramatist widely regarded as the greatest writer of all time. His plays are being performed more continually than that of any other dramatist.

55. Edmund Spenser (1552–99), British poet famous for his *The Faerie Queen* (1596) for which he invented the Spenserian stanza.

devising," having composed it at the age of twenty-eight. Milton[56] was twenty-six when he wrote his *Comus.* But Cowley[57] was writing poems of mythology at twelve. When Pope[58] "first began to talk, it was in verse." His health was wretched and his body deformed, but no matter how much his head ached, good poetry came out of it in profusion. The one who was to conceive *The Dunciad* came home from school one day, having been thrown out because of a satire he wrote against his teacher. Samuel Johnson[59] says that Pope wrote his *Ode to Solitude* at twelve and his *Pastorals* at sixteen. Between the ages of twenty-five and thirty he translated the *Iliad.* The unhappy Chatterton[60] succeeded in deceiving with a marvelous literary misrepresentation the most famous learned men of his time; his *Ode to Liberty* and *Songe of Aella* overflow with genius. But he was rude and arrogant, with an insolent and faulty character, and he rebelled against the laws of life. He died at seventeen before having commenced to live.

Robert Burns,[61] the Scottish poet, was already writing his enchanting songs of the highlands at the age of sixteen. At thirteen the Irishman Moore was composing fine verses to his

56. John Milton (1608–74), one of England's finest poets, famous for *Paradise Lost,* published in 1667.

57. Abraham Cowley (1618–67), poet and essayist who helped establish the ode in English literature.

58. Alexander Pope (1688–1744), outstanding poet and satirist of the first half of the eighteenth century in England.

59. Samuel Johnson (1709–84), British poet, essayist, critic, journalist, lexicographer, and conversationalist, regarded as one of the outstanding figures in English eighteenth-century life and letters.

60. Thomas Chatterton (1752–70), chief poet of the eighteenth-century "Gothic" literary revival who was also England's youngest writer of mature verse and precursor of the Romantic movement.

61. Robert Burns (1759–96), Scottish folk poet whose poems made him the national poet of Scotland and one of the best-loved poets of all time.

famous Celia, and at fourteen he had started to translate Anacreon from the Greek. His household wondered about the meanings of those nymphs, winged pleasures, and songs in praise of wine. Moore soon discarded these dangerous models and achieved a better fame with the rich lines of his *Lalla Rookh*[62] and the exemplary prose of his *Life of Byron*.

Keats,[63] the greatest of England's young poets, died at twenty-six, already famous. But nobody had been able to predict that this ferociously studious poet, who was always involved in quarrels and fisticuffs, was to become well known for his poetic genius in his youth. It is true that he read without stopping; although he was apparently unaware of his vocation until at the age of sixteen he read Spenser's *Faerie Queene*. From that time on, he lived for poetry alone.

Shelley[64] was extremely precocious indeed. While studying at Eaton, at fifteen, he published a novel and gave a banquet for his friends with the money he earned from it. He was so original and rebellious that everyone referred to him as "Shelley the atheist" or "Shelley the madman." At eighteen he published his poem *Queen Mab;* at nineteen he was thrown out of college for the boldness with which he defended his religious doctrines; at thirty he drowned, with a volume of Keats' poetry in his pocket. Shelley's poetry is marvelous for its lyricism, its elegant construction, and the depth of its ideas. He was a bundle of constantly vibrating nerves, and had such illusions and peculiarities that his fellow students considered him out of his head. But his intelligence was

62. *Lalla Rookh,* the narrative poem published in 1817 by Thomas Moore. Set in an atmosphere of oriental splendor, it gave Moore a reputation rivaling that of Byron and Scott. Martí translated the poem into Spanish for a Boston publisher, but it was never published.

63. John Keats (1795–1821), one of the greatest of the nineteenth-century English lyric poets, recognized for his vivid imagery, sensuous appeal, and rich classical themes.

64. Percy Bysshe Shelley (1792–1822), one of the greatest of the English romantic poets and advanced thinkers of the period.

intensely acute and subtle, his frail body trembled at the slightest emotion, and his poems are incomparably beautiful.

Byron[65] was another extraordinary and wandering genius contemporary with Shelley and Keats. Even in his school days he was known to have had an excitable and impetuous character. He gave little attention to his schoolbooks, but before the age of eight he was already suffering the pangs of humanity. One of his legs was shorter than the other, although this did not rob him of courage, and he became master of his schoolmates by dint of his fists, like Keats; he himself tells us that out of seven scuffles he lost only one. While a student at Cambridge he kept a bear and several bulldogs in his quarters, and every day some scandalous story was told about him. Yet he was a sensitive boy who at twelve had praised one of his girl cousins in sensitive verse. He eagerly read the works of literature and at eighteen published for his friends his first book of poetry: *Hours of Idleness*. The *Edinburgh Review* criticized it severely, and Byron replied with his famous satire: *English Bards and Scotch Reviewers*. At the age of twenty-four the first canto of his *Childe Harold* reached the public. "At twenty-five," says Macaulay,[66] "Byron was at the pinnacle of his literary glory, with all the famous Englishmen of the times at his feet. Byron was already more celebrated than Scott, Wordsworth, or Southey. There is scarcely an example of such a rapid rise to such dizzy heights." He died at thirty-seven, a fatal age for so many men of genius.

At twenty-five Coleridge[67] wrote his hymn to *Dawn* in which sublimity and energy are wholly merged. Bulwer-

65. George Gordon Byron (1788–1824), British poet and satirist, whose poetry and personality captured the imagination of Europe. His death in the fight for Greek independence made him a legend.

66. Thomas Babington Macaulay (1800–59), famed British historian author of *History of England* (5 vols., 1849–61).

67. Samuel Taylor Coleridge (1772–1834), a leading English Romantic poet, famous for his *"Rime of the Ancient Mariner."*

Lytton[68] had written his *Ismael* by the time he was fifteen. At seventeen the poet Elizabeth Barrett[69] had published her first volume; she had been writing verse and prose since the age of ten. Robert Browning,[70] her husband, published *Paracelsus* at twenty-three. At twenty Tennyson[71] had written some of the melodious poems which have made his name famous. You can see, then, that the tumultuous fervor of youth has given birth to much of the noblest music, painting, and poetry. Poetic genius usually diminishes with the years, although Goethe says that poets improve with age. It is true that if the precocious poets had not died so soon, they might later have conceived more perfect works than those of their youth. The force of genius does not end with youth.

But the special endowments which later make men famous are almost always revealed between the ages of seventeen and twenty-three. Poetic talent develops little by little, but the true poet will always show it in some way. Crabbe[72] and Wordsworth,[73] who discovered their genius late, had been writing poems ever since they were children. Crabbe filled a whole drawer with his verses when he was an apprentice to a surgeon; and Wordsworth, who was bitter and melancholy as a child, began to write heroic quatrains at fourteen. Shelley's opinion of him was that "he had no more imagination than a

---

68. Edward George Earle Bulwer-Lytton (1803–73), British politician, poet, and critic, and most famous as a prolific novelist.

69. Elizabeth Barrett Browning (1806–61), English poet, most famous for her *Sonnets from the Portuguese,* love poems, who married Robert Browning.

70. Robert Browning (1812–89), one of the greatest British poets of the Victorian age, noted for his mastery of dramatic monologue.

71. Alfred, Lord Tennyson (1809–92), poet laureate of England, who is regarded as the chief representative of the Victorian age in poetry.

72. George Crabbe (1754–1832), British writer of verse tales memorable for their realistic details of everyday life.

73. William Wordsworth (1770–1850), greatest poet of the English Romantic movement.

clay pot," which did not prevent Wordsworth from being an immortal poet. He was not as precocious as Shelley, but he grew slowly and with stability, like an oak tree, until he achieved his majestic stature.

Walter Scott[74] was not a precocious child either. His teacher said that he had no head for Greek, and he himself admitted to being a very mischievous and lazy boy, but he enjoyed good health and was very fond of games suitable to his years. His genius was first shown by the pleasure he took in the ancient ballads, and in his extraordinary facility for making up stories. When his father found out that he had been wandering through the country with his friend Clark, butting in everywhere and staying in farmers' houses, he said to him: "I doubt very much, Sir, that you're good for anything but a horsetail!" Referring to his facility with stories, Scott himself says that in leisure time in the winter, when there was no way of being outside, he spent many hours amazing his schoolmates with his narratives, and they would fight among themselves to sit near the one who told such beautiful stories that never ended.

Carlyle says that in a class of an Edinburgh grammar school there were two boys: "John—always spruced up, correct and ducal; and Walter—always slovenly, plodding and stuttering. As the years went by, John became Alderman John in a wretched neighborhood, and Walter became Sir Walter Scott of the entire world." Carlyle says, and rightly so, that the most precocious and perfect vegetable is the cabbage. When Scott was thirty, nobody could say for certain that he was a literary genius. At thirty-one he published the first volume of his *Minstrelsy of the Scottish Border,* and his *Waverly* was not printed until he was forty-three, although he had written it nine years earlier.

74. Sir Walter Scott (1771–1832), Scottish novelist and inventor of the historical novel, which made him one of the most popular novelists of all time.

The Paris Exposition

All the nations of the world have come together in Paris this summer of 1889. Up to a hundred years ago, men lived like the slaves of kings who refused to let them think and took away much of what they earned from their work to pay the troops they used in fighting other kings, and in living in gold and marble palaces with servants dressed in silk and white-plumed ladies and gentlemen of the court, while the real gentlemen—those who worked in the countryside and in the city—could only dress in corduroy and could not afford feathers in their hats. And if they said that it was unjust for the idle to live upon what the laborers earned; if they said that an entire country must not be deprived of bread so that one lone man and his friends might have carriages and gauze and lace clothing and dinners with fifteen wines, the king ordered them beaten or shut up in the Bastille until they died, mute or insane; and they put an iron mask upon one man and held him prisoner all his life, never removing the mask. Men lived like this in every nation, with king and nobles as their masters and working people like beasts of burden, never able to talk or think or believe or own anything, because the king took away their children for soldiers and their money in taxes, and gave all their lands to the nobles. France was a courageous nation, the nation that rose up in defense of man, the nation that robbed the king of his power.

That was a hundred years ago, in 1789. It was as if one world had come to an end and another was beginning. All the kings banded together against France. The French nobility helped these kings. The working people, alone against everyone, fought the nobles and everyone else, and killed the nobles with the blade of the guillotine. Then France bled the way an animal does when it is cut open alive and its entrails are pulled out. The workers were infuriated, accused each other, and ruled badly because they were not accustomed to rule. A daring and ambitious man came to Paris, saw that the French were not united, and when he had won all the battles against their enemies, ordered that he himself be proclaimed emperor, whereupon he governed France like a tyrant.[1] But the nobles no longer returned to their lands, nor did that king in silk and gold ever return. The working people divided the nobles' lands and those of the king among themselves. Neither in France nor in any other country have men become slaves again as before. This is what France wanted to commemorate a hundred years later with the Paris Exposition. For this reason France summoned every nation in the world to Paris, in the summer when the sun shines more brightly.

And it is this Exposition that we are going to see now, as if it were before our eyes. We are going to the Exposition, to see the visit which the races of man are paying each other. We are going to see in one single grove the trees of every nation upon earth. On the banks of the Seine we are going to see the history of houses, from the troglodyte's cave in a hollow of a rock to a granite-and-onyx palace. Along with the red-bearded Norwegians, the wooly-haired Senegalese Negroes, the turbaned and pigtailed Annamese, the slippered and burnoosed Arabs, the silent English, the suspicious Yankees, the courteous Italians, the elegant French, the lighthearted

1. The reference is to Napoleon Bonaparte (1769–1821), the Corsican who became one of the greatest military leaders in history and who had himself crowned emperor of France in 1804.

Spaniards, we are going to climb higher than the tallest cathedrals to the cupola of the iron Tower. We are going to see our beloved nations of America in their strange and magnificent palaces. We shall see—among lakes and gardens, in iron and porcelain monuments—the life of all mankind, and all he has discovered and created since the days when he walked naked through the forests till now when he navigates high in the air and deep under the sea. In an iron temple—so vast and handsome that it resembles a gilded heaven—we shall see all the wheels and machines in the world working at the same time. From below the ground, we are going to see, like a volcano erupting jewels, three hundred fountains spouting colored sprays of water that look like sparkling precious stones raining down upon a lake of fire. We are going to see how the Javanese live in their reed houses in their lands of light, the Egyptian singing behind his donkey, the Algerian embroidering woolen cloth in the shade of his palm grove, the Siamese working wood with his hands and feet; the Sudanese Negro with his pointed spear, eyeing from his patch of land the Arab firing his Moorish gun as he gallops along the palm-bordered streets, his white burnoose billowing in the wind. There is dancing in a Moorish café. The Javanese dancers go by in their plumed headdresses. The actors from Cochin-China,[2] dressed as tigers, come out of their theater. In amazement the men of all nations go through the Moorish streets, the Negro villages, the bamboo hamlets of the Javanese, over the reed bridges of Malaysian fishermen, through the Creole orange groves and banana plantations, and around the place where rises the serpent-ringed tower of a pagoda, its roof carved like a fine piece of furniture. And for us children, there is a palace of toys and a theater where crafty Bluebeard and pretty Little Red Riding Hood look as if they were alive. The rogue's beard is a fiery red and he has lion's eyes. The little girl wears a red cap and a woolen apron. Every day one

2. Cochin-China is a southern part of what is now Vietnam.

hundred thousand people visit the Exposition. On top of the Tower waves the tricolored flag of the French Republic.

You enter the Exposition by twenty-two gateways. The most beautiful entrance is through the Trocadero Palace, built in the shape of a horseshoe, left there from a former exposition and filled with those exquisite designs which in cloak-and-dagger days the jewelers used to make out of silver for the churches and the tables of royalty when dinner plates were made of gold and goblets were like chalices. And from the palace you go out into the garden, the first marvel. It has nothing but roses, but there are four thousand five hundred varieties, one almost blue. In a red-and-white-striped tent some young women are selling sharp-bladed pruning shears, shiny steel rakes, watering pots like the toys you use when you work in a garden. The ground is divided into small garden patches surrounded by irrigation ditches running with clear water, making the patches look like little islands. One of them is full of black pansies, another of coral-colored strawberries hidden among their green leaves, and another of peas and asparagus with its pretty, fernlike foliage. There is a red-and-yellow-bordered patch filled with tulips. One corner is planted with climbing vines, and beside it some gigantic ivy with leaves like feathers. Water lilies, the rose-colored nelumbo of Hindustan, and lyre-shaped lotuses from the river Nile float upon the water of a maze. One grove has trees with pointed tops: pine and fir. Another has trees pruned into odd shapes: they bear poor fruit because their branches are deprived of their natural freedom. Within a cane enclosure are Japanese lilies and cherries in their big blue-and-white porcelain jars. By a palm grove is the log Pavilion of Woods and Streams where you can find out how to care for the trees that give the land happiness and beauty. In the shade of a Japanese maple, in rustic containers, are the Wellington pines from the north—the tallest of the pine family—and the Araucaria, the pine of Chile.

You cross the famous river Seine over a bridge, and you

can see groups of astonished people everywhere; they come from the buildings along the river where the Hall of Labor is located, in which biscuits are baked in an enormous oven and liquor is distilled in a red-bronze still and cacao beans are ground in a cylindrical machine, with sugar to make chocolate, and white-hatted candy makers make caramels and meringues upon hot trays. Everything to eat can be seen in this hall—a mountain of sugar, a tree of prunes, a pillar of hams. And in the wine room there is a cask so large that it can be used as a table to seat fifteen guests, and a relief map that everyone wants to see at the same time, explaining the art of the vine—the vinestock with its bunches of grapes, the men gathering them into baskets in the vintage month, the trough in which the mature fruit ferments, the cold caves where the grape juice rests, and finally the pure wine and the bottles out of which you pour the champagne with its aromatic bubbles. Nearby is the entire story of farming in embossed models and pictures and books; and a pavilion of shining steel plows; and a hive of honeybees together with the downy leaf upon which the silkworm is raised; and fisheries where the eggs in tanks of water produce thousands of fish to stock the sea and rivers. The most amazed people are those who come to see the Forty-three Habitations of Man. The life of man is there from the time he first appeared upon earth, fighting the bear and the reindeer to protect himself from the terrible cold with their skins, huddled in his cave. Some people live like this today. The savage imitates grottos in the woods or clefts in the rock; then he sees the beautiful world around him and affectionately feels a desire to entertain, and so he looks at his reflection in the river and copies on the stones and timbers of his house all that he considers beautiful—man's body, the birds, a flower, the trees. And all peoples grow by imitating what they see around them, making their own houses like those their neighbors make, learning about their neighbors from their houses—if they are from a cold climate or hot, if peaceful or

fond of fighting, if artistic and natural or vain and ostentatious. There you can see the houses of the first men, made of
roughly hewn and then polished stone; and the lacustrine city
of the days when houses were built upon stilts in the lake, to
be safe from the attacks of wild animals; you can see tall
houses, square and fragile, with a continuous unbroken
mirador, of the peoples of the sun who used to be great
nations—wise Egypt, commercial Phoenicia, warring Assyria.
The Hindustan house is just as tall. The Persian house is a
castle with elegant blue tiles, because precious stones leap out
of the ground in Persia, and that country has brightly colored
flowers and birds. The Hebrew, Greek, and Roman houses
seem to belong to the same family—all of them low and made
of stone, with flat roof or terrace; and you can see by their
similarity that the Etruscan and Byzantine houses had something in common. In those times the barbarous Huns lived in
the north of Europe, as you can see there, in their nomadic
tents; and the Germans and Gauls in their first houses made
of wood with a thatched roof. And when wars brought
nations together, the Russian houses were fancy and gaily
colored, like the Hindu houses, and the barbarians put the
gracefully carved stonework of the Italians and Greeks in
their houses. Afterward, at the end of the age between that
struggle and the discovery of America, the former tastes of
Greece and Rome returned in the gracious and wealthy
houses of the Renaissance. In America the Indians lived in
stone palaces adorned with gold, like those of the Aztecs in
Mexico and the Incas of Peru. You can see the African Moor
by his house of decorated stone, for he knew the Hebrews,
and he lived among the palms, defending himself against his
enemies from his tower, as he watches the gazelle in his rose
garden and the capricious wavelets breaking upon the sands.
The Sudanese Negro, whose white house has a roof rimmed
with bellflowers, looks Moorish. The agile Chinese, who lives
on fish and rice, builds his house of boards and bamboo. The
Japanese earns his living by carving ivory in his house of

rice-straw and narrow boards. There you can see how the savage lives now—the Eskimo in his round igloo of ice blocks, and the North American Indian in his tepee of animal skins painted in a childlike manner with strange animals and men with round faces.

But what draws the crowds in respectful silence is the Eiffel Tower,[3] the tallest and boldest of man-made monuments. It serves as a gateway to the Exposition. Surrounded by palaces, its four iron feet spring out of the ground, coming together in an arch and almost meeting near the second stage of the Tower, high as the pyramid of Cheops. From there—delicate as lace, brave as a hero, slender as an arrow—it climbs higher than the Washington Monument, which used to be the tallest structure made by the hand of man, and plunges out of sight into the blue, its domed top crowned with clouds like the mountaintops. And all of it, from top to bottom, is a fabric woven of iron. It rises through the air with scarcely any means of support. The four feet take hold of the sandy soil like enormous roots. Two of them are near the river, where the ground was unstable, so two huge containers were sunk there, the shifting sand removed, and the containers filled with stabilizing cement. The four strong feet rose from the four corners to come together high above; scaffolding supported the higher parts, which sloped downward; four heavy wooden pillars raised the first platform, upon which were inscribed the names of the great French engineers all around it, like a crown. There in the air one fine morning those four feet were inserted into the platform like a sword in its scabbard, and the Tower was supported without props.

---

3. When the French government was organizing the Centennial Exposition of 1889 to commemorate the French Revolution, the noted bridge engineer Alexandre Gustave Eiffel was chosen to build a symbolic structure. Eiffel built a 984-foot tower of open-lattice wrought iron, a structure which began a revolution in civil engineering and architectural design.

From there, like spears pointing to the sky, projected the slender booms; from each hung a derrick, and the new pieces were hoisted high up there, dancing in the air. Those workmen, clinging to the booms with their legs like sailors to the rigging of their ship, affixed the metal trimming as if running their country's flag up the enemy's flagpole—the men leaning backward, facing emptiness, clinging to the booms, which the wind tossed about like a branch of a tree. Clad in fur jackets and caps because of the winter blizzard, those men adjusted the corner pieces, crossbars, and supports, and raised that delicate openwork above the world as if it were to hang from the sky. The painters were swinging back and forth on their scaffolds, holding their brushfuls of red paint. The whole world is now surging ahead as if upon the sea, with the nations of man on board, and rising from the world's ship is the Eiffel Tower mast! The winds swirl around it as if to blow down that structure defying them, and flee through the blue spaces defeated and shattered. There below the people enter like bees into a hive. They ascend and descend by way of the Tower's feet, by the spiral staircase, by the inclined elevators, two thousand visitors at a time. Like worms the people swarm within the iron network; between the upper girders you can see the sky in big blue triangles with sharp or blunted points. By a spiral staircase you climb from the first open platform, with its four curious way-stations, to the second rest stop, where a newspaper is being written and printed at the height of the top of St. Peter's in Rome. The press cylinder goes round and round; the newpapers come out still damp; the visitor is given a silver medal. Courageous people go up to the third level, three hundred meters above the land and sea, where you no longer can hear the bustle of life, and where at that altitude the air seems to be washing you clean and kissing you. The city spreads out below, silent and deserted, like a relief map; twenty leagues of sparkling rivers, illuminated valleys, dark green mountains, can be seen with the spyglass. Above the platform rises the cupola where two men, in their glass enclosure, are studying the birds, the course of the stars, and the path of the winds. From one of the Tower's legs, climbing snakelike through the vibrating wire, electricity illuminates in the dark sky the beacon that sheds over Paris its rivers of red, white, and blue light, like the country's flag. On top of the cupola a swallow has built its nest.

Unable to speak from astonishment, you can see fountain-filled gardens surrounded by palaces, the largest one of all in the background where samples of all the works of man are displayed, the palace's wrought-iron gate in designs of wreaths and garlands of the kind formerly wrought in gold for the use of the wealthy; and above the entrance, imitating the vault of heaven, the gleaming enameled cupola surmounted by a woman with an olive branch in her hand, spreading her wings as if ready for flight; at the entrance to the portico, one of her hands on the head of a lion, stands a bronze Liberty. And in front of the great fountain stand the men and women whom the poet of long ago said inhabited the seas—the Nereids and Tritons—bearing upon their backs, as if in triumph, the ship in which, in figures of heroes and heroines, Progress, Science, and Art are hailing the Republic, the latter seated higher than all the rest and holding her lighted torch high above her wings. At either side of the garden, from the great palace to the Eiffel Tower, there is another gold and enameled palace—one of them for statues and paintings where there are English landscapes of mountains and animals, graceful Italian paintings of peasants and children, Spanish paintings of war and death with their figures that seem to be alive, and the tasteful history of the world in the paintings of France. This is the Fine Arts building. And on the other side is the Palace of Liberal Arts—those arts which are of practical value, and all that is not merely decorative. There you can see the history of everything: engraving, painting, sculpture, schools, the press. All is so fine and perfect that it seems to be running like clockwork. There you can see, in wax miniatures, the Chinese in his tower observing the heavenly bodies; Lavoisier the chemist, with his silk stockings and blue waistcoat, blowing into his retort to find out the composition of a meteorite that fell to earth from a cold and shattered star. There, among the figures of the various races of man, are the powerful Bronze Age men with their big heads, seated upon the ground and working the rough stone, like those excavated in Denmark not long ago.

And now we are at the bottom of the Tower; there are two groves of trees, one on each side. One of them is greener, like a woods we go to for recreation, with its Swedish house of pine, full of flower-filled window boxes, standing beside a lake; and the log house of the Russian peasant, with its decorated doorway and pointed roof; and the pretty wooden house with triangular windows in which the Finn spends the snowy months, teaching his children to paint and to think, to love the poets of Finland, and to repair the harpoon for the catch and the sleigh in the outbuilding, while the grandfather polishes granite so it shines like an opal, or carves boats and figures of people out of a dry branch, and the women in their tall caps and their aprons make fine lace beside a carved wooden hearth. You will find a theater there, and dairies, and spacious dining rooms whose waiters wear black jackets and pass to the diners bottles of wine in baskets, while birds sing in the trees. But to the other side is where our hearts go, because there, at the foot of the Tower, like sprouts of banana plants around the main stem, stand the famous pavilions of our lands of America, light and graceful as an Indian warrior. Bolivia's is like a headpiece, Mexico's like a belt, Argentina's like a multicolored crest. People seem to look at them the way children look at giants! It is a good thing to have some new blood—the blood of industrious nations! The Brazilian pavilion is there too, like a church on Sunday in a palm grove, with everything that grows in its dense forests, and the rare urns and vessels of the Marajo

Indians of the Amazon, and floating in a fountain a huge water-lily leaf upon which a child can maneuver, and rare flowering orchids, and sacks of coffee beans, and heaps of diamonds. A golden sun shines there above the trees and pavilions; it is the Argentine sun on top of the cupola, blue and white like the country's flag. Among the other four cupolas, with groups of statues at the roof corners, this sun crowns that gilded iron palace with its stained-glass windows. This is the building in which the country of America's new man invites the astonished world to see what a newborn Spanish-speaking nation can accomplish in a few years—a nation with a passion for freedom, a passion for work! Better to die burned by the sun than to travel over the world like a solid rock, with folded arms! At the door a statue points to a relief map that shows the Republic with its river by which steamships filled with people ready for work arrive there, and the mountains that produce its metals, and the vast pampas covered with cattle. The model city of the Plata, suddenly appearing on the uncultivated plain, is also there in relief, with its railroads and port and forty thousand inhabitants and palatial schools. And there you can see all the products of sheep and oxen, and all that courageous man can make from the animals he raises: a thousand industries; fresh meat in the refrigeration room; horsehair, animal horns, cocoons, feathers, woolen cloth. All that man has made, the Argentinian attempts to make. At night when the crowds knock on the door, all the thousand electric lights in the palace turn on at the same time, in their blue and white and red and green glass globes.

The steel temple of Mexico is girdled with a frieze of gods and goddesses, with its stately flight of stairs leading to the entrance, and on top of it the sun god Tonatiu looking down to see how the goddess Cipactli, the earth, buds forth in its warmth. And all the gods of Indian poetry—those of the chase and the fields, those of commerce and the arts—are on the two walls flanking the doorway, like two wings; and also the last of the braves: Cacama, Cuitláhuac and Cuauhtémoc who died in the fight, or were burned on the grills, defending the independence of their country from the conquistadors. Inside, in the exquisite wall paintings, you can see what the Mexicans of those days were like—their labors and festivals, the widowed mother giving her opinion to the city's rulers, the peasants extracting the unfermented juice of the maguey, the kings visiting each other on the lake in their flower-decked canoes. And two Mexicans supervised the building of that steel temple at the foot of the Tower so that those who had not known Mexican history as children might come to know it, for history is like a country's mother! That is how you must love the country of your birth—fiercely and tenderly! The beautiful curtains, the mahogany showcases decorated with silver filigree, the weavings, sweet-smelling perfumes, enameled plates and highly glazed jars, the opals, wines, harnesses, sugars—everything adorned with Indian figures and inscriptions. Manikins of the wealthy plantation owner, and the elegant young man who looks after his fortune and can "throw" a bull, in their fringed and laced leather suits, broad-brimmed hats with silver-and-gold-braided hatbands, and their serapes of colored silk slung over their shoulders, seem to be as alive as if they were about to mount their horses. At one side of the doorway are colossal tree trunks of highly polished fine wood; at the other, a pyramid of the country's rose and sea-green translucent marble, and onyx that looks like a cloud frozen by a sunset. From the roof flies the red, white, and green flag with the eagle.

And there are other pavilions standing together like sisters: the pavilion of Bolivia, daughter of Bolívar,[4] with its four

4. Bolivia gained its independence from Spain in 1825 under the leadership of Simón Bolívar and José Antonio de Sucre and was named in honor of Bolívar, liberator and "George Washington of Latin America."

graceful towers and its golden cupola, displaying many chunks of quartz from the choicest mines, the remains of savage man and the mountain-size animals that used to roam over America, and coca leaves that fortify the weary so they may continue walking. The pavilion of Ecuador is an Inca temple with drawings and decorations like those which the ancient Indians put upon their temples to the sun, and inside are shown the famous metals and chocolate and weavings and needlework of great delicacy, all exhibited in glass and gilded showcases. Then there is the Venezuelan pavilion with its cathedrallike facade, and in its vast hall so many samples of coffee, loaves of unrefined sugar, books of poetry and volumes on engineering, and fine, delicate shoes. The Nicaraguan pavilion has a red roof like the roofs of that country's houses, and on both sides of the center hall are rooms full of chocolate and aromatic vanilla and birds of gold-and-emerald plumage and metallic stones with glints of the rainbow and woods that ooze fragrant sap. And in the center hall, among other ruins, is a map of the canal that will join America's two oceans. El Salvador's pavilion has wide windows like that country's houses, and a very handsome wooden balcony. El Salvador is a workers' nation, inventive and industrious, and it cultivates fields of sugar cane and coffee, and makes furniture as fine as that of Paris, and silk to equal Lyon silk, and embroidery to match Burano's, and gaily colored woolen cloth as fine as England's, and very graceful wood carvings and engravings in gold. By an imposing porch, among sacks of wheat and samples of minerals, you enter the iron palace of Chile. There you find the hard woods of the Araucanian Indians' forests, the red and topaz wines, the bars of silver and dull gold—all the arts of a nation that has no desire to lag behind, and the salt and the red bushes of the desert; in the rear, in a garden setting, the walls are filled with paintings.

And there beside the Chilean building we would now enter the Children's Palace, where the little ones may swing and play "horsie" and watch the glassblowers make boats out of

Venetian glass, and see how the Japanese make dolls by winding soft paste of different colors around a stick with a rough little twig, and how they make a feudal Japanese prince with his sword, and a present-day Mikado in his French frock coat. Oh, and the theater! And the man making bonbons! And the dog that knows how to multiply! And the gymnast riding a horse in the ring! That palace is filled with toys from the front door to the little flags on the roof! But if we have no more time, how are we children of America going to stop and play when there is still so much to see, if we have not yet seen all the pavilions of our American lands? And this wooden building that is so open and friendly, inviting people to come inside and see everything that the volcanic soil of its country produces, such as grapes and coffee, climbing plants and tigers, coconuts and birds, and invites people to its curtained shelters to drink foaming chocolate out of carved cups? This hospitable building is the Guatemalan pavilion. And that other elegant one with so much timber is from the land that knows how to defend itself with branches against outsiders who come to rob them of their country: Santo Domingo. And that one over there is the Paraguayan pavilion with its belvedere tower, its doors and windows like what you would expect from a country of many forests, for Paraguay's houses imitate the arches and grottos of trees. And that other sumptuous building, gay as a parlor, with towers like spears; that building which has given part of its halls to two nations of our family—to Colombia, which has much to do now, and Peru, which is sad because of a recent war—that one is from the brave and cordial nation of Uruguay that works happily and artistically, like France, and for nine years fought against a bad man who wanted to rule it; a country that has a poet of America named Magariños. Uruguay makes its living by raising cattle, and no nation in the world has invented as many ways of preserving fresh meat: by drying, pickling, wrapping it in the dark dough of Liebig, and baking it in delicious biscuits; and from the spearlike tower, as if calling to all good men, flies the blue-and-white-striped flag of the sun.

What a shame to have to go so quickly through the palace of a midget country like Holland, where not one Hollander is unhappy! The Dutch live as if they were in a big nation—working as sailors, engineers, printers, lace makers, and diamond cutters; or the pavilion of a country like Belgium, that knows so much about farming, building houses, making carriages, guns, chinaware, tapestries, and bricks! We cannot see the Swiss pavilion with its model school, its cheeses that look like wheels, and its clock workshops; or that of Hawaii, a country where everyone knows how to read, and where men of the island work at the foot of a volcano that spews streams of lava; or that of the Republic of San Marino—who knows where San Marino is? —with its famous stained-glass windows and its families of sculptors. The building with the carved and painted doorway is the pavilion of Serbia, near Russia, where they make fine tapestries and mosaics, and that dining room with the overhanging roof is from Romania, where the poorest person wears embroidered clothes and eats meat that is almost raw, seasoned with lots of pepper, on wooden plates, and drinks buffalo milk. The Siamese house with two roofs is filled with embroidered silks in designs of birds and flowers, and with palanquins and elephant tusks—Siam, the country of ceremonies and rice. And who does not know about China, whose pavilion has three towers, and so many curtains with pictures of trees and golden demons on them, and ivory boxes carved in relief, and the tapestry woven with the six colors of the rainbow, where birds from the court fly through the air, in the month of May, to greet the king and queen, which are two nightingales that flew to the sky to find out who is seated among the clouds, and brought back a nest made of sunbeams? Oh, there is so much to see! And the Hindu palace, dark red with white decorations like the braid trimming of a woman's dress, and everything so finely carved—the little windows and the tower, the marble fountain, the porphyry columns, the bronze lions adorning the hall hung with tapestries! And the Japanese pavilion which is like the Chinese, only more graceful and delicate, and has some old gardeners who are very fond of children! And the Greek pavilion, with a low doorway and a wall on each side, one bearing a legend of that country's ancient history from before the Romans conquered it when it was vice-ridden, and its modern history telling about its work today—in antiquities, red marbles, fine silks, fragrant wines; and now Greece has cities such as Piraeus, Syracuse, Corfu, and Patras, as valuable to the workers as were the four famous cities of ancient times: Athens, Sparta, Thebes, and Corinth! And the Persian pavilion with its mosquelike entryway and its bright blue roof; and inside, among the green and yellow wall hangings, the chased incense burners, silk shawls so fine that they can be pulled through a finger ring, jewel-hilted cutlasses so sharp that they can slice through iron, sugared violets and rose-petal conserves! And the Moroccan bazaar with its series of white arches shining in the sun, and its slippered and turbaned Moors polishing knives, dying softened pelts, braiding straw, working and hammering copper, and embroidering velvet with gold thread! And the Cairo street copying a street in Egypt, where some people are buying burnooses, others weaving wool on a loom, some selling confections and crying out their wares, and others working as jewelers, turners, potters, toymakers—and everywhere men with donkeys for hire and ass keepers selling asses' milk; and over there, covered with veils, the lovely Moorish woman looking out from behind the openwork blinds of her balcony!

We have no more time! We must go to see the greatest marvel of them all, and feel the daring that melts when we see the human heart and makes us want to embrace all men and call them brothers. Let us return to the garden. We enter through the portico of the Palace of Industry. With our eyes shut we go through the gallery of the fourteen doors where every country exhibits its finest work, and where every industry built the door to its own section—the silversmith's shop with its gold and silver and two blue stone columns, the potter's shop with its porcelains and tiles, the cabinetmaker with his woods carved in leaf designs, the iron worker with his pickaxes and hammers, the gunsmith with his wheels, gun carriages, bullets, and cannons; and that is all. By way of a corridor that makes you think of great things, you climb the stairs that lead to the monument's balcony. You look up and see, bathed in sunlight, an iron hall in which two thousand horses could move about all at one time, in which thirty thousand men could sleep. And filled with machines that turn, crush, whistle, shed light, quietly move through the air, and rumble below the ground! The principal machines stand in four rows in the center. Their power comes from a red furnace. It comes by driver belts so slender that you cannot see them move. From four rows of posts hang the belt wheels. Connected to one another, all the machines in the world are there—from those that make steel dust to those that sharpen needles. Some women in red aprons are making fine-quality Dutch paper. A cylinder that looks like a moving elephant is cutting envelopes. Grains of wheat are being removed from the chaff in a mortar. An iron ring is kept in the air by electricity, with nothing else to hold it up. There, they fuse metals for making type for printing presses; there, they make paper out of rags or wood; there, the press prints the daily newspaper, expels it from the other side, and returns it while it is still wet. One of the machines pumps air into mine shafts to keep the miners from being asphyxiated. Another crushes cane and pours out a stream of molasses. Seeing all those machines from the balcony makes you want to cry! They roar, they hum softly; it is like the sea. Plenty of sun comes in. At night a man presses a button, two wires come together, and above those machines that look as though they are kneeling in the dark, comes electric light from the vaulted ceiling. Far away, where Edison has his inventions, twenty thousand lights, like a crown, can be turned on with a flying spark.

There are panoramas of Paris; of Naples and its volcano; of Mont Blanc, which makes you feel cold merely by looking at it; and of Rio de Janeiro's bay. There is another in the center like a ship's bridge, and the painting gives the illusion of seeing the entire ship and the sky and sea. The delicate art of the water colorists is shown in one palace, and in another, with mirror decorations, the art of those who work in pastels. Then there are the two Paris pavilions, where one learns how to run a great city. Along the outskirts of the Exposition there are workshops where you can see—so the self-centered person learns to improve himself! —how men work in the bituminous coal mines, or in deep water, or with tanks where gold bubbles like boiling mud. Far away there are huge, black, and ugly furnaces into which smudge-faced men stoke the coal for making steam. But everyone is bound for the open space in front of the palace where one-armed and crippled soldiers stand guard at Napoleon's stone tomb surrounded by torn battle flags. And high atop the palace the golden cupola! Everybody goes to the Esplanade des Invalides to see the foreigners. In passing, all we see is the palace containing everything having to do with war: the balloon that sails through the air to keep track of the enemy, the pigeons that know how to fly so high with their messages that they cannot be struck by the bullets, except when one hits the mark and the white pigeon falls to the ground, bathed in blood! In the pavilion of the Republic of South Africa, we see in passing the imperial diamond mined there—the biggest diamond in the world. We see the soldiers' tents, their guns by the doorway, and the attractive houses that good men want to build for the workers, so they may see daylight on Sundays, and relax in their clean homes when they come home tired. There, with its magnolia-blossom tower, is the pavilion of Cambodia, the land where the Khmers—who make temples higher than mountains—no longer live, because they died for freedom. There, with its wooden columns, is the palace of Cochin-China, its door frames carved with a pointed knife, and in its courtyard a pool with goldfish; in the rear, on the stairs, are two open-mouthed dragons made of gleaming porcelain. The Annamese palace looks Chinese with its red and blue timbers and in the courtyard a giant god cast in Annamese bronze, which is like very fine filbert-colored wax, and its roofs and columns and doors delicately carved, as if with a razor's edge, in designs like birds' nests or little leaves or bowers. And beyond the Hindu temples with their colorful towers and forest of bronze gods at the door—gods with golden bellies and enameled eyes—stands the Central Palace, where the products of all of France's possessions in Asia are displayed; there you can see an abundance of silks and ivories, cloth of silver edged with sapphires, and in one of the halls, when you lift a blue curtain, an elephant offering an opium pipe. There among the palms shines the white, lacelike minaret of the Algerian row of arches under which, like imprisoned kings, walk the handsome, tight-lipped Arabs. With flat roofs and doors studded with nailheads stands a group of Tunisian houses in a grove of date palms. These are built of ancient stones and broken tiles from Carthage, and are filled with Tunisian Moors and black-bearded Hebrews drinking golden wine in their coffee and buying daggers inscribed on the blades with sayings from the Koran. One lone squatting Annamese is looking with half-shut eyes at the Angkor pagoda, the one whose tower resembles a magnolia bloom, and that has a four-headed Buddha on top.

Among the palaces there are entire villages of mud and straw where you can see the New Caledonian Negro in his round hut, the man from Futa-Jalón melting iron in his earthen oven, the man from Kedugú with his feather breeches in the round tower from which he defends himself against the white man. And next to it, built of stone with loopholes, is the square tower from which twenty-six Frenchmen drove back twenty thousand Negroes, who were unable to pierce the hard rock with their wooden spears! In the Annamese village, with its delicate houses of galleries and peaked roofs, you can see the Cochin-Chinese seated on a straw mat and reading his book, which is one long page rolled around a stick; and another, an actor, painting his face vermilion and black; and the Buddhist priest praying, his cowl over his head and his hands on his lap. The Javanese, wearing a loose-fitting blouse and white trousers, lives happily, breathing plenty of clear air, in his *kampong* of bamboo houses. Everything is made of bamboo: the village fence, the houses and chairs, the granary where the rice is stored, the row of seats where the elders meet to rule on village affairs, and the musical instruments that follow the barefoot dancers with their feathered headdresses and gold bracelets. The Kabyle, in his white burnoose, goes back and forth by the door of his low, dark mud house, to prevent any daring stranger from entering to catch sight of the women of the house who are seated upon the floor, weaving on a loom, their foreheads painted in different colors. In the rear is the Kabyle's tent which he carries with him when he travels; his donkey wallows in the dust; his brother tosses into a corner a leather chair decorated in pure gold; the old man in the doorway lifts his grandson onto a camel as the youngster pulls his beard.

And outside in the open air it is like some kind of madness. Those people in their colorful clothes look like walking jewels. Some go to the Moorish café to watch the Moorish girls dance, in their gauze veils and violet skirts, moving their arms slowly as if drowsy. Others go to the *kampong* theater where there are rows of conical paper puppets, their porcelain eyes watching the Javanese dancers moving as if they never touched the floor, and with their arms spread like butterfly wings. In a café with red tables and Arabic lettering on the walls, the Aissawas, who are like religious fanatics, gouge out their eyes and leave them hanging, and chew on glass, and eat live scorpions, because they say their god talks to them at night from Heaven and orders them to do those things. And in the Annamese theater the actors—dressed as panthers and generals, leaping and howling, pulling each other's head-feathers and whirling about—tell the story of the prince who went to visit the palace of a greedy man and drank a cup of poisoned tea.

Now it is night and the time to go away and think. The buglers sound the retreat with their brass bugles. The camels start running. The Algerian climbs up to his minaret and calls to prayer. The Annamese bows three times before the pagoda. The dark-skinned New Caledonian native raises his spear to the sky. The Moorish dancers go by, munching on sweetmeats. And suddenly the sky lights up in a blaze of scarlet—now blood-red, now like a sunset, now the color of the sea at dawn, now blue as if the sky were entering a thought, now white, now silver, now the violet of a bouquet of lilacs, now with a yellow glow; the palace cupolas shine like golden crowns. Down yonder, from within the fountains, colored crystals leap into the air among the light and water that fall in streams of color and hurl to the flaming sky their giant sparkling flowers. In the light of those fountains the Eiffel Tower glows in the night sky like red lace as all the nations of the world pass below its arches.

The Rose-Colored Slippers

To Mademoiselle Marie

The sand is fine by the choppy sea,
The sun shines as brightly as fire;
Pilar wants to show off her fine feathered hat
For all to observe and admire.

"An enchanting child," her father says,
And kisses her on the hand.
"Go to the beach, my captive bird,
And bring me some of that sand."

"I'll go with my pretty daughter,"
Pilar's good mother decides.
"But don't let those rose-colored slippers
Get soiled by the sand or the tides!"

So both went out to the garden
By the laurel-bordered way;
The mother plucked a carnation,
Pilar picked a jasmine spray.

Pilar with her gay purple pail,
Her shovel and bright red hoop,
Is ready to play on the beach now
And some of that sand to scoop.

The people crowd round as they leave;
Not a one wants to bid them good-bye;
Then Pilar's *mamá* starts laughing
And an old man begins to cry.

The breezes muss Pilar's neat hair
As she runs to and fro, still quite clean.
"Mamá, would you tell me just how it feels
To be and to act like a queen?"

Pilar's good father has ordered the coach
Just in case the darkness should come
Unawares from over the wide blue sea,
For he wanted them safely home.

The beach is so lovely this afternoon
And everyone seems to be there;
Florinda, the French girl's nursemaid,
Wears her glasses to guard against glare.

The soldier Alberto is there today;
He seems to be off on a spree
With his tricorne hat and his walking stick,
As he launches his boat in the sea.

Magdalena is such a naughty girl
With her ribbons and bows so grand,
For she takes her doll without any arms
And buries it deep in the sand!

In beach chairs arranged along the beach
Some couples go chatting for hours;
Beneath their colorful parasols
The ladies resemble flowers.

But those strange ways make the sea quite sad;
Their manners and customs offend;
All the joy is there by the cliffs far away—
Out there with the crowds round the bend.

The waves sleep more soundly, the people claim,
Over there with the crowds, they say,
And the sand is far whiter and finer, too,
Where none but the little girls play.

Pilar runs right back to her mother now:
"Mamá, I shall do as I should;
Let me go and play alone in the sand
Over there; you can see, I'll be good!"

"Pilar, you're so very capricious!
Not a day when you don't make me fret!
Go and play, but do not let the water
Get those rose-colored slippers all wet."

The wavelets creep up to their feet
And both of them cry out with glee;
The girl in her feather-trimmed hat
Waves good-bye as she runs by the sea.

She runs off to where, far away,
The waters are heavy with brine,
Away where the poor are relaxing,
Away where the aged spend time.

Pilar goes to play by herself
As the wavelets slip back to their bed,
And time goes by and an eagle
Soars high in the sky overhead.

And quite a while after the sun sank
O'er the golden hills beyond reach,
A modest little feathered hat
Could be seen coming back o'er the beach.

Pilar walked as if deeply troubled;
Her gait was like one who is lame.
Oh why does that child walk like that,
With her head hanging low and in shame?

Her pretty *mamá* knows full well
Why she walks in that shamefaced way:
"I don't see your rose-colored slippers;
Where are they, my child, do say!

"Oh foolish girl, did you lose them?
Tell me, Pilar," said she.
"Señora," a woman in tears replied,
"I have them right here with me!

"I have a sick little daughter
Who cries in her dismal room,
So I carry her here for the sea air
And to sleep in the sun, not the gloom.

"Last night she dreamed about Heaven;
Heard a song, do you understand?
This filled me with fear and foreboding,
So I brought her to sleep on the sand.

"I saw her two tiny arms folded
As if in a close embrace,
And noticed her poor little feet so bare
And the look on her sad little face.

"When the surf crept up to my body,
I looked up and saw your daughter—
Your child with her new feathered hat
As she stood between us and the water.

" 'Your child looks just like a picture;
Is she made out of wax? ' asked Pilar.
'And tell me, why has she no shoes on?
Can she play? We will not go too far.

" 'But see, her hands are on fire
And her feet are as frozen as ice!
Oh, take all my things, please do take them;
I have others at home just as nice! '

"After that, pretty lady, what happened
Is something I can't quite recall,
But I saw some rose-colored slippers
On my little girl's feet, that is all!"

Two women—one English, one Russian—
Removed their fine neckerchiefs then;
And Florinda, the French girl's nursemaid,
Removed her eyeglasses again.

The sick girl's *mamá* spread her arms
And enfolded Pilar to her breast,
Unbuttoned her daughter's frayed dress
(Lacking ribbons and bows, though her best).

Now Pilar's *mamá* wants to know
Every detail about that sick child;
She cannot abide to see anyone weep,
To illness and need reconciled.

"Yes, indeed, dear Pilar, you may give them!
Your cloak and your ring—and that too!"
Pilar gave the woman her purse then,
The carnation, a kiss: "They're for you!"

At night they returned in deep silence
To their home with its garden in bloom,
Pilar perched atop a soft cushion
And both with no signs of past gloom.

And a butterfly poised on a rose bush
In a looking glass claimed it observed
A reflection of rose-colored slippers
Held therein and forever preserved.

Advice to a Young Girl
on What She Should Read:
A Letter to María Mantilla[1]

And my little daughter, what is she doing up there in the north so far away? Is she thinking about the world's realities, about knowing and loving—knowing in order to be able to love, about loving with the will and the affections? Is she fondly sitting beside her sad mother? Is she preparing for life, for the virtuous and independent work of living to be the same as, or better than, those who will come later, when she is a woman, to talk to her about romances—to take her away to the unknown, or to grief, with the deception of a few pleasant words or a pleasant appearance? Is she thinking about some free and virtuous work so that good men will desire her, bad men respect her, and so that she will not have

1. This letter was written as Martí was departing for Cuba to participate in the Second War for Independence, a movement to liberate Cuba from Spanish domination that he had so effectively organized and in which he was soon to meet his untimely death.

María Mantilla was the daughter of Manuel and Carmita (a Venezuelan) Mantilla, who ran a boarding house for Spanish Americans passing through New York. It was at 51 East 29 Street, and Martí, who was very poor, moved in with them. He became extremely fond of Carmita and her two daughters, María especially, and treated her as his own child. Later, the Mantillas moved to Brooklyn and Martí went to live with them for a time.

to sell her beauty and the freedom of her heart for food to eat or clothes to wear? For that is what the enslaved women of this world call "love"—women enslaved by their ignorance and inability to protect themselves. Love is a wonderful thing, but it is far from this. I love my little daughter. Whoever does not love her as I do does not love her at all. Love is sensitivity, true hope, merit, and respect. What is my dear daughter thinking of? Is she thinking of me?

Here I am in Cabo Haitiano when I ought not be here. I thought I would have no means of writing to you for a long time, and yet I am writing to you. Today I set out again, and I am again bidding you farewell. When someone is good to me and good to Cuba, I show him your portrait. I yearn to have you live close to one another, you two and your mother, and to have you spend your days purely and well. As long as you know that I am alive, wait for me. Know the world before giving yourself to it. Grow in stature by thinking and working. Would you like to see how much I am thinking of you—of you and Carmita? Everything gives me a reason to talk about you: the piano I hear, the book I see, the newspaper that comes. Here I am sending you, on a sheet of green paper, the announcement of the French journal Dellundé subscribed to for you. You never read *Harper's Young People,* but it was the journal's fault, not yours, for there were things in it of pure fabrication, neither felt nor seen, and with more words than necessary. This *Petit Français* is clearly written and useful. Read it and then teach. To teach is to grow. I am sending you two books by post, and with them a task you will perform if you love me, and refuse to do unless you love me. So, when I am suffering, I will feel as if there were a hand upon my shoulder, or affection upon my brow, or the smiles with which you used to understand and comfort me doing so now, and it will mean that you are working at that task and thinking of me.

One of the books is *L'Histoire Générale,* a very short book that tells very well, in pure and simple language, the entire history of the world from earliest times to the things men are inventing today. It has 180 pages. I want you to translate a page a day, in winter or summer, but done so that you and others can understand it, because my desire is that you will put this history book into good Spanish so that, in addition to helping you and Carmita understand the world's progress in a short but complete manner and enabling you to teach it, it may be printed as a salable book. Therefore you will have to translate the entire text, including the summary at the end of every chapter and the questions at the bottom of every page. But since these are to help the teacher to ask questions, you will translate them so that you will put at the foot of every page only those questions that pertain to that page. The summary should be translated at the end of each chapter. The translation must be natural, so that it seems as if the book were written in the language of your translation, for this is the sign of a good translation. French has many words that are unnecessary in Spanish. You know, they say *il est* when there is no *he* or *it*, except to go with *is*, because in French the verb does not stand alone; and in Spanish a repetition of those personal pronouns—*I* and *he* and *we* and *they*—before the verb is neither necessary nor pleasing. It would be a good thing if while you are translating, although of course not at the same time, you would read a book written in a simple and useful Spanish, to attune your ear and thought to the language in which you are writing. I cannot remember if among the books you have at hand there are any written in this pure and simple Spanish. I attempted to write that way in *The Age of Gold.* The French of *L'Histoire Générale* is concise and direct, just as I would like the Spanish in your translation to be. So you must imitate it as you translate, and try to use the same words except when the French manner of expression, the French sentence, is different in Spanish.

For example, upon page 19 in paragraph 6 I have this

sentence in front of me: *"Les Grecs ont les premiers cherché a se rendre compte des choses du monde."* Naturally, you cannot translate sentences like this word for word: "The Greeks have the first tried to recognize the things of the world." That makes no sense in Spanish. If I were to say: "The Greeks have tried the first . . ." I would be wrong, for that is not Spanish. If I were to say further: "to recognize," I would also be wrong, for this is not Spanish either. So you can see how careful you must be when you translate; the translation must be understood and be in good style so that the book, like so many translated ones, does not seem to remain in its original foreign tongue. And the book will entertain you, especially when you go back to the times when the personnages referred to in the poems and operas lived. It is impossible to fully understand an opera—or the romance of Hildegonda, for example—if nothing is known about the historical events the opera relates, and if one does not know who Hildegonda is, and where and when she lived, and what she did. Your music is not like that, my María; it is the music that understands and feels. Study, my María; work and wait for me.

And when you have made a very good translation of *L'Histoire Générale,* clearly written in even lines upon pages with good, clean, imposing margins, then how can that clear and finished text of the history of man—better and more attractive and pleasing than any history textbook in Spanish now in print—fail to be published and sold for you and your household? One page a day then, my dear little daughter. Learn from me. I have life at one side of my desk and death at the other, and a nation behind me, and see how many pages I am writing to you.

The other book is for reading and teaching; it has 300 pages, María dear, aided by drawings of the best of what is known about nature today, and it is all factual. You have already read Appleton's *Cartillas,* or perhaps Carmita has read it first. Well, this book is much better; it is shorter, more lighthearted and complete, with clearer language, all written as things are. Read the last chapter: *La Physiologie Végétale*— plant life—and you will see such poetic and interesting history. I am reading it now and will read it again, and I always find it new. I do not read many poems, because almost all of them are exaggerated or artificial and use forced language to express false sentiments, or sentiments with neither strength nor honesty—bad copies of those that are truly felt. Where I find greater poetry is in scientific books, in real life, in the world's order, at the bottom of the sea, in the truth and music of trees, in their very strength and affections, in the vault of heaven with its family of stars—and in the unity of the universe embracing so many different things, for it is all one and rests in the starlight of night from the productive work of the day. It is beautiful to look out from a balcony and see the world living—see it be born, grow, change, improve—and to learn in that continuous majesty the pleasure of truth, the disdain of riches and the false pride to which they are sacrificed; inferior and useless people sacrifice all of it. It is like the elegance that lies in good taste, my María, and not in cost. The elegance of clothing, great and true elegance, lies in the pride and strength of the soul of the wearer. An honest, intelligent, and free spirit gives the body more elegance, and the woman more dominance, than the most elaborate fashions from a boutique. Much boutique but little soul. Women with much within need little outside. Those who wear much on the outside have little within and wish to conceal that little. She who feels her beauty, her inner beauty, does not seek borrowed beauty outside; she knows that she is beautiful and her beauty shines forth. Try to appear joyful and pleasing to the eye, for it is a human duty to cause pleasure instead of pain, and whoever knows beauty respects and cares for it in others and in herself. She will never put jasmine in a large Chinese flower vase; she will put a sprig of it by itself in a glass of clear water. True elegance consists in the flower not being overshadowed by the container. And this true and natural way of living, compassionate toward the vain and pompous, is charmingly learned in the history of the earth's creatures. You and Carmita must read Paul Bert's[2] book, and in two or three months reread it; read it over again and always have it at hand for an occasional page in your spare time. That is how you will become teachers, telling your pupils those true stories instead of all those common fractions and decimals and useless names of capes and rivers that should be taught by the map, rather incidentally, in order to locate where the story takes place or where lived the man whose history is related. Explain some things upon the blackboard, but not every day. Let your pupils love school and learn pleasant and useful things in it.

For I will see you and Carmita this winter sitting in your school from nine to one every day, working both at the same time if the girls are of different ages and there must be two groups, or working one after another in a class where the same lessons are taught to all. You could teach piano and reading and perhaps Spanish after having done a little more reading in it, and Carmita could teach a new class in spelling and composition together—a grammar class with everything taught upon slates by dictation, and then writing upon the blackboard what was dictated, making sure that the girls correct their mistakes. And you could teach a geography class, more physical geography than mere names: how the world is made and how its surroundings contribute to its existence. And you could teach the other kind of geography, the major land masses, and those well, without being too fussy or pausing over too many Yankee details. There could be a science class consisting of Carmita's talking to the

2. Paul Bert (1833–86), French physiologist and politician, minister of public instruction and worship (1881–82). In politics he was an anti-clerical leftist.

students as if she were telling a real story, in Paul Bert's style if you can understand it fully; if not, then something of your own devising together with what you know about the *Cartillas* and with the aid of what you do understand of Paul Bert. You might consider a class in astronomy; for that, a book by Arabella Buckley called *The Fairyland of Science* would be very helpful, as would the books of John Lubbock, two of them especially: *Fruits, Flowers, and Leaves* and *Ants, Bees, and Wasps.* Imagine Carmita telling the girls about the friendship between bees and flowers, and how flowers turn their coquetry upon bees, and about the intelligence of leaves that sleep and love and protect themselves, and about the visits and voyages of the stars, and about anthills. Few books and continuous conversation. The girls may find history still very new to them. And on Fridays a class in dolls—how to cut out and stitch dolls' dresses—and a review of music, and a long class in penmanship, and a drawing class. Start with two, three, or four girls. Others will come. As soon as they hear about that happy and beneficial school with classes conducted in English, those who have children in other schools will send them to yours. And if they are our people, you will teach them by means of patient coaxing in a class of explanatory readings, explaining the Spanish meanings of the words. No more grammar than that; children gradually discover what they read and hear, and that is the only useful method. And what if you were to make extra efforts and teach French the way I taught it to you, by translating from books that are natural and afford pleasant reading? If I were where you could not see me, or where it was impossible for me to return, it would make me tremendously proud and happy to see you from there, wise with your enlightened little mind among the schoolgirls who would go forth from your spirit as enlightened as you. It would be an enormous source of pride and joy to see you established there, free of the world and working independently. Train yourself in summer; start your work in winter.

Go silently among the conceited; your soul is your adornment. Take care of your mother and indulge her, for it is a great honor to have come into the world from that woman. When you look inside of you and at what you are doing, you will find yourself like the morning earth, bathed in light. Feel clean and gay like the light. Leave the frivolous world to others; you are worth more than the frivolous. Smile and go forth. And if you do not see me again, do what that little toddler did at Frank Sorzano's burial: put a book—the book I ask of you—upon the grave. Or upon your breast, for it is there I shall be buried if I should die someplace where men cannot find me. Work. A kiss. And wait for me.

Your *Martí*
Cabo Haitiano, April 9, 1895

Index

DATE DUE